Karate Masters

Volume 2

Karate Masters

VOLUME 2

Jose M. Fraguas

P.O. Box 491788, Los Angeles, CA 90049

Disclaimer
Please note that the author and publisher of this book are NOT RESPONSIBLE in any manner whatsoever for any injury that may result from practicing the techniques and/or following the instructions given within. Because the physical activities described herein may be too strenuous in nature for some readers to engage in safely, it is essential that a physician be consulted prior to training.

Copyright © 2006 by Empire Books.

All rights reserved. No part of this publication may be reproduced or utilized in any form or by any means, electronic or mechanical, including photocopying, recording, or by any information storage and retrieval system, without prior written permission from Empire Books.

EMPIRE BOOKS
P.O. Box 491788
Los Angeles, CA 90049

First edition

05 04 03 02 01 00 99 98 97 1 3 5 7 9 10 8 6 4 2

Printed in the United States of America.

Library of Congress: 2006012533
ISBN-10: 1-933901-20-9
ISBN-13: 978-1-933901-20-9

Library of Congress Cataloging-in-Publication Data

Fraguas, Jose M.
  Karate masters / by Jose M. Fraguas. -- 1st ed.
      p. cm.
  Includes index.
  ISBN 1-933901-20-9 (pbk. : alk. paper)
  1. Karate. 2. Martial artists--Interviews. 3. Large type books. I. Title.
  GV1114.3.F715 2006
  796.815'3--dc22
                                    2006012533

"And I tell you that you should open yourselves to hearing authentic artists, of the kind whose bodily senses were shaped in a world that is not our own and that few people are able to perceive; artists closer to death than to philosophy, closer to pain that to intelligence. Closer to blood than to ink."

—**Federico Garcia Lorca (1898–1936)
Spanish poet and dramatist**

Dedication

To my mother, an extraordinary person of unending forgiveness, deep understanding, and limitless giving and patience, who over the years has used all those qualities—and then some—in dealing with my martial arts and writing addiction.

A mi madre, una persona extraordinaria de infinita bondad, profunda comprensión y de paciencia ilimitada, quien durante muchos años ha tenido que usar estas cualidades—y alguna que otra más—para soportar mi adicción a las artes marciales.

Acknowledgments

A lot of people gave their time and mind to help me write this book, and so I gratefully acknowledge their expertise, charm and wit. I thank not only the people I interviewed for the book, and those who supplied great and extremely valuable pictures to illustrate the work, but the others who were always on the lookout for me. Special thanks go to designer Patrick Gross, whose flights of logic and guidance in the artwork of this book were always on the wings of excitement; Australian publisher and friend Silvio Morelli, an enthusiastic supporter of this project from the very beginning; France's Thierry Plee, long-time friend and president of *Sedirep* and *Budo Editions*; photographer Norma Harvey of England; Billy Bly, founder and editor of *American Samurai*; Germany's publisher Schlatt (director of *Schlatt Books*); John Cheetham, dear friend and editor of *Shotokan Karate magazine*; wado-ryu stylist Salvador Herraiz from Spain, who delved deep into his collection of photos to find some that could be included in this book; Michael Lorden, friend and dedicated karate-do practitioner from Colorado; great karate-ka, writer and friend Terry O'Neill of England; Kent Moyer, goju-ryu stylist from Los Angeles; Steven Heyl, director of Doshin Martial Arts, of Los Angeles, California, who kindly supplied additional information to complete some interviews; Don Warrener, director of Rising Sun Productions; Okinawa karate great and master calligrapher Tetsuhiro Hokama; Jean Paul Maillet of France, for his support and help with some of his great photographs; Harold E. Sharp, a true legend in the world of martial arts and who kindly supplied great photos from his personal archives; Martha Engber for her kindness and additional photographs; Isaac Florentine, film director and passionate karate-ka; Arthur Tansley of Tokyo, Japan … your amazing talent as photographer is only surpassed by your kindness as a human being; Lance Douglas, editor of the work, and finally to my wife, Julie, whose discernment is always tempered with kindness.

A word of appreciation is also due to my good and dear friend Masahiro Ide, President of *JK Fan* and *Champ* videos, for his generosity and cooperation in this project; I also want to thank Okuma-san from the JKA Honbu Dojo in Tokyo for his assistance, kindness and supply of great photographic material for some of the chapters; and I must acknowledge the cooperation and help from the publishers of *Gekkan Karate-do* magazine [Fukushodo, Ltd., Japan]. Without their support, kindness and commitment to preserve the art of karate-do, this book would not exist.

I would foremost like to give my most heartfelt gratitude to all the masters appearing in this book. Not only did they generously give me an enormous amount of personal time for the long interviews, but they also provided me with great pictures to illustrate the work.

You all have my enduring thanks.

—Jose M. Fraguas

About the Author

Born and raised in Madrid, Spain, Jose "Chema" Fraguas began his martial arts studies with judo, in grade school, at age 9. From there he moved to taekwondo and then to kenpo karate, earning black belts in both styles. During this same period, he also studied shito-ryu karate under Japanese Masters Masahiro Okada and Yashunari Ishimi, eventually receiving a fifth-degree black belt. He began his career as a writer at age 16 as a regular contributor to martial arts magazines in Great Britain, France, Spain, Italy, Germany, Portugal, Holland and Australia. Having black belts in three different styles allowed him to better reflect the physical side of the martial arts in his writing: "Feeling before writing," Fraguas says.

In 1980, he moved to Los Angeles, California, where his open-minded mentality helped him to develop a realistic approach to the martial arts. Seeking to supplement his previous training, he researched other disciplines such as jiu-jitsu, escrima and muay Thai.

In 1986, Fraguas founded his own publishing company in Europe, authoring dozens of books and distributing his magazines to 35 countries in three different languages. His reputation and credibility as a martial artist and publisher became well known to the top masters around the world. Considering himself a martial artist first and a writer and publisher second, Fraguas feels fortunate to have had the opportunity to interview many legendary martial artists. He recognizes that much of the information given in the interviews helped him to discover new dimensions in the martial arts. "I was constantly absorbing knowledge from the great masters," he recalls.

"I only trained with a few of them, but intellectually and spiritually all of them have made very important contributions to my growth as a complete martial artist."

However, there were some drawbacks to his position as a publisher, Fraguas acknowledges, that directly affected his personal martial arts development. "Of course, some people taught me because of my position as a publisher and not because who I was as a person. Even though I recognize that, I'm still grateful for the knowledge they shared with me."

Steeped in tradition yet looking to the future, Fraguas understands and appreciates martial arts history and philosophy and feels this rich heritage is a necessary steppingstone to personal growth and spiritual evolution. His desire to promote both ancient philosophy and modern thinking provided the motivation for writing this book. "If the motivation is just money, a book cannot be of good quality," Fraguas says. "If the book is written to just make people happy, it cannot be deep. I want to write books so I can learn as well as teach. Karate-do, like human life itself, is filled with experiences that seem quite ordinary at the time and assume a fabled stature only with the passage of the years. I hope this work will be appreciated by future practitioners of the art of the *empty-hand*."

Originally from Madrid, Spain, he is currently living in Los Angeles, California. He can be contacted at: **mastersseries@yahoo.com.** O

Introduction

Some of my best days were spent interviewing and meeting the masters in this book. There is little I enjoy more than reading a great interview while time slows and sometimes even seems to stop. Having the opportunity to meet and interview the most prestigious martial artists of the past four decades is something that every martial artist doesn't have the chance to do. Hopefully, in some small way, this will help make up for that.

Meeting the masters and having long conversations with them allowed me to do more than simply scratch the surface of the technical aspects of their respective styles; it also allowed me to understand the human beings behind the teachers. Some of the dialogues and interviews began by simply commenting about the superficial techniques of fighting, and ended up turning into a spiritual conversation about the philosophical aspects of the martial arts. Although these masters are all very different, they share a common thread of traditional values such as discipline, respect, positive attitude, dedication and etiquette.

For more than 25 years I've interviewed these martial arts masters, one-on-one, face-to-face, with no place to run if I asked a stupid question. Many times it was a real challenge to not just talk to them, but to make the questions interesting enough to bring out their deepest knowledge. I tried to absorb as much knowledge as I could, ranging from their training methods, to their fighting methods, to their philosophies about life itself. Their different cultural backgrounds never prevented them from analyzing, researching or modifying anything they considered important. They always kept their minds open to improving their arts and themselves. From a formal philosophical point of view, many of them followed classical philosophies and religions—but they all tempered that with vast amounts of common sense.

They devoted themselves to their arts, often in solitude, to the exclusion of other "normal" pursuits. They worked themselves into extraordinary physical condition. They ignored distractions and diversions and concentrated on their mental and physical training. They got as good as they could possibly get at performing and teaching their chosen art while the rest of us watched them, leading our "balanced lives," and wondering how good we might have gotten at something had we devoted ourselves to it as ferociously as these masters embraced their arts. In that respect, they bear our dreams.

If you read carefully between the lines, you'll see that none of these men were trying to become a fighting machine, or create the most devastating martial arts system known to man. They focused, rather, on how to use martial arts to become a better person. There are many principles that once discovered open a wide spectrum of possibilities, not only to martial arts, but to a better existence as individuals.

The interviews often lasted as long as three or four hours. I would begin at their school and finish the conversation at a restaurant or coffee shop. Much of this information had never been published before and some had to be trimmed either at the master's request or edited to avoid misunderstandings. It is not the questions that make an interview. An interview is either good or bad depending on the answers. Considering the masters in this book, I had an easy job. My goal was to make them comfortable talking about life and training—especially those who trained under the founders of original systems. In modern times, there are not many who have had the privilege of living and learning under these legendary founders.

"The masters are gone," many like to say. But as long as we keep their teachings in our heart, they will live forever. To understand martial arts properly, it is necessary to take into account their philosophical methods as well as their physical techniques. There is a deep distinction between a fighting system and a martial arts. Unfortunately, the roots of the martial arts have been de-emphasized, neglected or totally abandoned today. Martial arts are not a sport. Someone who chooses to devote himself to a sport such as basketball, tennis, soccer or football—which is based on youth, strength, and speed—chooses to die twice. When you can no longer do that sport, due to the lack of their required attributes, waking up in the morning without the activity that has been the center of your life for 25 years is troubling and unsettling. In contrast, the martial arts can and should be practiced for life—they never leave you.

A true martial artist is like a musician, painter, writer or actor—their art is an expression of themselves. The need to discover who they are becomes the reason for an endless search for the perfect technique, great melody, inspiring poetry, amazing painting or Academy Award performance. It is this motivation to reach that impossible dream that allows a simple individual to become an exceptional artist and master of his craft.

Many of the greatest teachers share a commonly misunderstood teaching methodology. They know the words they could use to teach their students have little or no meaning. They know that to try "self-discovery" in quantitative or empirical terms is a useless task. A great deal of knowledge and wisdom comes from oral traditions, which martial arts, like every other cultural expression, has. These oral traditions have always been reserved for a certain kind of student and considered "secrets," given only to a special few who have the minds and attitudes to fully grasp them.

Alexandra David-Neel wrote: "It is not on the master that the secret depends but on the hearer. Truth learned from others is of no value, the only truth which is effective and of value is self-discovered ... the teacher can only guide to the point of discovery." In the end, "the only secret is that there is no secret." As Kato Tokuro, arguably the finest potter of the last century, a great art scholar, and the teacher of Pablo Picasso said: "The sole cause of secrets in craftsmanship is the student's inability to learn."

To find out what karate-do means to you, what it does for you, and what it holds for you, is a deeply personal process. Each path is different and we all have to find a personal rhythm that fit us individually, according to what surround us.

As human beings, we are always tempted to follow linear logic towards ultimate self-improvement—but the truth is that there are no absolute truths. You have to find your own way in life whether it be in martial arts, business or cherry picking. Whatever path you pursue, you have to distill the personal truths that are right for you, according to your own nature. The quest for perfection is very imperfect, and not in tune with human nature or experience. To have any hope of attaining even a single perfection, you have to concentrate on a single pursuit and direct all your energy towards it. In this sense, perfection comes from appreciating endeavors for their own sake—not to impress anyone—but for your own inner satisfaction and sense of accomplishment.

It is important to have a feeling of responsibility; and putting yourself into an art as genuinely as you can, without any sense that you are going to get something back in return, reverberates throughout time and space. We need to honor those who came before us, as well as nurture those who will come after, so the art can grow and expand—you've got to send the elevator back down.

Martial arts are a large part of my life and I draw inspiration from them. I really don't know the "how" or the "why" of their effect on me, but I feel their influence in even my most mundane activities. All human beings have sources or principles that keep them grounded, and martial arts are mine. That is when the term "way of life" becomes real. In bushido, the self-discipline required to pursue mastery is more important than mastery itself—the struggle is more important than the reward. A common thread throughout the lives of all the masters is their constant struggle towards self-mastery. They realized that life is an ongoing process, and once you achieve all your goals you are as good as dead. But this process is not all driven by action. Often the greatest action is inaction, and the hardest voice to hear is the sound of your own thoughts. You need to sit alone and collect yourself, free from technology and distraction, and just think. This is perhaps the only way to achieve mental and spiritual clarity.

I don't believe that books are meant to be read fast. I've always thought that writing is timeless and that reading is not a detraction. So take your time. Approach this book with the Zen "beginner's mind" and "empty cup" mentality and soak up the words of these great teachers. They will help you to not only grow as a martial artist but as a human being as well. O

Contents

1
Yoshiaki Ajari
The Peaceful Warrior

11
Keinosuke Enoeda
The Tiger of Shotokan

21
Randall Hassell
No Finish Line

37
Yashunari Ishimi
The Internal Serenity

49
Richard Kim
The Classical Man

61
Yukiyoshi Marutani
Karate's Mastermind

71
Shinpo Matayoshi
The Heritage Keeper

81
Val Mijailovic
Knowledge Does Not Belong to Me

95
Yoshinao Nanbu
Walking His Own Path

105
Yuishi Negishi
A Modern Samurai

115
Seiji Nishimura
A Critical Reflection

131
Tsutomu Ohshima
Strict Eyes

147
Yoshiharu Osaka
Karate's Perfect Form

空手道

159 Eihachi Ota	**171** Mas Oyama	**183** Shigeru Oyama
A Man of Ethics	The Divine Fist	In the Footsteps of the Master
197 Wally Slocki	**209** Alex Sternberg	**229** Masahiko Tanaka
A Straight Shooter	A Focused Determination	The Legend
241 Keiji Tomiyama	**257** Dominique Valera	**271** Tamas Weber
The Challenges of Budo	Long Live The King!	Budo on The Battlefield
285 Goshi Yamaguchi	**297** Kiyoshi Yamazaki	**317** Koss Yokota
Protecting the Legacy	The Perfect Balance	A Balanced Spirit

Yoshiaki Ajari

The Peaceful Warrior

In a karate world full of self-interest and self-importance, Sensei Ajari has selflessly spread the art of Wado-ryu karate in a very open and humble manner. Born on July 4, 1933, in the village of Minato Kawaguchi, near Wakayama City, Yoshiaki Ajari began training in the goju-ryu style of karate-do under Shozo Ujita Sensei. He eventually became a direct student of the founder of Wado-ryu karate, Hironori Ohtsuka, when he went to Meiji University to further his studies. An architect by profession, and a graduate of both Meiji and Berkeley universities, Yoshiaki Ajari is one of the leading teachers of the Wado-ryu style around the world, and an active member of the World Karate Federation. As a Chief Instructor of the U.S. Wado Kai, he travels extensively to spread the "art of peace" as the founder advised. His restless spirit and inquiring mind have made him very critical of those who do not teach the art in the proper and traditional way. His lifelong dedication and commitment to spread the art of the late Sensei Ohtsuka has definitely paid off.

Q: How did you begin in the martial arts?
A: Right after the war, Shozo Ujita Sensei from the goju-ryu style of karate started to teach a group of young people. He came from the same city as me so we became very close. Ujita Sensei was a very nice human being. He worked as a military policeman and after the war decided to get involved in teaching. I was just 13 years old at that time, and I really enjoyed watching the training. I can't remember the reason why I decided to join, but I instantly felt attracted to it. At the dojo in Minato Kawaguchi we used to train in Ujita Sensei's warehouse. The light supply after the war was very limited, so when we couldn't use the lights anymore we all moved to the outside and trained on the gravelstreets. Later on, the dojo moved to another location in Wakayama City and started to expand very fast due to the reputation we got from giving demonstrations. The training under Ujita Sensei was physically very demanding. Coming from a goju-ryu background, we used to do a lot of physical conditioning exercises for the body.

Karate Masters

"At the university, the training was very hard compared to regular dojo in the cities. The idea was give them a hard time so they would leave. That way we had more room for training."

The idea was to make the body strong to take a blow and to deliver a powerful strike of your own. It was very hard on the body.

Q: What happened as you grew up?
A: I went to Meiji University in Tokyo to study, and I found out that they had a karate class, which I decided to join. But it wasn't goju-ryu at all. Their karate was very different than what I had learned before, but I really wanted to keep training and that's how I started training in wado-ryu. For a long time I kept doing both styles at the same time—six days a week for two hours I did wado-ryu, and on Mondays and Saturdays I went to Gogen Yamaguchi Sensei's dojo to train in goju-ryu. At his dojo, I was not only training but working as an assistant teacher as well. For more than two years, I was using a white belt in the wado-ryu classes while I was already a *nidan* in goju-ryu. At the university the training was very hard compared to regular dojos in the cities. In the university dojo there was not enough room for everybody, so the seniors students put a lot of pressure on the beginners to make them quit. The idea was give them a hard time so they would leave. That way we had more room for training.

Q: Did you visit other universities during your college years?
A: Yes, I did and I had the opportunity of meeting many great karateka. Ujita Sensei used to get a group together during the summertime and send us to other universities to train and spar. I remember that two other students, juniors Yoshida and Iwai, would join the group. It was then that I met people like Mikami Sensei and Kanazawa Sensei. I used to meet Kanazawa Hirokazu more often because we used to exchange practice sessions between Takushoku, Keio and Meiji universities. To be honest, I have to say that Kanazawa Sensei was probably the only one in the shotokan group who could actually fight at that time.

Q: Was it difficult to adapt from one style to another?
A: In the very beginning, it was easy, because all we did was punching and kicking. After all, a basic technique is a basic technique—there are limited variations. As time went by and I became more skilled in the wado-ryu way of moving, I began to find some difficulties trying to adapt a very offensive style like wado-ryu to another more defensive system such as goju-ryu. Wado-ryu uses a lot of lateral and side-stepping maneuvers and goju-ryu bases its actions on short snapping techniques. They don't move the body around too much. Goju-ryu works in close distance and wado-ryu operates more in middle distance —similar to shito-ryu. Eventually, I believe that you can take elements from both and combine them so you get a more complete approach to fighting—but that time for me was a little bit confusing since the tactics of the style determine the way you do the techniques and the way you move.

"Wado-ryu uses a lot of lateral and sidestepping maneuvers and goju-ryu bases its actions on short snapping techniques. I believe that you can take elements from both and combine them so you get a more complete approach to fighting."

Q: Why did you decide to stick to wado-ryu and Ohtsuka Sensei?
A: The main reason was Ohtsuka Sensei explained in detail the way the body moves. He explained how to use the body to move and develop power and momentum in every single action. Wado-ryu movements are very fluid and relaxed, but powerful at the same time—because when you hit your opponent you have to be sharp. He had the ability to teach and explain details in every point of the technique. I truly enjoyed this and decided to stick to him instead of going back to goju-ryu.

Q: How was your training under Ohtsuka Sensei?
A: He was a very special individual. He was gentle and quiet and was always into the practice of karate. He trained under Funakoshi Gichin, but after a few years Ohtsuka Sensei began to move more into the *kumite*, or fighting aspect, and this approach was not shared by Funakoshi Sensei. They remained friends but took separate ways in their personal expression of the art. His martial arts background was comprised of different methods, but in

Karate Masters

"The main idea behind his teachings was to flow with the attack, re-direct the incoming force and avoid it. Never crash or use force against force. That's the reason why he stressed the tai-sabaki so much since it is an important part of the ten tai principle. One curious aspect is that I didn't see Ohtsuka Sensei practicing with the makiwara."

his style of karate you can see a big influence of his early training in shindo yoshin-ryu jiu-jitsu under Shinzaburo Nakayama Sensei, the third grandmaster of this style of jiu-jitsu.

The jiu-jitsu influence is not as obvious in the external movements, but you can see it in the application and *bunkai* of the kata. It's here when we can see all the subtle details of locking and throwing from his jiu-jitsu training. Once he closed the distance, he would grab your arm and throw you onto the ground, applying a lock or immobilization to finalize. I would say that he had a special ability to rotate his hip and apply that into any particular actions he performed. It was really amazing. He was always very busy teaching at different colleges and had lots of students because of that.

Technically he developed the principles of *noru*, *nagasu* and *inasu* and took them to another level of application. He always stressed the aspects of *ten-tai*, which means to move the body away from the line of attack, and *ten-gi*, or changing techniques. The main idea behind his teachings was to flow with the attack, re-direct the incoming force and avoid it. Never crash or use force against force. That's the reason why he stressed the *tai-sabaki* so much since it is an important part of the *ten-tai* principle. One curious aspect is that I didn't see Ohtsuka Sensei practicing with the makiwara.

Q: You met the legendary kyokushinkai founder Mas Oyama, right?
A: Yes, I did. He was a very interesting individual. He used to practice all these tricks that the audience enjoyed. He was very close to Gogen Yamaguchi Sensei and they trained together many times. In fact, Yamaguchi Sensei granted him a high rank in goju-ryu and this was not well accepted by some of the seniors there. As a result, he decided to pursue his own way. His approach to karate was very combative and you can see that in the method he developed afterward and named kyokushinkai.

Mas Oyama really enjoyed things like bending coins, breaking bottles and the famous fight with the bull. I saw him to do some very amusing things. I really can't tell you how much truth there was in every one of those things, but he was a very enjoyable person to be with. He had a lot of charisma when talking in front of an audience. He knew how to keep the audience interested in what he was saying and doing. His lectures were extremely interesting and were followed by a lot of people.

Q: When did you decide to move to the United States?
A: It was in 1957, and the reason was not to teach karate but to further my education. I got involved in teaching because some people asked me to do it. I only did it locally and I had no intention of expanding the group. At that time I had the opportunity to meet other people like Hidetaka Nishiyama Sensei and Tsutomu Ohshima Sensei. They were already established to a certain degree and their names were known among the practitioners. I remember I met Nishiyama Sensei in San Jose, California, and one or two years later I met Ohshima Sensei.

"If you combine the body evasion with the principle of using your strong-side forward, your counterattacks will be faster (as your strong side is closer to the opponent's body) and you will be very elusive since you are moving from one of the blind spots in your opponent's vision."

Q: Why is wado-ryu the only karate style that emphasizes the use of the strong-side forward?
A: It has to do with Ohtsuka Sensei's *budo* background. He was very well-versed in the use of the sword and in kendo. In kendo, you always grab the *shinai*—or "sword" in iaido—with your strong-side forward. Ohtsuka Sensei used this principle in the empty-handed art of karate and ended up using his strong-side forward. You can also see this influence in the type of *kamae* we use. On the other hand, wado-ryu is a karate style that focuses on middle distance—we like to enter and crash inside. This is more safely done using your strong side. If you combine the body evasion with the principle of using your strong-side forward, your counterattacks will be faster (as your strong side is closer to the opponent's body) and you will be very elusive since you are moving from one of the blind spots in your opponent's vision. Structurally, it is a faster method than those using the strong-side in the back, although there are many more elements involved.

Karate Masters

"Ohtsuka Sensei was always looking for quality and not quantity in everything he did. He never looked for a lot of kata because you can't really master 50 or 60 kata. With that kata collector mentality, the practitioner won't go very far in his karate training."

Q: Why does wado-ryu have a limited number of kata compared to other styles?
A: Ohtsuka Sensei was always looking for quality and not quantity in everything he did. This approach conditioned his point of view and therefore his mentality in karate-do. He never looked for a lot of kata because you can't really master 50 or 60 kata. You may be able to memorize them but not master them. Other styles like goju-ryu only have a dozen of forms; however, they are very effective and very rich in their *bunkai* and self-defense techniques. The amount of kata doesn't mean anything. Other masters like Mabuni Kenwa dedicated his whole life to preserving and codifying the traditional kata. Mabuni Sensei became a living encyclopedia of kata, but he was a real exception in *budo* history. He was a very talented and dedicated man. Unfortunately, today we don't have the time to train 60 kata every single day.

As far as the beauty of the movements of wado kata compared to other karate styles, I would say that we try to keep the movements very natural and within the confines of the technical common sense. This means that we don't modify the techniques to make it look more impressive in front of judges or spectators. Nowadays, I see students all over the world trying to collect as many kata as they can from different styles, rather than spend time and energy internalizing the information. With that kata collector mentality, the practitioner won't go very far in his karate training. Knowledge is very important, but going around accumulating forms and kata is not the best idea. It means nothing in the true way of karate-do.

Q: Would you describe Ohtsuka Sensei as a rebel?
A: He was a very special individual, but I don't think "rebel" is the right word. Ohtsuka Sensei was the living example of the *budo* principle of *shu-ha-ri*. He did learn from different masters to achieve a high level of skill and understanding of what those masters were teaching. This is *"shu."* He kept that and experimented with his own research to modify things according to

his own way of thinking and doing. He broke from that tradition, which is called *"ha."* And finally he transcended. This is *"ri."* These three principles are the reason why you can see differences in top teachers of the same style. It's part of budo and not against it.

Funakoshi Gichin did the same thing. He didn't keep the art the way he learned it in Okinawa. In fact, Funakoshi Sensei, changed—to a large degree—almost everything to better suit the Japanese mentality. Kenwa Mabuni from shito-ryu did the same. He learned from many masters—mainly Higashionna Kanryo and Itosu Anko—and modified things to later formulate the shito-ryu style. To gain a deep understanding of any martial art system requires many years, not only in technique, but also in spirit. This is the reason why it seems childish to me when someone with two years of training criticizes a martial art system and decides to create his own.

Some styles really differ one from each other because they have special techniques and different approaches to the physical movements. It's their own particular flavor that sets them apart from each other. If you try to combine two or three styles, you really need to know those methods and have a high level of understanding of how they work. Most likely you'll end up integrating elements and principles and not simply mixing techniques. You need a strong foundation and direction of where you are going. Learning multiple martial arts styles or karate methods can become an obstacle to reaching a high skill level of mastery.

"Some styles really differ one from each other because they have special techniques and different approaches to the physical movements. It's their own particular flavor that sets them apart from each other. If you try to combine two or three styles you really need to know those methods and have a high level of understanding of how they work. Learning multiple martial arts styles or karate methods can become an obstacle to reaching a high skill level of mastery."

Q: What is karate-do for you?
A: Karate teaches you more than fighting and combat. It teaches you discipline—both mentally and physically. Through the physical training of pushing your body to do things in a well coordinated way, you learn how to apply the force that lies inside your body in a very natural way. The movements may

Karate Masters

"Karate teaches you more than fighting and combat. It teaches you discipline—both mentally and physically. Through the physical training of pushing your body to do things in a well coordinated way, you learn how to apply the force that lies inside your body in a very natural way."

look simple at first sight, but there is a tremendous complexity behind all the physical actions of a simple straight punch. It's only through constant training that your body can develop the necessary pathways to use your body force in the more appropriate way.

For instance, one of the typical karate training methods is a constant repetition of the same movement. If your instructor makes you to do this, please don't be a fool and assume that he doesn't know more or is trying to rip you off. Let's say that you do a *gyaku-tsuki* 5,000 times. Well, you have to look inside and try to feel your body doing the perfect technique, because maybe only three or four of all those 5,000 punches were correctly done. These three or four punches are the ones your body has to remember. That feeling, that sensation, is what you have to try to duplicate every time you punch. Then, when you are capable of recalling that correct sensation, you'll be setting a foundation for success. Many people punch and kick for 20 or 30 years without knowing what to look for. They don't improve the quality of what they are doing. All they do is repeat a physical action. And that in karate-do is not enough. You have to keep pushing your technique to the limit—and in order to do that you have to keep a constant interest and desire to learn and improve yourself. It's only through proper training that an individual can reach his highest goals. There are no shortcuts of any kind in the true art of karate.

Q: What do you get out of your karate training?
A: I'm retired now, so I get to kill a lot of time! Kidding aside, I get a lot of things from practicing and teaching the art of karate. I get immense enjoyment doing it. Karate allowed me to develop myself not only physically but also mentally and spiritually in a manner that I never would have been able

"Karate-do is not only physical techniques but a philosophy of life. Age is not important for someone who really wants to train in karate. Karate is a life journey, not a destination. It's only when we look at it as a destination that we'll stop training."

to without it. I don't have anything to prove, so I just do it for myself. Karate-do is not only physical techniques but a philosophy of life. Age is not important for someone who really wants to train in karate. Karate is a life journey, not a destination. It's only when we look at it as a destination that we'll stop training. Unfortunately, this is what happens when you focus too much on competition. Once your competitive years are over, you have no motivation to pursue the real karate-do.

Q: What is the philosophy behind your training?
A: During all my years of involvement in karate, I have met many individuals. Despite the diversity of these encounters, each has left a mark on my memory. All your training must be based on deep honesty of what you are doing. Don't think you are superman because you know karate-do and you walk around quoting some *budo* philosophy—because one day you'll have a rude awakening. Don't lie to yourself. Life is a repetition of confidence and emotions. I believe that through karate training we can find the way to spiritual and physical exercise and exertion. That you will believe in yourself and have a life based upon solid links of confidence. O

Keinosuke Enoeda

The Tiger of Shotokan

KEINOSUKE ENOEDA WAS A TRUE CELEBRITY IN THE WORLD OF KARATE. HE GRADUATED FROM TAKUSHOKU UNIVERSITY WHERE HIS MAIN INSTRUCTOR WAS THE LATE MASTER NAKAYAMA. SENSEI ENOEDA MASTERED ALL KARATE TECHNIQUES THROUGH HIS TOTAL DEDICATION TO THE ART—BUT EVEN MORE IMPORTANTLY CAPTURED AND UNDERSTOOD THE PHILOSOPHY AND SPIRIT OF KARATE-DO AS LAID DOWN BY MASTER GICHIN FUNAKOSHI. AS A FORMER ALL-JAPAN CHAMPION, HE WAS RESPECTED AND FEARED AS A FIGHTER. SUCH PROWESS EARNED HIM A REPUTATION OF HIGH STANDING AND MADE HIM ONE OF THE MOST FAMOUS AND RESPECTED KARATE-DO INSTRUCTORS IN THE WORLD. HE WAS ONE OF THE FITTEST, MOST POWERFUL KARATE TECHNICIANS—BUT HE HAD ANOTHER, LESS DEFINABLE QUALITY. HIS AURA OF ENERGY AND CHARISMA WAS SOMETHING SPECIAL. HE HAD THAT ABILITY TO BRING OUT THE BEST IN A STUDENT, FORCING HIM TO PERFORM BETTER KARATE. LIVING IN THE UNITED KINGDOM SINCE 1966, HE DEVELOPED COUNTLESS NUMBER OF FINE KARATE-KA AND MANY LEADING CHAMPIONS IN THE ART. MASTER ENOEDA WAS INSTRUMENTAL IN MAKING GREAT BRITAIN ONE OF THE STRONGEST KARATE NATIONS IN THE WORLD. HE ALSO FOUND TIME, OVER THE YEARS, TO COACH MANY CELEBRITIES FOR FIGHT SCENES IN FILMS, INCLUDING LEE MARVIN, MICHAEL CAINE AND SEAN CONNERY. SENSEI ENOEDA TAUGHT REGULARLY AT HIS FAMOUS LONDON DOJO AND TRAVELED THE WORLD TEACHING HIS UNIQUE BRAND OF DYNAMIC KARATE UNTIL THE LAST DAY OF HIS LIFE. SIMPLY SAID, HE WAS "THE TIGER" OF SHOTOKAN.

Q: Would you tell us about your beginning days in karate?
A: I was born in Fukuoka on the island of Kyushu in Southern Japan on July 4, 1935, and I practiced the martial arts from an early age. While my brother and sister played games, I began judo at the age of seven. I continued my training through high school, where I regularly entered judo competitions and was runner-up in the All-Japan High School Championships. At the age of 17, shortly after I gained my second degree black belt, I watched a demonstration given by two members of the Takushoku University Karate Club in Tokyo. I was won over. Aside from any academic merits, Takushoku University was well known for its strong martial arts, particularly its tough

Karate Masters

"After two years of training, I passed my shodan examination, and then two years later, at age 21, I was made captain of the karate club. It was during my university training that I received instruction from the great master, Funakoshi Gichin."

karate team, and this was my main reason for enrolling at the university.

After two years of training, I passed my *shodan* examination, and then two years later, at age 21, I was made captain of the karate club. It was during my university training that I received instruction from the great Master, Funakoshi Gichin. Master Funakoshi was very old when I met him, but one thing that I still recall is that once he put the gi on, his whole attitude and body movement changed immediately. It was like he received some kind of external energy by wearing the karate *gi*. The transformation in his physical movements was amazing.

After graduating in 1957 with a degree in Commerce, I was invited to take the special instructor's course at JKA headquarters. I accepted, and for the next three years, studied long and hard on a daily basis under Masatoshi Nakayama, the chief instructor of the JKA, and Hidetaka Nishiyama, a leading senior. I regularly entered various tournaments and achieved several victories, including the East University Karate Championships. Then, in 1961, I won third place in the *kumite* division of the JKA All-Japan Championships and also finished high in the *kata* event. The following year I repeated my kata placing and moved another step up in the kumite by finishing second—losing to Hiroshi Shirai, a fellow JKA instructor. Then in 1963, after another year's hard preparation, I turned the tables on Shirai in the kumite finals and became the All-Japan Champion, and again placed as a kata finalist.

Q: When did you begin to travel abroad to teach?
A: Up until my 1963 triumph, I had only taught locally at the Tokyo Art College and a military university. Among the spectators at that year's championships was President Sukarno of Indonesia, and he negotiated for my services. Together with Master Nakayama, I spent four months in Indonesia teaching his personal bodyguards and also at various police and military establishments. Following the JKA's policy of sending its best instructors out from Japan to spread shotokan karate, I began my worldwide travels that were to culminate in my settling in Great Britain as the shotokan chief instructor.

Enoeda

Q: Who gave you the nickname "The Tiger"?
A: Nakayama Sensei watched one of my fights, and he mentioned that I fought like a tiger. So, after that moment, everybody started to use the term when referring to me and my attitude in *kumite*.

Q: Did you include the makiwara in your training sessions?
A: Of course! In those days, the training was very intense. Every morning I would do 500 punches on the makiwara. It was not something I did to impress anyone. It was simply a single-minded attitude necessary to develop power and *kime* in my techniques.

Q: You always emphasize the importance of kata in the art of karate. Why?
A: The importance attached to kata makes it one of the most recognizable features in all of martial arts. Kata was the creation of the most important teachers of each style of karate in the past. They formalized their knowledge and made a set of practical techniques to pass to their students. They systematized this huge amount of knowledge in forms that have been preserved throughout the years. They recorded for posterity the physical movements that came as a result of them risking their lives in actual contests.

When studying kata, we can see a model for a particular method of certain techniques. There is a formalized way of doing things but kata also offers freedom of expression. Not only the techniques of the creator, but also the acquisition of the right state of mind, which is called *kokoro*. Kata must be memorized, incorporated into one's own being and then mastered to perfection. It is essential to break into areas of techniques that are original. Kata training offers a way of understanding other aspects of human existence, that's why is so important not to study the form from a strictly structural point of view. All traditional kata are greatly respected in the martial arts, and you can search your entire life to find the deeper meanings of a particular form. Moreover, the beauty of refinement (*kohga*) and the elegant simplicity (*sabi*) are also important kata training elements.

"Kata must be memorized, incorporated into one's own being and then mastered to perfection. It is essential to break into areas of techniques that are original. Kata training offers a way of understanding other aspects of human existence; that's why is so important not to study the form from a strictly structural point of view."

Karate Masters

"Bunkai is the practical application of the kata. It is very important that the student understands the application of the technique. Many times students do not understand kata because they cannot see the meaning of the movement they are doing. Bunkai shows them the purpose."

If we simply focus on training the external movements (*waza*), without also analyzing the state of mind behind the form, it will be impossible to practice the true art of karate-do. Kata has dignity in its severity and is extreme in its beauty. Simply said, kata is physical movements by each individual. Due to this fact, it is possible to continue to train for the acquisition of technique and mind even when we are old. People tend to be really attracted to sparring, but a true karate-ka must stop and look very careful about the role kata plays in the art.

Q: What is your personal approach to kata?
A: When doing kata you must live the form. Each kata must be done full-out. If done correctly, the karate-ka will reach his physical limits and not be able to continue. He'll be near his end. You shouldn't endlessly repeat a kata. To do so is to show that you are not living the kata. Only on certain occasions will you repeat a kata a number of times—and that is for mental and spiritual purposes—to force you to go beyond the body, the mind and the art. You have to live the kata. Use all your power as if in life or death. This is something that sport karate does not have. This is why kata is important. The body is trained, the mind is trained and the understanding of the technique deepens.

Q: What about *bunkai*?
A: Bunkai is the practical application of the kata. It is very important that the student understands the application of the technique. Many times students do not understand kata because they cannot see the meaning of the movement they are doing. They see slow, broad movements and tend to think that kata has no purpose. Bunkai shows them the purpose. As the student advances in his study, his understanding of the techniques becomes deeper and more profound. Each technique improves his precision and kime. Kata helps karate-ka to understand the many uses of the techniques and how to apply them. Without kata training, one is not following the way of the martial arts. Profound technique is one of the main benefits of kata training. Other important facets are the artistic aspects and the individual self-expression.

Q: Do you have a favorite kata?
A: Yes. My favorite kata is *jitte*. Sensei Nakayama suggested that I should practice this kata. It translates as "10 hands" and is the kata I enjoy the most. It is heavier and more solid that some other forms derived from the *shorei* style of Okinawa. The name means that one who is proficient in this kata can fight with the strength of ten men.

Q: How does sport sparring relate to self-defense?
A: Sport sparring is not self-defense and has very little to do with it. Sparring is a test of ability, but ability of a different kind.

"A good karate-do student would never show off—and even in combat was expected to not use the art unless completely necessary. Winning competitions is not the true meaning karate—it is not enough just to do the techniques correctly. Those whose execute the techniques without true heart cannot call themselves true karate-ka."

It is in kata again, in which we can find the answer. The kata keeps the meaning of the technique deep. It makes one fresh to respond. Knowledge of the art increases because self-defense is found in kata. Without kata training, the body cannot properly understand the technique. There will be no calm and no confidence. With kata training, one is capable at all times—and calm and confident of his ability. With the self-assurance gained from kata, there is little need to ever use karate for self-defense.

Q: Is karate-do a composition of many different elements?
A: A long time ago, karate-do was an art practiced by a select few under the founder of a particular style. In those days, the art had a great deal of morality and dignity. A good karate-do student would never show off—and even in combat was expected to not use the art unless completely necessary. Of course, things have changed today, but the essence and heart of the art should still be the same. Too many people today tend to train simply for competition. Winning competitions is not the true meaning of karate—it is not enough just to do the techniques correctly. Those whose execute the techniques without true heart cannot call themselves true karate-ka. Karate-do is many things at once. It is budo. It is being fit and calm. It develops good character and confidence. It is crisp and powerful physical movements. It can be a sport and at the same time be a complete self-defense

Karate Masters

"If you train hard and consistently, one day you are going to come face-to-face with what is called a 'brick wall.' Only by destroying this obstacle will you succeed. Only then can you reach a higher level of technical mastery. Unfortunately, many reach this wall and do not succeed in breaking through."

method. Karate competition has become increasingly popular, and gradually the true heart of karate has almost been forgotten. Modern karate-ka must think about the true root of the art and try to understand the essence of it deeply. Without this deep understanding, it will be difficult for future generations to know what the real art is about.

Q: Why do so many students quit karate after a few years of practice?
A: If you train hard and consistently, one day you are going to come face-to-face with what is called a "brick wall." This stage is also known as "hitting the wall," or reaching a "plateau." In order to progress and follow real karate-do, you must be able to break through the wall—one step at a time and brick by brick. Only by destroying this obstacle will you succeed. Only then can you reach a higher level of technical mastery. Unfortunately, many reach this wall and do not succeed in breaking through. Thus, they limit themselves. This not only happens in the martial arts, but in many other aspects of life. After you have succeeded in conquering your "brick wall" in any field, you will have a feeling of true achievement. This is because you met a challenge and broke out of a difficult period. This will build confidence and bring about great results. This is when karate-do becomes a practical way of life and not merely a physical exercise.

Q: Is sport competition bad for karate?
A: Sport karate is a definite aspect of karate-do. Competition is not bad. It is good for the spirit. It is specifically good for the spirit when the proper etiquette—win or lose—is present. Sport karate is also a demanding test of one's individual ability. It is also a good test of the mind and one's control of power. And if etiquette and sportsmanship is present, it is always good for the spirit.

Q: Are there any drawbacks?
A: There are some. Technique, because of the tournament training, can become weak. The practitioner's techniques can become shallow because certain moves work best in sport karate. This means that one can devote all his time to practicing these techniques. This works against the true spirit of karate and all martial arts. There are many techniques in karate-do. In budo karate-do, not sport karate, one must know and develop all these techniques—not just two or three. The way to avoid this is intensive kata training. This is how I trained in my youth in Japan. Before competition we would train kata, kata and more kata. Only at the end of the session would there be one-step sparring. Don't focus excessively on sparring before a tournament; train kata. Then, immediately before the tournament, move to one-step kumite, and then, just a few days before the tournament day, concentrate on free-sparring. You'll be amazed by the results—especially when you win the kata division the same day!

Q: How much contact should be allowed in sport competition?
A: The important concept here is control. Good karate-ka should have good control, so there is no need for excessive contact. If there is too much contact, then there is a chance of injury if the technique is delivered with power. It is necessary to develop good control so that you can control the amount of body contact when you reach the target. The problem occurs when the competing karate-ka doesn't have control, due to insufficient training at the dojo. Then, as a referee, you have to deal with the problem in the competition. What the teachers should do is train students correctly and don't allow them to compete until they have the proper skill to control their punches and kicks.

Q: How is kata related to budo?
A: True budo is many things. Sport karate is OK, but you must practice kata as well. Kata training is very necessary for taking part in sport karate. This keeps techniques fresh, and it is also important because it develops the body properly. It is necessary to keep fit for the art. Kata teaches how each technique is to be performed in terms of body movements. It conditions the body and the mind. With kata training you reach a higher level of fitness. All you techniques are sharp and fresh. You have been drilling and exercising the body, extending your knowledge of tactics, techniques and applications. This keeps one fresh and also insures that all the techniques will have the right amount of power and precision.

Karate Masters

Q: What do you look for when refereeing a sport karate match?
A: I must always see a clean and powerful technique to award a point. This is the danger in practicing only sport karate. Punches end up looking weak and without proper *kime*.

Q: Should a fighter compromise karate-do principles in order to win?
A: In every karate match, victory is of prime importance; however, since a karate match is based on budo, you cannot use any means to defeat your opponent. In a karate match, you must fight strictly under the true spirit of budo and play fair in order to be victorious. This is the right way to win.

Appropriate rules for karate match play are currently being developed, in hopes of karate being accepted as an Olympic sport. A great amount of research and study has been done for this. The ideals of rules development are that mind, body and *waza* will be naturally perfected and combined for all styles—and consequently the karate match itself will be improved. A karate match is not only a place for testing your daily training, but also the culmination of numerous fights and experiences that have helped each practitioner progress in the art of karate-do— this is the true essence of a karate match.

Taking part in a match is a big responsibility as well as a great opportunity for both yourself as an individual and the organization to which you belong. In your journey through life, it is important to study and learn how to seize an opportunity and gain victory by displaying your own powerful ability. Composure, courage, sharpness, precision and courtesy must all be present in your waza when you move your entire body—not merely your hands and feet. In an instant every part of you moves in unison.

In order to win the match it is of great value to know your opponent and to know yourself. If your opponent is unknown to you, you should get to know him before your fight—paying attention to his strong points and favorite techniques. Then, after accumulating vast experience in the course of many matches, you will become very sharp in your observations and be able to recognize your opponent's strong and weak points at first sight.

When the time comes to fight, you must not think in terms of simply winning, but you should feel delighted that you have attained your long-cherished chance to compete. This will help you to focus and to defeat fear. When you have vanquished your own fear, then you will be ready to fight against your opponent—whoever he may be.

When you stand face-to-face with your opponent, the first thing you want is to make him feel that your energy will overwhelm him. The second thing is not to miss any of his movements—even slight ones—and at the same time, act as if you were engulfing the opponent's whole body with the inside of your hands and feet. Even if your opponent is a strong and experienced practitioner, you must not fear him. By the same token, if your opponent is weak and inexperienced, you must not underestimate him. Always fight every match with your maximum power.

When you attack, do not forget to protect yourself with defensive maneuvers, but just remember that defense alone won't win the fight. Attack with the right posture, correct spirit and precise techniques. Strive to be the one who always takes the initiative. If you act before your opponent moves, you will go on to victory. This is, I think, the most important point of all.

Q: What do you think about your own journey in karate-do?
A: I come from a very traditional background and karate is part of my nature. It affects the way I look at things and how I lead my life. Karate taught me discipline, and with discipline a person can continue karate practice for many years. My objective was and still is, to train everyday, regardless of the weather or the condition I'm in. I never neglect my daily training. I haven't missed a day's training since a very young age. I believe my everyday effort, plus my judo and kendo practice when I was very young, helped to develop my mental and physical strength. This strength as a human being has helped me to achieve my goals throughout my life.

All practitioners should remember to train in true budo karate-do. Do sport karate if you like, but always focus your mind and body on the perfection of yourself as a human being. This is true karate-do. And no matter where your interests lead you, remember that kata is the vehicle that will allow you to reach a true understanding of real karate. O

"In budo karate-do, not sport karate, one must know and develop all these techniques—not just two or three. The way to avoid this is intensive kata training. Don't focus excessively on sparring before a tournament; train kata. You'll be amazed by the results—especially when you win the kata division the same day!"

Randall Hassell

No Finish Line

RANDALL HASSELL IS A MEMBER OF THE FIRST GENERATION OF AMERICANS TO PIONEER SHOTOKAN KARATE AND, ALONG WITH SENSEI RAY DALKE, SENSEI LESLIE SAFAR, SENSEI DICK GOULD, AND THE LATE A.R. ALLEN, WAS AN ORIGINAL FOUNDER OF THE AMERICAN JKA KARATE ASSOCIATION. HE IS A WORLD-RENOWNED AUTHOR AND AUTHORITY ON SHOTOKAN KARATE. HE HAS WRITTEN, EDITED, OR SIGNIFICANTLY CONTRIBUTED TO 28 BOOKS ON KARATE, AND HAS PUBLISHED MORE THAN 100 MAGAZINE ARTICLES. HIS WORK OFTEN FOCUSES ON THE HISTORY AND UNDERLYING PHILOSOPHY OF KARATE-DO AS A WAY OF LIFE.

AS A TEACHER, SENSEI HASSELL IS KNOWN FOR CONCENTRATING ON THE FUNDAMENTAL PRINCIPLES OF KARATE AND FOR THE APPLICATION OF KATA TECHNIQUES AND PRINCIPLES TO SELF-DEFENSE AND KUMITE. ADDITIONALLY, FOR THE PAST TWO DECADES, HE HAS FOCUSED ON INSTRUCTOR TRAINING AND HAS DEVELOPED A HIGHLY SUCCESSFUL, NATIONWIDE INSTRUCTOR TRAINING AND BLACK BELT DEVELOPMENT PROGRAM FOR HIS ORGANIZATION, THE AMERICAN SHOTOKAN KARATE ALLIANCE (ASKA). IN 2001, HE WAS INSTRUMENTAL IN FOUNDING AN INTERNATIONAL, PROFESSIONAL SOCIETY OF SHOTOKAN TEACHERS, THE INTERNATIONAL KARATE SOCIETY. CURRENTLY, HE IS CHIEF INSTRUCTOR OF THE AMERICAN SHOTOKAN KARATE ALLIANCE AND PRESIDENT OF DAMASHI PUBLICATIONS, A BOOK PUBLISHING AND VIDEO PRODUCTION COMPANY IN ST. LOUIS, MISSOURI.

Q: What got you interested in the art of karate-do?
A: When I was 11 years old, my mother would take me to a big department store and leave me in the book department while she shopped. There I found the book, "*Karate: The Art of Empty-hand Fighting*," by Hidetaka Nishiyama and Richard Brown. It intrigued me from the instant I saw it. I think, in retrospect, that the book appealed to me so much because it said that anybody could do karate, and I sure wanted to do what I saw those men in the pictures doing. I hadn't had much success in other sports because of my eyes. I was born with eyes that did not focus together, so I had no depth perception at all. This made it very difficult for me to participate in sports because I couldn't tell, for example, how far away a ball was when I was trying to

Karate Masters

"After more than 40 years, I have so many good memories of so many fine sensei that I couldn't begin to relate all of them here. It would take a whole book to do that, which I might write one of these days."

catch it. As a result, I was always getting hurt. When my family saw my interest in karate, they bought me the book, and I started studying from it in 1960.

It is interesting because initially, I had no regular teachers. There were only two karate dojo in St. Louis at that time, and one of them was affiliated with Matsubayashi shorin-ryu. My friends and I would go to that school as often as we could, but we couldn't afford to join. Still, the instructors there treated us very nicely and invited us to attend whenever a visiting instructor was coming in, and they invited us to their tournaments. So we got to train with numerous people from goju-ryu, shorin-ryu and even taekwondo. My primary teachers over the ensuing years, though, once I was able to make contact with Nishiyama Sensei's new AAKF, were Hidetaka Nishiyama, Takayuki Mikami when he was stationed in Kansas City, and beginning in 1965, Shojiro Sugiyama of Chicago. But it was very difficult to obtain regular instruction, so my friends and I self-trained every single day, year after year. It was like an obsession with me, and since the age of 12, my life has been structured around karate.

From 1966 on, we were able to bring many different instructors to St. Louis for two- or three-day clinics. Throughout the 1970s, Nishiyama Sensei came to teach and conduct grading at least twice a year, and we also learned from Senseis Miyata, Okazaki, Mikami, Koyama and others. I traveled to seminars all over the country, too, where I eventually met and trained under virtually every JKA international instructor. In recent years, I have hosted numerous clinics with the late Osamu Ozawa, Ray Dalke and Stan Schmidt. Sensei Schmidt, in particular, has been very instrumental in my personal development.

After more than 40 years, I have so many good memories of so many fine sensei that I couldn't begin to relate all of them here. It would take a whole book to do that, which I might write one of these days. Overall, though, my memories of my teachers are extremely positive.

Q: Do you think going to Japan to train is highly necessary?

A: Perhaps I am biased because I personally never trained in Japan; but no, I wouldn't characterize training in Japan as "highly necessary." Many of my friends, seniors, and students have trained there, though, and they have given me great insights into the Japanese training experience. From what they tell me, I would say that training in Japan is highly desirable but not highly necessary. Some of the most extraordinary karateka I have met have never trained there.

Q: How do Westerners respond to traditional Japanese training?

A: It depends on what you mean by "traditional" and to what time period you are referring. When I started training in 1960, a lot of what we now call "traditional" was actually just brutal. Training was often a macho thing in some dojo then, and people routinely got teeth knocked out, broken bones and worse. I don't call that "traditional," though. I call it *stupid*. But society was different then, so a certain amount of *gung-ho* brutality was accepted as part of the training. Thankfully, people in general won't accept that kind of training today, and I think that shows progress. It was not necessary, and it drove a lot of people away from karate. To be very clear on this, though, many people today think of that period as brutal Japanese instructors beating up on Americans. That was not the case. The instructors certainly set the tone for the training, but it was gung-ho Westerners, in my opinion, who always pushed the envelope and competed harder and harder against each other. The instructors did not, by and large, willfully injure their students. The students did it to each other.

"When I started training in 1960, a lot of what we now call "traditional" was actually just brutal. Training was often a macho thing in some dojo then, and people routinely got teeth knocked out, broken bones and worse. I don't call that "traditional," though. I call it stupid."

Karate Masters

"Free-fighting looks a lot more like boxing, in terms of distancing and application, than it did when I first learned it, but that's a natural progression to make the sport aspect of karate more appealing to the spectators. Fundamental techniques, though, have not changed much at all."

Q: What is your perception of changes in the art throughout the years?
A: It has become a more accessible art for a broader spectrum of society. Good principles of fitness and physical training are now apparent in almost all shotokan dojo, and people of all ages and both sexes can now benefit immeasurably from karate training, which was not the case when I first started. It is a much safer art to practice than it was in 1960, primarily because of the incorporation of scientific principles of physical education.

Technically, the changes have been very few and far between. I have seen changes in performance of various kata, and it seems to me that, for the most part, these changes have been implemented to make the kata more appealing to competition judges. That's not true in every case, but in many. Free-fighting looks a lot more like boxing, in terms of distancing and application, than it did when I first learned it, but that's a natural progression to make the sport aspect of karate more appealing to the spectators. It used to be that free-fighting was much slower and much more serious with the intention of theoretically killing the opponent. Because of that, the contestants stood farther apart and moved less, waiting for that one, split-second chance to deliver a decisive blow. Of course, this made it extremely boring to the untrained eye, which is why it has evolved the way it has. Fundamental techniques, though, have not changed much at all. Overall, I would say that there have been major improvements in the art, rather than major changes.

Q: Do you think it is necessary to engage in free-fighting to achieve good fighting skills in the street?
A: I think it is important in terms of timing, distancing and experience, but not absolutely necessary. There are many styles of karate that do not engage in free-fighting, and they have produced a number of people that I would consider to be very formidable fighting machines in the street.

Q: How important is understanding Zen to fully absorb the meaning and essence of budo and karate-do in particular?
A: I think it is beneficial for a person to have an intellectual understanding of what Zen is about, to better understand the nature of Japanese martial arts in general, but I don't think that practicing Zen is necessary for success in karate. Studying the history and development of Zen and how it has influenced Japanese martial arts will give the student a better understanding of how his art developed and why certain things are done in certain ways, but it is not necessary to go farther than that.

Q: When teaching karate, what is the most important: self-defense, sport or tradition?
A: To me, they are all the same. I don't teach "self-defense karate," or "sport karate" or even "traditional karate." I just practice and teach shotokan karate, and all of those things are part of it. Daily purposeful training will sharpen all of those things, naturally. Your question is phrased in a way that makes each of those elements sound like a different pie. As I see it, karate-do itself is the pie, and those things are slices within it.

My advice for the beginner is to find a good teacher and to stick with that teacher. Don't be distracted by others' claims of superiority, and don't focus on your teacher's personality. Focus on what the teacher has to teach you, and try to learn it every day. Also, try to see your karate training as a pleasant respite from the problems of everyday life. Being challenged by the art is fine; but if it becomes a chore, it's probably not worth pursuing.

I understand that keeping the motivation going throughout the years is hard, but any dedicated practitioner needs to find his own way to keep training. Karate has been the focus of my life since I was a child, so I don't really think in terms of "motivation." It simply is what I do—and I enjoy it. It has become a natural part of my everyday life, like brushing my teeth and combing my hair. It doesn't require any special motivation.

"My advice for the beginner is to find a good teacher and to stick with that teacher. Don't be distracted by others' claims of superiority, and don't focus on your teacher's personality. Focus on what the teacher has to teach you, and try to learn it every day. Being challenged by the art is fine; but if it becomes a chore, it's probably not worth pursuing."

Karate Masters

"I have practiced shotokan karate for more than 40 years, and I am still challenged by it every day. I have never felt a need to study another style and cannot imagine that I would have the time. Of course, I have studied various aspects of other styles of karate, and have gained a better understanding of them as a result, but to actually enroll in a dojo to seriously study another style is beyond me."

The student needs consistency of practice and an unwavering dedication to learning what the sensei is trying to teach.

Q: What is your perception of full-contact karate and kickboxing ?
A: I think it's wonderful for people who want to do it and for people who like to watch it. I think the point has been made pretty clearly that full-contact and kickboxing have nothing to do with budo or the development of the human self that we strive for in karate-do. But that doesn't mean there's anything wrong with them—certainly not. They are sports in which the youngest, fastest and strongest win, and that's fine. That is not the case with karate-do, though, which is an art in which we keep trying to develop physically, mentally and emotionally until the day we die. I think most people understand the difference between sport and art.

Q: Do you think that the West has caught up with Japanese quality standards?
A: Absolutely, but it is more than just "catching up," in my opinion. I agree with my friend, the late Osamu Ozawa, who said that today there is absolutely no difference, technically, between Japanese and Western practitioners. What he predicted would happen next, though, is that each country or each area of the world will develop its own karate, just as the Okinawans did and the Japanese did again when they imported karate from Okinawa. I think he was right about this, and I don't think it's necessarily a bad thing, as long as the essence of karate as a martial art is not lost.

Q: What's your opinion about mixing karate styles?
A: I have practiced shotokan karate for more than 40 years, and I am still challenged by it every day. I have never felt a need to study another style and cannot imagine that I would have the time. Of course, I have studied various aspects of other styles of karate, and have gained a better understanding of

them as a result, but to actually enroll in a dojo to seriously study another style is beyond me. I am very happy with the effectiveness of shotokan karate.

Q: Modern karate seems to be moving away from the bunkai in kata practice. Do you think understanding bunkai is necessary to learning kata and karate-do in general?
A: I think that understanding bunkai is very important to an understanding of kata. However, I disagree with the statement that modern karate is moving away from bunkai. Bunkai simply means "analysis," and it has always been a part of karate training, both inside the JKA and outside. Mr. Nishiyama's *International Traditional Karate Federation,* for example, has two complete kata divisions that require powerful demonstrations of bunkai. I'm not a member of that organization, so I can't speak with authority about their competition, but that's hardly moving away from bunkai. I don't believe I was ever taught a kata without being taught the basic meaning of its techniques. Further, I was always taught to think about the movements of the kata and to try to devise applications of them in as many ways as possible. I have always taught this way, too. I teach that applications of kata movements are limited only by the limits of one's imagination.

"I was taught, and I always teach, that the techniques of shotokan karate should be practiced within the framework of 'ikken hisatsu,' which means, 'one-punch death blow.' That is, every movement hinges on life and death, and practicing the basics and kata are what prepare you for that eventuality."

It seems to me that what has happened recently is that bunkai has become a faddish way of re-arranging karate training to make it more appealing as a self-defense system. If one subscribes to the notion that shotokan karate is not an effective form of self-defense using only punches, blocks, kicks and strikes, then this idea makes sense. I personally do not subscribe to that notion at all. I was taught, and I always teach, that the techniques of shotokan karate should be practiced within the framework of *"ikken-hisatsu,"* which means, "one-punch death blow." That is, every movement hinges on life and death, and practicing the basics and kata are what prepare you for that eventuality. Rather than relying on intricate appli-

Karate Masters

"Practicing the kata as art forms that symbolize and develop the fundamental principles that prepare the individual for any eventuality, is the most productive way to practice them. Breaking them down and applying each technique in as many ways as possible is physically and intellectually stimulating."

cations of each technique in the kata—which may or may not prepare you for a fight—the concept of *ikken-hisatsu* teaches you to develop a punch and kick so strong that they cannot be blocked and a block so strong that it cannot be penetrated.

In my view, practicing the kata as art form that symbolizes and develops the fundamental principles that prepare the individual for any eventuality is the most productive way to practice them. Breaking them down and applying each technique in as many ways as possible is physically and intellectually stimulating. But when we do this in my dojo, I tell the students that no matter how many ways you practice a single technique, a real attack will always come in a way that will not be covered by individual practiced responses. Real attacks are thwarted by mastery of the core principles of awareness, timing, distancing, conditioned reflexes, strong technique and stable emotions under attack, among other things. Kata are excellent for developing these things.

In my early days of training, we often practiced responses to specific attacks, such as grabbing, choking, shoving, tackling, arm twisting, headlocks, and so on. We learned how to defend ourselves against such things using techniques from the kata. This, as I understand it, is what some teachers are emphasizing again now. I applaud that, because it is a move away from an emphasis on competition and toward an emphasis on self-defense—and I think that's good. But I worry that some will emphasize this bunkai training over actual practice of the kata itself, and I think that's bad. A balance between the two is very important.

I say this because trends often become fads, and fads often lead away from the original intention of the trend, and things get confused. The interest in *kyusho*—vital points—in recent years is illustrative of this. From my very first day of karate training, I was taught that vital points on the human body

"I was taught to attack areas of the body where nerves were exposed, and particularly nerves that crossed bones. I was also taught how to generate shock against arteries, such as the carotid artery on the side of the neck. My teachers were very specific about where these points were and how to attack them."

were the targets of karate techniques—both in blocking and counter-attacking. Aside from the obvious points such as eyes, solar plexus, testicles and the like, I was taught to attack areas of the body where nerves were exposed, and particularly nerves that crossed bones. I was also taught how to generate shock against arteries, such as the carotid artery on the side of the neck. My teachers were very specific about where these points were and how to attack them.

So it came as somewhat of a surprise to me to read in martial arts magazines in the 1990s that *kyusho* was a "lost art" and was being "rediscovered." As the trend progressed to a fad, it got intertwined with the old idea of vital points lying on energy meridians in the body and that energy flow could be interrupted with taps to specific points. This, of course, led to the old idea of harnessing *ki* and using it as a special force against opponents. A further extension of this was that an opponent's ki could be intercepted and

Karate Masters

"I believe that shotokan karate-do is a very valuable and beneficial activity for human beings to engage in, so I practice it. I also believe that it is worth passing on to others, so I teach it. It obviously is not for everybody, but it is just right for me."

used against him. The final stage of this trend/fad was the declaration that any of us old-timers who weren't teaching this way had learned inferior karate and just didn't know what we were doing.

The facts of the matter, though, was that 1) there was absolutely nothing new about any of this "rediscovery," and 2) the majority of people in my generation who were not teaching that way simply did not believe in the foundational premises of the "new" *kyusho*—ki malleability, energy meridians and so on. So what began as a good trend ended up expending its energy on secondary arguments rather than purely on the study of vital points. I hope this doesn't happen to the current trend of *bunkai*-based kata study, but I'm pretty sure that it will. It's the nature of trends and fads. It would be as bad for the trend as those who say that only a specific application is acceptable for a particular kata technique. That notion is utterly ridiculous.

Q: What is the philosophical basis for your karate training?
A: It's rather simple, really. I believe that shotokan karate-do is a very valuable and beneficial activity for human beings to engage in, so I practice it. I also believe that it is worth passing on to others, so I teach it. It obviously is not for everybody, but it is just right for me.

I see karate-do as an art of virtuous people and a tool that people can use to become better human beings—physically, mentally and emotionally. It's important to note that I use the word, "tool," because I don't believe that karate training, in and of itself, can make people more virtuous or improve their character. On the contrary, I see it as a tool that virtuous people can use for those purposes. Karate training won't guarantee, for example, that kids who study it will get better grades in school. But it can be a very useful tool to encourage kids to concentrate and be more self-disciplined. Sometimes good grades follow from that. I don't think that teaching karate to a criminal will make that person a model citizen, but I do believe that if that criminal sincerely wants to change, karate-do can be of great benefit in helping them focus on change, responsibility and disciplined thinking.

"Karate training won't guarantee, for example, that kids who study it will get better grades in school. But it can be a very useful tool to encourage kids to concentrate and be more self-disciplined. Sometimes good grades follow from that."

Q: Do you have a particularly memorable karate experience that has remained with you as an inspiration for your training?
A: I remember exactly when I decided that I was going to abandon other martial arts and karate styles and concentrate on shotokan. It was in the mid-1960s, and I witnessed a demonstration by Taiji Kase, Keinosuke Enoeda, Hirokazu Kanazawa and Hiroshi Shirai. Those men gave the most astounding demonstration of advanced karate that I had ever seen, and by the time Kanazawa had finished demonstrating the kata, *unsu*, at the end of the demonstration, I was hooked. More than anything else in my life, I wanted to be able to do what those great men had just done. In my mind's eye, I still can't do it the way they did it, and that will challenge me for the rest of my life.

Q: How do you think a practitioner can increase his understanding of the spiritual aspects of karate?
A: I prefer to use the word, "spiritful," rather than "spiritual," because I don't believe there is anything inherently spiritual about karate-do. The spirit resides inside the human being, and disciplined training can polish and improve that spirit according to the individual's personal beliefs. The staunchest atheists and the most devoted ministers can benefit equally from karate-do.

Q: How much training should a senior karate-ka be doing to improve in his art?
A: As much as possible. But "possible" varies greatly from person to person, and individual lifestyles really dictate how much time a person can spend practicing. Also, training comes in many forms. Teaching is a form of training, and after a person has been training for many years, the simple act of walking becomes training, too, because everything the human body does can be seen through the filter of karate training and thought of in terms of body mechanics, posture awareness, and so on.

Q: Is there anything lacking in the way karate is taught today compared with the way it was taught in your day?
A: I can only speak for shotokan karate, but I would say no, nothing is lacking. In fact, the training today is much better than when I started. Understanding of body mechanics is better, physical conditioning is better, and karate athletes are much more sophisticated in their movements, coordination and agility. I know some of us old-timers rue the loss of "spirit training," which supposedly forged an indomitable spirit, but I don't think that has really been lost. I think that fewer people seek to find it in modern society, and that makes it seem like it's been lost. But I see extraordinary young karate-ka all over the world dedicating themselves to forging strong spirits, so I'm not worried.

Q: What advice would you give to students on the question of supplementary training?
A: I teach my own students that the best way to improve an individual technique is to practice that technique itself. There is nothing at all wrong with supplementary training for strength and conditioning. In fact, it is very beneficial to the body. But I always stress to practice the karate techniques more than anything else.

Q: Why do many students start falling away after two or three years of training?

A: My experience has been that many students quit shortly after starting training because the training is not what they expected it to be, and they don't like it. Another fallout occurs around brown belt level—I think because the black belt looks so far away. Those students consciously or unconsciously decide that they don't want to put in the extra effort to get there. A major reason people fall away, though, is that at the *shodan* (first-degree black belt) level, they really have to come to grips with the fact that karate training requires a lot of time, effort and dedication. It is a never-ending process, and that sometimes seems like too large an obstacle to overcome. Really, though, I think that the majority of people who quit just have other things going on in their lives and don't feel that they can devote enough time to training to do it the way they want.

Q: Have you felt fear in your training?

A: Yes, many times, and I think fear is sometimes a good thing. Facing fear is a valuable tool in developing stable emotions under attack. If we never feel fear in the dojo, how will we know how to respond to it in a life-and-death situation? What we learn in the dojo is that the violence there is controlled, and although we are sometimes fearful, we are going to come out of it OK on the other side. We also learn how our systems respond to fear, and we can learn to adjust our systems to

"Facing fear is a valuable tool in developing stable emotions under attack. If we never feel fear in the dojo, how will we know how to respond to it in a life-and-death situation? What we learn in the dojo is that the violence there is controlled, and although we are sometimes fearful, we are going to come out of it OK on the other side."

Karate Masters

"Cling to your roots, no matter what style you practice, and work together with your classmates and friends to create a good atmosphere in your dojo. I believe that people who train together, sweat together, experience fear together and experience achievement together will be stronger people than those who do not."

that. I still feel some fear when I face some of my seniors, or perhaps "trepidation" would be a better word. I am not afraid that they will hurt me, but I'm afraid that I will get hurt if I don't concentrate properly and move correctly. These are people with an extraordinary amount of power, and it is not easy to go toe-to-toe with them—even in a controlled atmosphere—without experiencing some butterflies. My job is to become more skillful and, therefore, less vulnerable to injury. I teach my students this, also. Become more skillful to conquer fear.

Q: Do you have any general advice you would care to pass on to the karate-ka?
A: Cling to your roots, no matter what style you practice, and work together with your classmates and friends to create a good atmosphere in your dojo. I believe that people who train together, sweat together, experience fear together and experience achievement together will be stronger people than those who do not. Strong, well-adjusted people will make society better for all of us, now and in the future. In other words, please use your training today to create a better tomorrow.

Q: What are your thoughts on the future of karate-do and your personal plans for the years to come?
A: First, I believe that any art changes day by day as people continue to practice it. This is natural and not a bad thing at all, as long as the essence of the art is not lost in transition.

Second, I believe that any great movement must go through the process of thesis, antithesis and synthesis. Using my own experience as an original JKA karate-ka in the 1960s, I believe that I, and my seniors and peers, were part of the great thesis of shotokan karate for America. In the beginning, we were all together and all going in the same direction. We thought we had a perfect karate world. As time went by, though, we started to drift apart. First we left the Japanese organizations, and then we left each other and went in our own directions. This was the antithesis of what we originally thought we had. We developed our own organizations and pretty much ignored each other. Now, in the new millennium, and after attaining mature ages, we have started to come back together again.

We are not starting any new organization, or anything even resembling that, but we have gotten together and decided to work together for the benefit of shotokan karate-do. We have agreed to freely and mutually recognize and support each other's efforts. In addition to any alliances we have with anybody else, we have come back together personally. We mutually recognize each other's rankings and technical qualifications, and we get together as a group to conduct clinics and camps.

This, I believe, is the first step toward synthesis in the JKA shotokan structure among American pioneers of the art. As time goes by, I suspect that others will join us in this movement toward synthesis. My personal energies are being spent on this, on teaching my own students in my own dojo, and on developing the next generation of shotokan instructors in the U.S. Beyond the U.S. borders, many top-level shotokan instructors worldwide are in the process of coming together in the same way in a professional society—the International Karate Society. We are starting to share with each other on an international basis, and we are mutually recognizing each other's efforts, rankings and qualifications. In time, we plan for the society to publish an Internet journal where we can share our knowledge, experience and ideas with the rest of the world.

Finally, I believe that karate will continue grow and change, and that there will still be many political wars before the dust settles—if it ever does. I believe that the antidote for this is for people to communicate with each other, train together, sweat together and keep their thoughts focused on being the best they can be in their art, regardless of style. Politics and organizations come and go, but karate training is for a lifetime, and that's where we should put our energies. O

Yashunari Ishimi

The Internal Serenity

THE PRECISION OF HIS MOVEMENTS IS OUTSTANDING. RHYTHM, POWER AND TIMING SYNCHRONIZED PERFECTLY IN THE FORM OF A HUMAN BODY. ISHIMI SENSEI HAS DEVOTED HIMSELF TO DISCOVER NEW LEVELS OF UNDERSTANDING IN KARATE SINCE HIS FIRST DAYS OF TRAINING. A DISTINCTLY UNORTHODOX PERSON IN SOME RESPECTS, THIS *SHITO-RYU* EXPONENT HAS LEFT HIS MARK FOR GENERATIONS TO COME. EXTREMELY POLITE AND FRIENDLY, HE WALKS WITH THE POSTURE AND BEARING OF A WELL TRAINED BUT RELAXED MILITARY MAN. DESPITE HIS SUPERLATIVE EMPTY-HAND TECHNIQUES, HE SHUNS THE TITLES OF MASTER AND TRIES TO STAY AT THE LEVEL OF A STUDENT. HE ALSO CRITICIZES THOSE WHO PLACE SUCH A STRONG EMPHASIS ON TITLES AND CERTIFICATES. AN ADVOCATE OF INTERNAL SERENITY, ISHIMI SENSEI REMINDS US THAT PHYSICAL ACTION IS MASTERED BY THE MIND AND THE FORM IS THE OUTWARD REFLECTION OF INNER QUIETNESS. "THE ART STEMS FROM A CALM MIND, FOR ONLY WITH A CALM MIND CAN INTELLIGENCE ENTER THE MOVEMENT AND STABILITY BE MAINTAINED PHYSICALLY." THIS IS YASHUNARI ISHIMI, A KARATE-KA WHO MANY HAVE DESCRIBED AS THE CLOSEST MAN TO A TRUE MAN OF BUDO.

Q: Did anyone in your family practice any martial art before you started?
A: Yes. My father was a kendo practitioner, and my brother was training in judo. I began training in kendo because of my father's influence, but I stopped when I was 15 because I didn't like the fact that he had imposed the training on me. Looking back, I truly think all that hard training was extremely valuable for my future education, not only in the arts of budo but for my life, as well. Now I understand. I decided to practice karate because I thought it matched better with my personality. Before getting into Kobe University, I used to train three times per week. Once I got into the university karate club, karate became my life. I was training every single day. My teacher was Tsujikawa Sensei, and he is a direct student of shito-ryu founder, Kenwa Mabuni.

Karate Masters

"Looking back, I truly think all that hard training was extremely valuable for my future education, not only in the arts of budo but for my life, as well."

Q: You also trained under Mabuni Kenei, right?
A: Correct. After hours of training under Tsujikawa Sensei at the University, I used to go to Mabuni Sensei's dojo and train some more. That was the perfect combination of training because they were both excellent teachers and great budoka. The lessons I received from them are priceless.

Q: What is your opinion of how the teachings of karate-do have been passed down onto the new generation of practitioners?
A: Much of what is taught in the Western world is based on techniques and information passed down from one person to the next. A lot of the verbal transmissions are translations from the old texts. Unfortunately, these translations are incorrect. Someone translates ancient information incorrectly and then teaches this to his students. Then, the students transmit this information to the next generation. Already something has been changed and lost. Then, the next generation gets a different version of the same facts. When you look at the end of the chain, the facts are totally different from what they were originally. That's why I think it is important to be familiar with the terminology and language of the original budo arts. It helps to understand things in a clearer way.

Q: What do you think of all the technical differences in kata?
A: It is true that today there are many differences in kata, and I honestly think that they are irrelevant because they display only the personal flavor incorporated by the teacher. A lot of the time the arguments are simply nonsense. It is true that some specific movements should be performed in a certain way and no modification should be done. But then, there are other movements that are not that important, and the way you express them is not that relevant. There is a certain idiosyncrasy or temperament to it. You can personalize the movement, but you have to be aware of the essential meaning and principle behind the technique. And this shouldn't be altered at all. A traditional master teaches his students according to the student's capabili-

ties, dedication, understanding and trustworthiness. All these elements may affect the way the student receives the knowledge. The problems arise when the student tries to copy the "teacher's idiosyncrasy," and he believes that this is the only way. This will create a problem in the future. The master taught the teacher in a very personal way, so the teacher performs karate in a very individualized way. That's the all-traditional format of transmitting the knowledge. He modifies things to adapt the movements to his body, but he never changes the essential meaning of the form. And this is the point that many people don't understand; there is no one correct way of doing a kata. What we need to keep constant is the principle of the kata and not necessarily the specific details of the minor technical movements.

"You can personalize the movement, but you have to be aware of the essential meaning and principle behind the technique. And this shouldn't be altered at all."

Q: In the old traditional way of teaching, after a student asks a technical question, an instructor has him repeat a technique over and over. Do you like this method?

A: It is the traditional way. The "old" teacher used to send the student to a corner and ask him to repeat the movement 10,000 times. Then his questions would evaporate. I know this is not an acceptable way of teaching in the Western world. In the West, when a student asks you a question, you simply answer. There is a downside to this. The student will go back to training thinking and believing that he knows [the answer], but he doesn't. He just listened to the answer, but he doesn't know it. By doing the technique, the student needs to feel [the technique] and understand why the movement is performed that way. He needs to go inside for the answer. The problem lies in the fact that this method requires a lot of time because the answer is not learned immediately. This method [teaching yourself] is very good for those students who have a strong will and are dedicated. But let me warn you here ... many instructors with very limited knowledge use this approach to avoid answering a student's questions when they don't know the answer. The student's passion to know becomes a threat to the instructor.

Karate Masters

"If you are not interested in sport competition because of your age or orientation, don't enter a school that mainly focuses on entering tournaments. Ask questions when you visit the dojo. Don't be afraid."

Q: It's always difficult to find the right dojo. What are your suggestions for a prospective student?

A: This is a tough question, and it requires many different answers. First, if a person gets involved in karate simply because he wants to exercise, I don't think he really knows or cares about the important things that should be known before entering a dojo. [In this case], the dojo where he ends up will [strictly] be an accident ... mostly because the school is conveniently located near his work, home or school.

If the individual has at least a little idea of what the art of karate-do is and represents, then let me explain a few things here. The art of karate-do includes a vast spectrum of styles and each one has a special orientation and characteristic. It is not the same to train in shito-ryu as it is to train in kyokushin-kai. This is obvious. The important thing here is to match your needs with the right instructor and style. If you are not interested in sport competition because of your age or orientation, don't enter a school that mainly focuses on entering tournaments. Ask questions when you visit the dojo. Don't be afraid. Once you know the kind of karate you want to do, then you have to find the right teacher. Visit several classes imparted by the same instructor. Make sure that he is consistent with the classes and he really cares for the students. It is very sad to spend not only money but also time with the wrong individual. You can make more money [if you throw it away on the wrong instructor], but you can't get the years back. Time is priceless. The problem for the inexperienced student is how to evaluate the authenticity and skill of the instructor. It is here where many so-called masters take advantage of good people. Try to learn as much as possible about the teacher's background. Nowadays we have the Internet and although there is a lot of incorrect information there, it can be also beneficial to verify and confirm some specific details. This process can be tedious and usually very few people follow it before enrolling in a martial arts school. Once you have found the right dojo and teacher, however, put yourself into it with heart and soul. Trust your teacher and make sure you receive the proper respect. Only then you'll be able to achieve your goals.

Q: Do you think traditional forms and techniques are really useful for modern self-defense?
A: First, let me remind you that traditional arts were taught by invitation. You couldn't step into a dojo and ask the instructor to teach you. The instructor knew the student's personality, physical capability and limitations when he decided to teach him. The art was taught to the student in a tailor-made format. The teacher had the time and motivation to make the art or style fit perfectly with the student's physical make-up and qualities.

Second, any physical movement performed as a reflex—which is the very basic essence of the self-defense—must be extensively trained to become a natural reaction. This only can be accomplished through tedious repetitive training of the basic movements of your style. Once you have these movements in your system like a reflex, you need to have the strength and knowledge to use these techniques. The body must support your technique; otherwise, your technical knowledge is useless.

"It is very sad to spend not only money but also time with the wrong individual. You can make more money [if you throw it away on the wrong instructor], but you can't get the years back. Time is priceless."

The final aspect of self-defense is [developing] the right fighting spirit or decisions to get you through a fight. This last aspect is the most important.

But don't fool yourself. Doing *sanchin* up and down a dojo floor won't be useful to defend yourself in a serious situation in the street in which your physical integrity is at stake. You have to take everything for what it really is and then you'll be at peace with yourself and happy doing whatever it is you are doing. And this applies to everything in life.

Q: You seem to be very traditional in your approach to kata. Why?
A: You can look at this from the perspective of karate-do and what you do in a competition. The art of karate and kata—as part of it—shouldn't be altered to the point that the essence of what the art is all about gets lost. As I said

Karate Masters

"The art of karate and kata—as part of it—shouldn't be altered to the point that the essence of what the art is all about gets lost."

before, the global meaning of kata is what counts, and I am talking about real and true traditional karate now ... not sport karate.

You have to focus on keeping the real essence of the form with the proper global rhythm and pace. That's what you should keep in mind. If you do that, then a little modification on the speed of a hand movement or sequence won't matter at all. What is wrong is when someone alters the essence of the form, which includes changing movements to make them more spectacular for competition, increasing or decreasing the general pace of the kata to look better when doing it, creating additional and unnecessary movements that are incorporated into the form to compensate for a lack of training and skill or spicing up a segment that doesn't seem too flashy. You can practice a traditional kata and perform it beautifully in a tournament without having to alter and modify the original form to look better in front of the judges.

Q: If a karate-ka knows a large amount of kata, does that reflect the amount of his technical knowledge?

A: Definitely not. Having five cars in your garage does not make you a better driver. Karate is not about quantity ... it is about quality. Those who think that a karate-ka is better than another because he knows a larger number of forms should re-evaluate their thinking. Old masters like Funakoshi Gichin, Miyagi Chojun and many of their predecessors never tried to learn or teach great amounts of kata. *Shito-ryu* founder Mabuni Kenwa Sensei, who was determined to accumulate many of the old forms to prevent them from being lost, is the only exception to this, but he never pushed his students to learn 60 kata either. The student has to go deeper into the meaning and application of every single movement and principle found in the forms. And this is a lifetime study because many of the real techniques are hidden in *onyo-bunkai*.

Q: Do you believe that shito-ryu has a more natural "flavor" to express kata than other karate styles?
A: Maybe. Shito-ryu has a strong influence from Okinawa's culture, and they [Okinawans] tried to make the practice of karate very natural for the human body. Karate is a part of the practitioner's life, and the Okinawans approach it like something that you will be doing for the rest of your life. Therefore, they don't train in karate like it is something you do when you are young but quit when you get older. This mentality influences the techniques of the art. If you practice a kata in which you have to jump 360 degrees in the air and land flat on your hands, are you planning to do that when you are 60? You have to be logical in your approach to karate. Using logic, you can practice the art for the rest of your life.

"Karate is not about quantity ... it is about quality. Those who think that a karate-ka is better than another because he knows a larger number of forms should re-evaluate their thinking."

Q: What is your opinion of kumite in modern competitions?
A: *Shiai-kumite* is not real kumite as it is understood in traditional karate. In a sporting event, the main thing organizers need to provide is a safe environment, and this is always based on rules and regulations. Shiai kumite is controlled sparring under safe sportive regulations. And that is what it is. To stay close to the true essence of traditional karate-do, the requirements to score a point should reflect the important points of any given karate technique. Otherwise, competitors will score with anything. Unfortunately, this is what is happening these days. A scoring technique should have the basic technical elements required by the art; a *tsuki* is always a tsuki and a *keri* always a keri, but a competitor needs to deliver the scoring technique with

Karate Masters

"Shiai kumite is controlled sparring under safe sportive regulations. To stay close to the true essence of traditional karate-do, the requirements to score a point should reflect the important points of any given karate technique."

balance, the right *ma-ai* (distance), *kime*, control, body mechanics and the correct fighting spirit. And finally, a perfect *zanchin* should be shown after the technique has been delivered and scored. If we ask the competitors to maintain these qualities and the referees strongly reward these technical elements, then sport kumite represents the true idea of fighting in traditional karate, which means displaying budo attitude. The problem arises when anything that touches, regardless of the way the technique has been delivered, is counted as a point. Then, it becomes a matter of touching the opponent instead of delivering a powerful, well-controlled technique.

Let's not forget that shiai kumite is an aspect of the whole kumite side in karate-do. It has regulations and many effective techniques have to be eliminated to prevent major injuries. Karate has many fighting techniques as eye attacks, elbow and knee strikes in close-range, kicks to the legs and knees, et cetera. These are highly efficient and powerful. Sport karate is good if we keep the essence of what the right attitude and real technique should be in a life-and-death situation. This is as close as we can get to budo.

Q: What is your opinion of the various forms of full-contact karate and fighting events practiced these days?

A: Full-contact karate, kickboxing and other types of sport fighting events are good for young people if they feel inclined to do them. [However], these kinds of activities are [only] good up until a certain age. If a practitioner has only focused on fighting, he has nothing left. That's why karate is for life. You can always train because the art will always have something for you.

Ishimi

Q: How should supplementary training such as running, weightlifting and other sports be balanced with pure technical karate sessions?
A: Runners run, weightlifters lift weights and karate-ka do karate. Now that I have said this, let me elaborate a little. Everything a karate-ka does—besides practicing the art of karate-do—should be specifically designed to supplement and help the technical element of the skill training. Don't lift weights like a bodybuilder does and don't run like a marathon runner because it won't help. Instead, a karate-ka should do intervals (sprints combined with recovery) because they duplicate the change of rhythm found in kumite and kata. The karate-ka should lift weights to balance the less-worked muscles in his body because this will strengthen and support those, as well as the ones used all the time in karate training. He shouldn't, however, try to develop huge mass, plus he should work on flexibility. In essence, he should be strong and supple.

If any additional training doesn't help the karate-ka improve his karate, why is he doing it? I have seen many practitioners run, lift weights and do other things because they think these activities will help them in karate. The truth is they don't do them to fit into the structure of the martial arts. Instead, they do them as an addition, and this prevents them from spending more time on the technical aspects that they really need to [focus on to] progress in their chosen art.

Q: How important is self-defense?
A: Very important. Karate is a self-defense method. Not only does it teach you how to use your body to protect yourself from an aggressor, but it also gives you the moral and ethical code to avoid confrontations. In combat, the highest level of skill is the ability to read and neutralize your opponent's actions before he moves. Similarly, the highest level of [skill in] self-defense is [the ability] to prevent a dangerous situation before it arises. You should be able to foresee how an irrelevant incident may escalate before it becomes a difficult situation. Feel it, see it before it becomes bigger and abort it. This is true mastery.

Q: Do you believe there are advantages to studying in Japan?
A: I really do, and it's not for the technical and mechanical aspects of the art. Instead, training in Japan will teach you a lot of the feeling of the land where karate was developed. The atmosphere, the ambiance, the etiquette, et cetera feels different if you train in Japan than if you follow the same rituals in another country. Of course, this is true for those who are interested in going deeper into the traditional and cultural aspects of budo and Japan. If

Karate Masters

"Karate has many fighting techniques as eye attacks, elbow and knee strikes in close-range, kicks to the legs and knee, et cetera."

you practice karate simply as a sport, then I don't think it is necessary. You can learn, perform and become a world champion without ever going there.

Q: Sensei, on a personal level, you had cancer and went through an extremely dangerous surgery. Nevertheless, you came out on top and you continue training in karate as you used to do. What is the secret?
A: There is no secret. When you face death with the true attitude of bushido, there is nothing to lose and everything to win. Karate-do helped me to maintain the warrior spirit and be ready for whatever came into my life ... good or bad. I have learned to simplify my life and stay close to my good friends and loyal students who have been training with me for more than three decades.

Q: Finally, what does it mean to you to practice the art of karate-do?
A: The martial arts and karate-do are a vehicle and a prescription for personal growth. They provide a useful tool to greater understanding and

Ishimi

"Everything a karate-ka does—besides practicing the art of karate-do—should be specifically designed to supplement and help the technical element of the skill training."

acceptance of many things in life. It is a perfect learning environment to test ourselves to the limit, deal with certain issues that can bring us closer to the life-and-death situations of the old samurai and stretch our conception of reality until the only impossibility is lack of change in what we are doing. Karate helps you to understand how simple life should be: strive to happy. Life is very simple, but we [human beings] tend to make it very complicated. Budo is a way to find life in the midst of death. In combat, we need mindlessness and acceptance of what is; therefore, we learn to be in peace with the outside world. In dealing with this paradox of life-and-death, and peace in the midst of violence, we teach our minds to accept the duality of existence and focus on the now rather than trying to evaluate everything and try to find a reason behind it. Karate-do is a valid vehicle to reach the higher levels of human existence. O

Richard Kim

The Classical Man

Considered one of the most knowledgeable men in the world of martial arts, he practiced different styles for most of his life. Studying both in Japan and China, Sensei Kim had the opportunity to learn from some of the greatest icons of his time. Most of his life was spent teaching and lecturing around the world, educating the masses about the ethical aspects of budo and the true meaning of martial arts. His extensive training made Kim one of the most sought-after instructors on the planet. From judo to shorinji-ryu to kung-fu to boxing, Sensei Kim was a true teacher in every sense of the word. To understand Richard Kim is to realize the intensity of his convictions. Knowledgeable in Japanese and Okinawan karate, as well as several Chinese internal styles, the memory and knowledge of this true gentleman of budo will survive in thousands of dedicated students and practitioners who had the good fortune to receive instruction from one of the greatest martial arts masters the world has ever known.

Q: When and where were you born?
A: On November 17, 1919, in Hilo, Hawaii. My mother was Japanese and my father was Korean. I began studying judo in 1925 when I was 6 years old, under Tatsu Bata. My mother owned a building that had a hotel upstairs and a Japanese judo club downstairs where she made me train.

Q: When did you start karate?
A: I saw a demonstration in 1927 by Yabu Kentsu and his assistant, Sensei Arakaki, at the Nuanu YMCA in Honolulu. Right after that I began training with Yabu Kentsu, who stayed in Hawaii for about a year. I received my black belt from the Dai Nippon Butoku Kai. Remember, before World War II this was the only organization that issued official dan rankings. There was no JKA or Kodokan in those days. These organizations only arose after World War II when General MacArthur closed the Butoku Kai down. He believed that the Butoku Kai was responsible for the war.

Karate Masters

"I never wanted to teach in mass. I always preferred to teach more in an individual or small-group format. I preferred to encourage my students to run commercial dojos."

The style of karate I learned and taught is shorinji-ryu, Yabu Kentsul's style. This is why my kata are named like Yabu Chinto's. Of course, over the years I have refined the kata, as karate in those early years was quite unsophisticated. There wasn't even any real names of styles in the early days—it was just called "*te*." It wasn't until quite some time later that the word "karate" was even invented. I moved to Japan in 1939 and came back to the U.S. in 1959 after the war was over.

Q: How did you become involved with the Butoku Kai?
A: When I was in Japan, and part of the Japanese military, I was trained in the *Busen* as part of the Dai Nippon Butoku Kai, and it was there that I met Ono Komo Sensei, a 10th dan in kendo. When I returned to the U.S. in 1959, he asked me to organize the Butoku Kai internationally, and I did so by teaching at the Chinese YMCA in the San Francisco Chinatown for years. I continued to organize the Butoku Kai until 1992 when Hamada took over. The Butoku Kai prior to Word War II was the only body allowed to award dan ranks in the martial arts. The Butoku Kai was mostly judo, and prior to and during World War II it was the only organization—all others had to belong to it. After the war, it never regained its status or its recognition by the government. It just isn't the same organization as it was back then.

Q: Why didn't you ever open a professional dojo?
A: I never wanted to teach in mass. I always preferred to teach more in an individual or small-group format. I preferred to encourage my students to run commercial dojo. I wanted to mix religion with martial arts because I really wanted to teach morality to the Western world and not just physical fighting. Some students did not understand this and left because they wanted high dan ranks, but I would not grant them. The highest dan rank I ever granted was a 6th dan, which I gave to Brian Ricci in Boston and only within the last few years.

Q: Did you have a problem going back to Japan when the war broke out?
A: Not really. I had dual citizenship because I was born before 1924 and the Exclusions Act allowed me to have citizenship.

Q: I've heard that you are the inheritor of the Menkyo Kaiden scrolls of Daito Ryu? Is this true?
A: Yes, it is true. I was given the Menkyo Kaiden from Yoshido Sensei. He was a great martial artist. He went with Ueshiba to Hokaido prior to World War II as part of a government program in which individuals from each prefecture went there to help populate Hokaido. While there, he trained with Hokaido Sokato and became the assistant instructor to him. Actually, he became the main instructor. I learned two main lessons from him: the first was that nothing is impossible; and the second was before you become a thief or any other type of criminal, you first become a liar. He stressed this lesson over and over and taught the importance of always telling the truth, no matter what. The physical training was very harsh, but it was a different from karate training. It was not kicking and punching but rather throwing and rolling around on the ground. We also did a great deal of work with swords and knives. The training was practically every day and I became like an apprentice under him.

"The master taught the student personally and this is the way the information was handed down — teacher to student. The student would never leave the sensei because the teacher would always hold back one thing from the student and he wanted that one thing."

Q: Who are some of the other great masters you have met?
A: Well, the first who comes to mind is Yoshido Kotaro; he was the epitome of the word "master," technically, mentally and spiritually. Ueshiba was another one of the great ones. In fact, I trained with Ueshiba for about a year, every day from 6 a.m. to 9 p.m. Then there was Sawai—he trained with Wang Xiang Zhay in China and became a master of the internal systems and wrote a book called "*Tai Ki Kae.*" He was one of the most impressive people I ever met. Wang Xiang Zhay, his teacher, could actually just touch you and send you flying. In fact Sawai, who was a 5th dan from Kano himself and a 5th dan in *kendo,* once tried to hit Wang but ended up on the short end of the stick and on his back. He even tried to hit him with a stick

Karate Masters

"Funakoshi was good but it was because of his ability to communicate with the Japanese that he was chosen to go to Japan and spread the art of karate."

and could not. During the first lesson with Wang, we would just stand there for three to nine hours a day—of course, not all at one time. It was 30 minutes here and 30 minutes there. All he said to us was, "Just don't think."

Q: From whom did you learn your tai chi?
A: I trained with a man named Chen Chen Wan in China. My style of *tai chi* is an offshoot of the Yang style. In fact, if you saw them both side-by-side you would think they were the same. I also met a man in Hong Kong whose named Charlie Tu Tai. He could do something no one else I have ever seen could do. He would let mosquitoes land on him and then, using his powers, they would fall off of him dead. I have never seen anything like this. I learned *pa qua* from him, and he is the one who told me that no pa qua fighter had ever lost. Then there is Nishiyama Sensei, who is alive today. He is the most knowledgeable man alive when it comes to *shotokan* karate. No one is equal to him. Oh, yes, then Mas Oyama. He was excellent as well. I remember in 1936 that he Sawai, and I were walking along discussing the martial arts when Oyama hit this telephone pole and put his fist into it at least 1/2 inch. He believed that nothing beat a good right hand. He and Kinjo used to come to my place in Yokohama at least once a week to train. I met Yamaguchi Gogen through Oyama—he, too, was very good.

Q: Why is it so difficult to get information from Chinese masters on the internal systems?
A: Because of their culture. The master taught the student personally, and this is the way the information was handed down—teacher to student—and in some ways, this is the best. The student would never leave the sensei because the teacher would always hold back one thing from the student, and he wanted that one thing. Once in a while, a great Chinese master came along

who influences many people, like general Yei Fei—he's the one who created the Eight Brocades of Silk and also the *suparimpei* kata. In fact, he created all the *goju-ryu* kata and also The Eight Gods Crossing The River. I think I am the only one who still teaches this form. But even Yei Fei fell victim to his own friend who turned on him and killed him.

Q: You mentioned that Mas Oyama believed that a good right hand is the best weapon. Do you believe that?
A: Let me put it this way: The defect of karate fighters is that they don't know how to use a good right hand like a boxer does. The good boxer will only use the right hand once he has feinted. It's important to understand this to fully apply a karate blow.

Q: How much boxing did you do?
A: I had 42 pro fights and became the champion of the Orient when I lived in Shanghai. I lived there for five years. I studied tai chi and pa qua as well when I lived in Shanghai.

Q: Did you ever meet Gichin Funakoshi?
A: Yes. I met him in 1957 at his final public performance. In fact, Bob Fusaro was there at the time, and he performed in front of Funakoshi Sensei. Funakoshi was good, but it was because of his ability to communicate with the Japanese that he was chosen to go to Japan and spread the art of karate. In fact, there were many more skillful masters like Miyagi, Yabu Kentsu and others, but Funakoshi was educated; therefore, he was chosen to go. Most of the other masters only spoke Hogan, a dialect used in Okinawa.

Q: Peter Urban. How and where did you meet him?
A: I was teaching karate and judo at the Black Friars Gym in Yokohama and this guy, Smith, was punching a kid around in the ring. I stopped Smith and said,"What do you want to do that for?" He said the kid told him not to pull back so he let him have it. That kid was Peter Urban. Peter was one of the few men I have ever met in my life who had absolutely no fear—I saw that in his eyes that day. He became my student and then one day he asked if he could go train with Mas Oyama. Then, he later became a disciple of Gogen Yamaguchi. In fact, he introduced me to them both.

Karate Masters

Q: How much value does kobudo have in modern society?
A: Weapons training is very important because it brings into focus the frailty of life. Without weapons, karate loses the concept of art and degenerates into a sport.

Q: How important is kata in the overall spectrum of karate?
A: Kata teaches fighting skills and living skills at the same time. The aim of kata is to make the individual one with the universe, attuned to the kata. Sparring and self-defense with partners are part of the instruction, but it is kata training that is most important. Kata is the primary path to self-mastery of the individual. Kata training is of foremost importance and adherence to the original form is a must. The masters who created the kata movements did so in a state of enlightenment, and it should be the student's goal to practice repeatedly in an attempt to attain that same state of awareness. The creators believed that a student should spend three years training a single kata. I'm amazed at the people who clamor for "another kata." Is it important to know more or is it important to know better?

Q: Have you ever felt fear in your training?
A: Yes. Fear is the culprit that makes our training unique from other systems, in that we put the emphasis on conquering fear, self and ego—defeating the opponent comes afterwards. Say we are in a life-and-death match with each other. At the moment of the actual confrontation, you may think you can beat me so there is no reason why you should die. That's the intellect taking over. The idea of letting go of life is too terrifying to think about. But that is the whole point! By not letting yourself think of death, you have lost your life. Our method of training is to face death with equanimity. The martial artist, the samurai, reached deep down into his subconscious, and through imagination, restructured his mind to view death as a passing phenomenon to the beyond, not to be feared, but to be welcomed as something natural to the scheme of things.

Q: What is the difference between Japanese karate students and the students of the Western world?
A: Physically, Westerners are just as good as the Japanese, but the Western student lacks the morality and ethics that a Japanese student has. On the other hand, I don't think any art is superior to another. The Chinese martial arts are rich in tradition, and the Japanese martial arts are deep in discipline. The Korean martial arts, although they do not like to admit it, are based on Japanese karate. In fact, in the beginning all their forms were Japanese kata

but with Korean names. They do have very beautiful kicks that are similar to the French, but all they did was incorporate their own kicking techniques with Japanese karate. What I am saying is that they do not have any history like the sword or spear, although they were exceptional in archery. But to give you a final answer, no one art is better than another. Mastery comes from the individual and not the style.

Q: Is Japanese or Okinawan karate superior?
A: Well, first off, Okinawan karate is true karate—the Okinawans are much more traditional than the Japanese. But the Japanese, especially those like Nishiyama Sensei, have refined the Okinawan karate to what it is today.

"I trained with a man named Chen Chen Wan in China. My style of tai chi is an offshoot of the Yang style."

Q: How did the martial arts change before and after the Boxer Rebellion?
A: The boxer rebellion of 1900 saw the loss of many great martial arts masters because they thought their chi could stop bullets. Obviously, they were wrong; bullets are a different type of weapon. The Okinawans in 1905–1906 lost the etiquette that was there prior to this—there was absolutely no commercialism before this point.

Q: In the martial arts, we talk about karate being physical, mental and spiritual. What do we mean when we say it is spiritual?
A: The root of all Japanese martial arts is Buddhism, and in Buddhism we do not kill anything. Let me share a short story about this with you. There was a young boy who was about to kill a cricket when a priest stopped him and said, "How important to you is your life?" The boy replied, "It is the most important thing to me." The priest then said to the boy, "It is just as important to the cricket."

Karate Masters

"One of the major problems is that, depending on the different sensei or associations, the requirements for each rank are totally different. This simple fact has created flaws in the organizations and some karate-ka have found an easier way to get their rank by moving to another association where the requirements are less demanding. These people are not interested in learning the art. They are interested in other things."

Q: If you could snap your fingers and change one thing in the martial arts, what would it be?
A: Etiquette—simply etiquette.

Q: Where would you like to see karate in the future?
A: First, I would like to see it in the Olympics. Second, I would like to see it taught in every public school in the world. If karate were taught in public schools, crime would be cut drastically as the students would learn respect.

Q: In the beginning of your classes, you often explain the purposes of the rei. Could you explain it?
A: The first lesson in martial arts is respect, compassion and gratitude. Every time you bow your head you are internalizing each of these words. You are showing respect to your seniors and compassion for your juniors, as you know what they have gone through over the years because you have gone through the same. Then, you are showing gratitude for your country, from which you reap benefits every day, your parents who gave you life, and the friends who support you every day in your successes and in your failures. Finally, you revere God, as it is he who will decide what will happen to you.

Q: Who do you think are currently the best karate masters in the world?
A: Without a doubt, Hidetaka Nishiyama is probably the best karate master in the world. I have seen the man in action, teaching, explaining and demonstrating the art. He is simply great. His attitude and mentality is pure Japanese and his technique is simply excellent. Another Japanese master I truly admire is Teruo Hayashi of shito-ryu. He is powerful, dynamic and very budo-oriented. His demonstrations are second to none and his knowledge of

the art simply amazing. He is one of the greatest teachers in the world. Even Nishiyama Sensei acknowledged Hayashi Sensei to be the top demonstrator in the world of karate. In goju-ryu, Yagi Meitoku is a great sensei and also I'm amazed with the historical knowledge and understanding of Kinjo Hiroshi, who unfortunately is not too well known in the Western world. Historically, I have to mention two legendary men: Mas Oyama, an extremely powerful man, and Gogen Yamaguchi. They set the standards for everybody else. In their prime, they were exceptional karate-ka.

Q: What is your opinion of the ranking system used all over the world? Do you think ranking has lost its meaning due to all the watered-down belts (dan) given by different associations?
A: Unfortunately, the ranking system doesn't have the same meaning anymore. This is not everybody's fault, only those who for personal interest and monetary ambition who have been giving high rank to unqualified people. For instance, if you have a fourth dan under Nishiyama Sensei, Hayashi Sensei or Mabuni Sensei, nobody is going to argue about your knowledge and skill. These men do not give rank away for personal interests. You have to earn the rank because they won't give it to you.

One of the major problems is that, depending on the different sensei or associations, the requirements for each rank are totally different. This simple fact has created flaws in the organizations and some karate-ka have found an easier way to get their rank by moving to another association where the requirements are less demanding. These people are not interested in learning the art. They are interested in other things. In order to solve this, I believe that the basic criteria should be the same all around the world. The problem is that this has not only affected the Japanese martial arts but all styles.

The Chinese started the belt system with the use of sashes and different colors, then judo and karate followed. To be very honest, belts are just another means of bringing dollars into the dojo—it is a form of commercialism in the dojo. Unfortunately, it has been greatly abused here in the USA—nobody needs to be told this. During the last 40 years, the overall quality of a black belt has steadily deteriorated to the point in which some instructors are selling their dan grades. In the Butoku Kai, there was no belt system; there was only trainee, assistant instructor, instructor and master.

Q: How could this problem be solved?
A: To begin with, increase the time a student spends training before he gets a shodan (black belt level). A shodan rank is not only about physical skill. This is the main mistake Westerners make. Black belt rank is about attitude, dedi-

Karate Masters

"The high-caliber requirements set by an instructor or association will give knowledge and foundation that is very different from what you can get in some other places with the same rank. It would be stupid, though, to have the opportunity to keep learning and gaining the benefit and decide to break away simply because you want to do your own thing."

cation and character. These three aspects are even more important than the physical skill. The technical skill is simply the basic element. I don't care how skillful a person may be; if he doesn't have the right attitude and character, I won't give him a shodan. Period. It's that simple. This goes against many people's belief that if you are skillful enough, then you deserve the black belt. Sorry, but not. Accepting the fact that a student can be extremely gifted and talented and his skill level reaches black belt standard in two years, there are some things that, no matter how good he is, can never be gained in only a couple of years of training—those things are maturity and perspective ... the kind of maturity and perspective that belongs to someone who has dedicated a minimum of five years to steady training in the dojo. It takes more than two years for a teacher to really know the student's character.

Q: What is the rank that is required to open your own school and teach?

A: Fourth-degree black belt (dan). That's the minimum to start to walk your own path. I'm very traditional and this is it. No other way around it. Please don't forget that a fourth dan under a true karate association or a sensei of the talent and knowledge of Nishiyama Sensei or Hayashi Sensei is very different from another instructor's fourth dan. The high-caliber requirements set by an instructor or association will give knowledge and foundation that is very different from what you can get in some other places with the same rank. Even a fourth dan under an instructor of the recognition and prestige of the men mentioned above will need to keep growing, but the foundation to grow by is already set. It would be stupid, though, to have the opportunity to keep learning and gaining the benefit and decide to break away simply because you want to do your own thing.

Q: What do you think of the practice of giving shodan rank to teenagers and kids?
A: I'm sorry, but I don't accept that. How can you give a black belt to a 12-year-old kid? He hasn't matured as an individual yet! It's impossible. Once again, the problem is that many teachers and associations only look at the physical side of the rank, and a shodan rank involves much more than just skill in punching and kicking. A 16-year-old teenager can intellectually absorb all the theory and information that a doctor needs to know to operate, but would you leave your son to be operated on by a 16-year-old kid, regardless of how much information he has memorized? The bottom line is how demanding you are with yourself and how much you value your own dignity. If you want a real shodan rank, then go to the men who can teach you well, but accept from the very beginning that the road will be harder and more difficult than getting it from those who simply are interested in making money and not in the quality of what they teach.

Q: What is your opinion of martial arts movies?
A: Chuck Norris is a true gentleman. He is great martial artist and a great human being as well. I truly respect him, and I know everybody else does too. That means a lot when you talk about an individual. People ask me about Bruce Lee. Well, he died too young to really go deep into other aspects of martial arts that a practitioner can only discover after a certain age. He opened the doors to mainstream martial arts acceptance due to the movies. That's his main contribution.

Q: Did the word "sensei" used to have a deeper meaning than it does today?
A: Again, the word "sensei" involves much more than someone who can just teach a technique. A sensei is someone who is ahead of you in life, not only in karate or martial arts. A sensei is someone who has been on this earth longer than you. He is a father figure. He is a leader because he has previous experience in life. He is hard and demanding with the students but compassionate and understanding at the same time. Unfortunately, today the word is abused and misused all over the world. Everybody seems to be a sensei. A true martial arts sensei never stops learning until he dies and meets God. Until that very moment arrives, he is trying to help people in their journey to a higher existence as individuals. O

Yukiyoshi Marutani

Karate's Mastermind

WITH A UNIQUE TEACHING PHILOSOPHY THAT STRESSES LEARNING KUMITE BEFORE KATA, SENSEI MARUTANI IS A THROWBACK TO THE EARLIER DAYS OF KARATE IN WHICH ONE'S ABILITY TO FIGHT WAS THE TRUE MEASURE OF A MAN'S MARTIAL ARTS SKILL. A SEVEN-YEAR MEMBER OF THE JAPAN NATIONAL KARATE TEAM, YUKIYOSHI MARUTANI HAS A WEALTH OF KNOWLEDGE FROM WHICH TO DRAW UPON. HIS KNOWLEDGE AND UNDERSTANDING OF KUMITE, BASED UPON HIS YEARS OF REPRESENTING JAPAN AT ALL THE MAJOR WORLDWIDE KARATE TOURNAMENTS, MAKES HIM ONE OF THE TOP COACHES IN THE WORLD AND AN ACKNOWLEDGED AUTHORITY ON KUMITE TACTICS AND STRATEGIES. HIS KNOWLEDGE AND UNDERSTANDING OF KUMITE ASPECTS PUTS HIM YEARS AHEAD OF MOST INSTRUCTORS AROUND THE GLOBE AND MAKES HIS SEMINARS AND CLASSES ONE OF THE MOST SOUGHT-AFTER FOR THOSE INTERESTED IN PURSUING THE TOURNAMENT ASPECTS OF KARATE-DO. THIS IS YUKIYOSHI MARUTANI, THE MASTERMIND BEHIND THE CHAMPIONS.

Q: When did you begin your martial arts training?
A: I started in 1967 with a college karate club. There were classes Monday through Saturday for three to four hours a day. In addition, you were expected to do personal training like hitting the *makiwara* during the lunch break. Many times my hands or feet were bloody. It was always my college *senpai*, or seniors, who led those early workouts. We did nothing but basics—again and again. I remember wondering to myself after three weeks if this was all that karate was. There was nothing new for three weeks, three hours a day! Interestingly enough, I failed my first kyu exam. There were about 30 students who tested that time. They split us into two groups and the upper group passed. But the lower group, my group, failed. My sempai told me I was a bad kicker and that my center of gravity was too high! They were always yelling at me. Later on, they were all amazed that I stuck it out and progressed as much as I have. My main instructor was Kunihiko Tosa.

Karate Masters

"'Gen' means the universe and 'sei' means control—so 'gensei' is to 'control the universe.' I think Mr. Shukumine had done research in body movements like gymnastics. I believe he was also involved in that sport. So the body movement in gensei-ryu was more natural, more reasonable."

Q: What made you stay with it?
A: You know, the first month I hated it. But the second month I began to like it. My mind and body became fixed on the simple acts of hitting and punching. I failed the testing but after that we had our first *gasshuku* training. It was long—about 10 days. Running in the morning and then punching until our hands were bloody. Afterwards, we had to clean up and cook. That was ten long days. After that, the feeling was so different. It was like being a new person. I became more involved with karate, working on my punching, working with *seiken-tsuki*. At night, I would train my eyes. I was a shy person. On the trains I would look into people's eyes, never moving my eyes from theirs—they hated it! I have since heard about the "Eye of the Tiger." So maybe I was practicing that.

Q: Your original training was in *gensei-ryu*. What is that?
A: I don't have a lot of details, it just happened to be that way. I learned through my instructors that Mr. Shukumine, the founder, started gensei-ryu after World War II. Mr. Shukumine's instructor was Soko Kushimoto, an Okinawan. We can see through the kata that it is very close to tomari-te. I only met Mr. Shukumine twice, but I understand that he had a very strong character and that he was a very philosophical man. "Gen" means the universe and "sei" means control—so "gensei" is to "control the universe." He wrote the *kanji* and analyzed it to more fully understand what it meant, physically and spiritually.

Q: What makes it different from the other more well-known Japanese styles?
A: I think Mr. Shukumine had done research in body movements like gymnastics. I believe he was also involved in that sport. So the body movement in gensei-ryu was more natural, more reasonable. He also figured out how

to incorporate certain movements from gymnastics like jumps, flips and handsprings into karate techniques. These sorts of techniques helped to make the movements faster and more surprising. I am always open to new things and new methods. This helps me to improve my karate. It is good to see that so many other karate-ka feel the same way.

Q: In your classes, you always talk about the need for confidence in your weapons. What do you mean by this?
A: Part of being comfortable with sparring is overcoming fear. A person becomes overly concerned about what the opponent can do to him. People should concentrate more on what they can do to the opponent. They need to develop their own weapons. You work on your skills, your technique, your power. You begin to understand that you can handle the situation because you know that your technique is strong and it works. Then you are in control of the encounter, not the opponent. I want to emphasize the need for realistic *kihon* as applied to sparring. I think people really need to become more comfortable when they spar.

"People should concentrate more on what they can do to the opponent. They need to develop their own weapons. You work on your skills, your technique, your power. You begin to understand that you can handle the situation because you know that your technique is strong and it works. Then you are in control of the encounter, not the opponent."

Q: Can you explain a bit more about this point?
A: People sometimes get caught up in the process of funtionalizing the basics of the art into actual sparring. You watch a class as they go up and down the floor, but you wonder how many of the students actually understand how to apply good *kihon* to live sparring. How many people can actually execute a proper technique in the heat of battle? I mean, does your punch or kick work? Does it stop the opponent?

Q: You stress distance control and body rotation/evasion in your seminars. These are much more sophisticated skills than what is normally taught today. Is this the next step for the typical American competitor?
A: Yes. A lot of these ideas came to me from my own competition days. Back then it was basically full contact. I would just fly at my opponent, and I didn't have any teeth! I went to the dentist, and he joked with me that I was too

Karate Masters

"If you analyze a punch, the fist is the fastest point and the shoulder is the slowest. If you stop the shoulder, you don't have to worry too much about the fist. It loses most, if not all, of its power."

weak—after every tournament, I showed up in his office! I started thinking about things and began to experiment. I would put pressure on the opponent, both physically and mentally. I never backed up. I pressed, I hit, I pushed—naturally. I lost some, but I won a lot more! About three or four years ago I began to train seriously with weapons. It changes the atmosphere. Everyone worries about getting hit with a weapon. It can be a *bo* or *nunchaku* or sword—it doesn't matter. It got me to think more and more about distance. When I moved in close, the opponent couldn't hit me. If you analyze a punch, the fist is the fastest point and the shoulder is the slowest. If you stop the shoulder, you don't have to worry too much about the fist. It loses most, if not all, of its power.

Q: Let's go back for a moment to your competition days. When did you qualify for the Japanese National Team?
A: It was in 1974. I was on the national team for about seven years. I retired from competition in 1981. I remember the first team selections were in 1972 or so. There were about 150 people in the selection pool. All of the top people from the tournaments except for the JKA. We ran, and we free-sparred. If you got hurt, there was no sympathy. "Good-bye. Thank you for coming!" You packed your bags and went home. No one was special. If your karate was bad and you couldn't survive, you went home. They started with about 150 of us —all championship caliber—and ended with seven or eight.

Q: What were some of the highlights of your time with the Japanese National Team and who were your teammates?
A: I was on the team for the World Championships in Long Beach, California, Tokyo, Japan; and Madrid, Spain. I took the bronze medal in 70 kg. at the World Games in Santa Clara, California. During the seven years, I trained alongside Mr. Murase, Mr. Nishimura, Mr. Maeda and several others.

Those three were at one time or another part of the coaching staff for the Japanese National Team.

Q: Can you tell us a little about those days and training with the team?
A: We met about seven times a year for three days. The first one was longer. It was a good time. We trained and trained, but then the coaches changed. They wanted us to be more like college students — younger. I was 32 or 33 at the end. Now, the maximum age is 29. I am not sure if this is good or not. Youth doesn't guarantee good and experienced karate. Time will tell.

"Some of the first coaches understood the concepts but couldn't explain it. They had no frame of reference because the rules were changing. Ippon-shobu has a different strategy than sanbon-shobu. You really need to experience and know it before you can actually pass it onto the new students and competitors."

Q: When were you first exposed to international competition?
A: My first memorable encounter was in Tokyo. I was matched against a big Italian. I couldn't move, and he couldn't move—we were both so nervous. It was the first time in the spotlight with 20,000 spectators watching me, especially the Japanese team. I managed to get past him and relaxed in the later rounds. I still remember it. The coaches were inexperienced as far as competition was concerned. They didn't understand how to coach for sport and how to use strategy to score a good point.

Q: Has this situation improved as seasoned competitors like yourself and your teammates, Murase Sensei and Nishimura Sensei, have moved into coaching?
A: That is right. They can explain concepts better to the new generations. They understand the point of competition, or at least can put themselves into the position of the competitor and explain it in those terms. Some of the first coaches understood the concepts but couldn't explain it. They had no frame of reference because the rules were changing. *Ippon-shobu* has a different strategy than *sanbon-shobu*. You really need to experience and know it before you can actually pass it onto the new students and competitors.

Karate Masters

"I think that sparring should be taught first in karate. After you've learned how to move that way, you should progress on to learning kata. I learned kata through the fighting when I was beginning. If you look at the really good kata competitors, you can see they have an understanding of kumite."

Q: I understand that you were also ranked nationally in Japan for kata. What kata is included in the curriculum for your dojo?
A: We do the mandatory kata used by the WKF.

Q: You have a rather unique approach to kata training. Can you explain it?
A: I think that sparring should be taught first in karate. After you've learned how to move that way, you should progress on to learning kata. I learned kata through the fighting when I was beginning. If you look at the really good kata competitors, you can see they have an understanding of kumite. Their kata is real and alive. If you don't have this understanding, it doesn't look right. It lacks soul.

Q: When did you come to the United States of America?
A: The first time I went to the U.S. was in 1981. I stayed for three or four months at Mr. Yamazaki's dojo in Anaheim., California. Later, in 1982, the Huntington Beach dojo in California sent me tickets to go there. I have been there ever since.

Q: Within a very short time, your students were ranked nationally and competing internationally. What was the training formula you used?
A: I didn't teach much as far as technique. Some Americans —and Westerners in general —get caught up in asking questions. I told them not to worry about the competition. Win or lose, it didn't matter; just go to the tournament and their bodies would understand. Back then we had mini-training camps two or three times a week. Every morning we ran 10 miles. After that, we would train. It helped to teach them about stamina. We wanted to push the competitor to make the preparation more difficult than the actual competition. It is like hitting a very heavy bag. When you switch to a smaller bag, it is easier, no problem! Unfortunately, most competitors are not skilled in basic things like distance control, body evasion, situational strategy and time management. These sorts of skills should be second nature to a competitor. I think that this is

the biggest weakness in some competitors, especially when compared to the stronger teams like Japan, France, et cetera. These teams had a better understanding of competition, even 15 years ago, and it is very hard to fight against opponents that are aware and control all these important elements of the sport.

Q: Can you tell us about the Japanese Instructor's Club?
A: When I first arrived in the United States of America, I was surprised to learn that there was no group already organized. I just assumed that one would exist as do similar groups in Japan or other countries. Once I got settled, I started to work on putting the club together. The initial idea was to form a club that could act as a sort of support group for all the Japanese instructors in the country. We all share a common life experience or situation. We are all Japanese-speaking karate instructors. We could all draw upon the common experiences of the group. Instructors such as Mr. Nishiyama, Mr. Kubota, Mr. Demura and Mr. Ohshima have already been in the United States for many, many years. They could offer invaluable advice on how to survive and prosper in the country. Right now there are more than 40 of us from all styles. We get together as often as we can, but it's difficult. Before the club, when we were at the tournaments, it was usually with six or seven competitors each, and it was difficult to discuss things. I want to learn what other people are thinking and saying about karate for the future. It gives us a place to pool our knowledge and be sure that things are passed on from one generation to the next. It's an easy concept to explain in Japanese, but very difficult in English. For my generation, it means passing on what we learned from the last generation to the next generation. It also means that the new Japanese instructors coming here should not expect to control American karate because there are already *senpai* here from whom they can get advice and guidance. It works both ways.

"I want to learn what other people are thinking and saying about karate for the future. It gives us a place to pool our knowledge, and be sure that things are passed on from one generation to the next. It's an easy concept to explain in Japanese, but very difficult in English. For my generation, it means passing on what we learned from the last generation to the next generation."

Karate Masters

"I want to research more into the relationship between basics—kata and kumite. I've seen too many demonstrations of karate that are basically the same thing and not done very well. I would like to be able to present demonstrations that really show what karate is about and are meaningful for future karate students."

Q: You continue to train and develop. Is there anything special you're doing?
A: I enjoy doing basics more and more every day—*kiba dachi*, forward stances, hit the makiwara, combinations—and I enjoy sparring with the kids. They hit me with all their power, and I learn how to absorb the impact better. I learn how they move and what to expect from them.

Q: Do you practice any other arts?
A: I'll watch boxing or anything else, but sometimes I don't have time to physically do it. During high school, I practiced *judo* as part of the physical education. I enjoy watching it. The movements are very similar to karate. I always want to learn something new. I want to research more into the relationship between basics—kata and kumite. I've seen too many demonstrations of karate that are basically the same thing and not done very well. I would like to be able to present demonstrations that really show what karate is about and are meaningful for future karate students. I was really impressed by some aikido demonstrations I've seen. It looks like dancing, but the fundamental movements and concepts are sound. Karate instructors have to prepare for the future—for when they are done. To pass onto the next generation what we have been taught and what we have learned, so that they can do the same in the future.

Q: You have mentioned the need for instructors to accept their own unique role in the teaching hierarchy. What do you mean by this?
A: Some instructors get caught up in the ego. Every other learning situation recognizes different levels of instruction. There are elementary schools, junior high, senior high, junior college, college, graduate school, et cetera. Each of these levels has corresponding instructors or teachers. Why is it that some karate instructors feel they can teach everything? Does that seem real-

istic? Is this attitude good for the student? Instructors should always try to improve their skills, be it technical or instructional. However, when the situation calls for it they shouldn't be afraid to refer a student to the best situation possible for that student. This way the student benefits and karate continues to develop and grow. We all win.

Q: Some people would say that one of the weaknesses of European and American karate schools today is that they have become businesses and that compromises have been made to keep the students from leaving.
A: Somebody told me once that it was bad if the students sweat too much after a workout and that you had to think about the students! I didn't change my workouts. People who join have to understand what they are getting into. To develop your mind and body you have to sweat. The school is not joining the student, the student is joining the school. I try to teach like this is a church, and people who join have to make a different kind of donation. If I taught like this was a college, with people coming for one semester and then leaving, I couldn't have the correct control to teach.

"Somebody told me once that it was bad if the students sweat too much after a workout and that you had to think about the students! To develop your mind and body you have to sweat. The school is not joining the student, the student is joining the school."

Q: Is it difficult because the Western culture is so short-term oriented?
A: Yes, and that's my problem. I have to communicate better. If I said something to the students, more would probably stay. Having a conversation to explain why I won't change the workouts would probably help. My English is getting better than before so probably that's why I have more students now!

Q: What are you plans for the future?
A: I love to teach anytime and anywhere. I enjoy sharing my experiences and am always open to learning new things. I'm immensely happy with that, and I plan to keep doing it for a very long time. O

Shinpo Matayoshi

The Heritage Keeper

HIS NAME HAS BECOME SYNONYMOUS WITH *KOBUDO* AND KARATE-DO. THERE IS HARDLY A KARATE-KA ANYWHERE IN THE WORLD WHO HAS NOT HEARD OF THIS CHARISMATIC LEADER OF THE OKINAWAN TRADITION. SHINPO MATAYOSHI WAS THE HEIR OF A VENERABLE KOBUDO TRADITION FOUNDED BY HIS FATHER SHINKO MATAYOSHI—THE MATAYOSHI-RYU METHOD OF KOBUDO. BORN IN 1921, AND SMALL IN STATURE AND WEIGHT, SENSEI MATAYOSHI LOOKED UNASSUMING ENOUGH. THIS MISCONCEPTION WAS FURTHER HEIGHTENED BY THE FACT THAT HE WAS RELUCTANT TO ELABORATE ON CERTAIN TECHNICAL ISSUES OF HIS EARLY TRAINING. BUT WHEN HE PUT ON A GI, HE BECAME MORE ARTICULATE THAN ANYONE EVER EXPECTED HIM TO BE WHEN HE WORE HIS STREET CLOTHES. OVER TIME, IT BECAME APPARENT THAT HE WAS EVERY BIT THE MASTER OF KOBUDO AND KARATE. FORTUNATE ENOUGH TO TRAIN UNDER SOME OF THE MOST LEGENDARY OKINAWAN MASTERS SUCH AS SEIKO HIGA, SHINPO MATAYOSHI EXEMPLIFIED EVERY ETHICAL AND MORAL PRINCIPLE A REAL WARRIOR SHOULD. WELL-RESPECTED FOR HIS KNOWLEDGE AND EXPERTISE INSIDE AND OUTSIDE THE LIMITS OF RYUKYU ISLAND'S WEAPONRY SYSTEMS, HE ALSO STUDIED SHORIN-RYU KARATE AS WELL AS FUKIAN WHITE CRANE KUNG-FU. SENSEI MATAYOSHI PASSED AWAY IN SEPTEMBER 1997 AT 77 YEARS OF AGE. HE WAS NOT ONLY A MASTER OF GREAT SKILL AND PRECISE TECHNIQUE, BUT ALSO THE MOST COMPASSIONATE AND UNDERSTANDING TEACHER ANY STUDENT COULD WISH TO HAVE.

Q: What was your training like under Master Kyan Chotoku?
A: My training under this great karate master began when I was only 7 years old. He was a very quiet man but also very disciplined and strict in everything he did. He didn't have many students because he didn't actively look for them. He wasn't anxious to increase the number of students at the dojo. He had his own dojo but was also at schoolteacher at the Prefectural Agricultural School in Okinawa. All I learned during the first year under Master Kyan was how to clean the floors and carry water from one place to another. There was no karate training at all—no punching or kicking—just cleaning. This was the way the old teachers used to find out how dedicated and loyal you were. Every student had a duty in the dojo, either cleaning or

Karate Masters

"The idea of a teacher accepting money for teaching karate was very unusual. Martial arts is a treasure—you can give it to anyone you want, but you should not sell it. Of course, times have changed and are different today."

buying supplies—everyone had a task to perform for Master Kyan.

Q: Did he charge fees or did students compensate him by buying things?
A: The idea of a teacher accepting money for teaching karate was very unusual. He would not be considered a real karate teacher , because according to the old bujutsu traditions, martial arts cannot be bought with money. Martial arts is a treasure—you can give it to anyone you want, but you should not sell it. Of course, times have changed and are different today. So he did charge money, but all the students also brought gifts to him. In Japanese culture, this is called *omiage*.

Q: Do you charge your students?
A: No, I don't. But they do contribute money so I can pay the electricity and rent and the regular expenses of having a dojo. It is a personal contribution and the amount depends on what the student can comfortably afford.

Q: Did you use the makiwara?
A: Very often. Makiwara training was something that we did almost all the time. The idea is to condition your body so your limbs become real weapons when hitting the opponent. Needless to say, makiwara training brings many other benefits, such as a perfect sense of *kime* at the moment of impact and perfect alignment of the body parts in the technique.

Q: What kata did he emphasize the most?
A: Probably *naihanchin*. This was the most important kata. *Chinto* was also practiced very often, but the fundamentals were gained from the diligent training of naihanchin. This kata is very difficult to master, but people today don't really understand it. They like the more flashy and acrobatic kata. It's a pity.

Matayoshi

Q: How was the training under Master Gogenki?

A: He was in his mid-40s when I met him. I trained under him until I went into the military. I began training when I was 12 and stayed with him for six years. Gogenki was a very unusual teacher, and I learned different things from him. I was really surprised when I heard he passed away because he was not really old. He probably had some malnutrition in his youth and this took its toll. After the war, there was not enough food and many people got sick for the rest of their lives. He influenced a lot of other Okinawan karate teachers due to his great knowledge and skill. Later on, many teachers started to spread certain rumors about the origin of their systems and their kata. If you look closely, you'll see that in the very end all the secret kata are no more than bad versions of authentic forms. It's sad, but many of these false masters are getting away with telling their fairy tales.

Q: Do you agree with the advertising used today to bring students into the martial arts?

A: Not at all. Unfortunately, too many instructors are trying to attract people to karate by presenting the art as an exotic thing. They use the mystical and mysterious aspects to intrigue people. I truly think this is not the right way because there is nothing secret or deadly in the art of karate-do—at least not in the way these people are trying to present it. All karate-do movements can be proven scientifically through physics and biology. Of course, when I started training, we didn't know anything about all this, but today we more aware of how the body works and how to generate the most power by using proper body mechanics.

Q: What is the proper attitude a true karate-ka should display?

A: There are certain ethical and moral qualities that a practitioner of true karate should display. Of course, if he practices karate like other people

"Gogenki was a very unusual teacher, and I learned different things from him. I was really surprised when I heard he passed away because he was not really old. He influenced a lot of other Okinawan karate teachers due to his great knowledge and skill."

Karate Masters

"Today, students have the opportunity to learn and get information about many different fighting arts to increase their knowledge. Magazines and videos allow this to happen. When I was learning we didn't have these luxuries. We had no time to study or analyze much. Everything had to be direct and to the point because our lives were on the line."

practice tennis or basketball, then you can't expect anything from him. Unfortunately, many modern karate practitioners don't trust or respect each other—not only in Japan or Okinawa—but all over the world. They are so proud of their own styles that they lose perspective on things. They reject anyone who doesn't use their type of punch or kick. Everything should be considered within its own context. Although we don't use certain techniques in the karate style that I practice, it doesn't mean those other techniques are not effective under certain specific situations or environments.

Q: Would you recommend for your students to look at other martial arts?
A: I believe that the more a practitioner knows about other styles, the more prepared he will be in case he faces someone who practices another method. Today, students have the opportunity to learn and get information about many different fighting arts to increase their knowledge. Magazines and videos allow this to happen. When I was learning, we didn't have these luxuries. The way we were taught was under pressure, and we had to learn to make the techniques work against any kind of opponent. We had no time to study or analyze much. Everything had to be direct and to the point because our lives were on the line. The good thing is that today, practitioners can learn how to adapt their techniques against other new methods of attack. For instance, in *kobudo* you use your weapon differently against a *bo* or a *sai*. Your attacker's weapon determines the way you'll use your own weapon. It's simple common sense. This is where the real understanding of the art and one's own self comes in. But this is not always something easy thing to do, let alone accept.

Q: Do you like the idea of mixing styles?
A: Knowledge is power. If you are a karate practitioner and you have to fight against another karate-ka, then you know what to expect. You know, more

or less, what he is going to do and what kind of technical arsenal he has. But if you fight against a boxer, and you don't know how a boxer moves, then you are in a very difficult situation. This is not to say that you should forsake your art for something else. But you'll find that it is harder to apply your techniques against someone who doesn't move the way you do. A real fighting art should be based on principles that allow you to use and interrelate all your techniques against any type of attack.

Q: Okinawa has maintained a very low profile compared to karate-do politics going on in Japan. How have they managed to do this?
A: In Okinawa, although we have different styles, we are all very much unified in form and spirit. There is a great deal of respect among the top instructors and masters compared to other places in the world. This is probably because Okinawa is a small island, and we have kept a lot of our traditions intact. Okinawans are humble people; we don't like to control others, and we don't brag about things. People have always been that way. Due to the influence of other cultures and the natural evolution of our society, the new generations began to look outside and began to copy other cultures. This created a social struggle between the old-timers and the younger generations. Kobudo and karate haven't escaped this struggle, and the way the arts are taught and spread today is very different from the methods and attitudes of the past.

"In Okinawa, although we have different styles, we are all very much unified in form and spirit. There is a great deal of respect among the top instructors and masters compared to other places in the world. This is probably because Okinawa is a small island, and we have kept a lot of our traditions intact."

Q: Why do you think Westerners are attracted to Eastern philosophy and culture?
A: I think Westerners want the culture of the Orient as a direct personal revolt against the impersonal, sterile materialism in the West. They really want the respect for rank and tradition that Eastern culture provides. Aside from the physical aspects of the martial arts as efficient self-defense systems,

Karate Masters

"The training in Okinawa is very different than Japan. The practitioners work by themselves and don't follow the militaristic structure used in Japan. Western students require an explanation for everything, even if they don't understand it. The arts have to be experienced to be understood and not just talked about."

Westerners want the serenity and imperturbability of the ancient cultures—an aspect of life that was one of the foundations of the Western world before the age of the machines. For this reason I believe that Western students, whether consciously aware of it or not, are seeking the security of permanency which is lacking in the Occidental culture.

Q: How does the Okinawan teaching method differ from that of Japan?
A: The training in Okinawa is very different from Japan. The practitioners work by themselves and don't follow the militaristic structure used in Japan. Of course, in America or Europe, the teacher has to explain and elaborate when the students ask why they are doing this or that. Western students require an explanation for everything, even if they don't understand it. Karate and kobudo have to be practiced by the body first, and followed by intellectualizing the action. You can explain how the body moves when you punch, but this doesn't mean you either know the technique or you are capable of using it against an opponent. The arts have to be experienced to be understood and not just talked about. I'd like to see people training more and talking less, respecting more and badmouthing less. Unfortunately, I don't think this will ever change.

Q: Why do you think many students drop karate after only a few years of practice?
A: Communication is one of the main reasons. Some Oriental instructors don't try to understand the Western way; understanding between teacher and student is a two-way street. The teacher must be aware of the student's comprehension problems, but at the same time it is the duty of the student to try to be knowledgeable and listen attentively. I believe the teacher should try to find out what benefit each student expects to gain from the art and try to help them to attain that goal. Every effort should be made to intro-

duce the trainee to the philosophy and culture of martial arts. In the art of *bujutsu* and *budo*, the difference between one whose mind wanders and the student who is attentive is much more apparent than any other field. Not only will the inattentive student get low marks, but he is more likely to have his bones broken during *kumite*.

Q: Have you ever felt fear in your training?
A: Many times. You should remember that I didn't train in *bujutsu* for fun. I trained for necessity—to learn how to survive. Fear is not bad if you understand where it comes from. A person must always confront fear head-on, otherwise it will overwhelm him. As President Roosevelt of America said, "The only thing we have to fear is fear itself."

Q: Do you think karate should be considered a sport?
A: I am not totally against karate being practiced as a sport, but don't be mistaken ... karate is not a sport. Certain technical aspects can be used and re-arranged for sportive competitions —that's all. There is a danger in the fact that the rules and regulations that must be observed by competitors may stunt the development of a real fighting attitude. Many students confuse tournament fighting with real fighting. Nothing could be worse than to have this false sense of security about one's fighting ability. If all one does is pursue sport, he will gradually lose interest in the psychological and philosophical background of the art. This is especially true if a beginner is taught on a competitive sport basis, instead of being exposed to the art in its totality. He never experiences the other, more valuable, aspects that the art has to offer. I must reiterate that in order for karate or kobudo to be understood, it must be experienced in their essence, and not singled out solely as a sport or self-defense method. Karate is everything together. It is similar to a movie. A movie is not only the leading actor and the acting, it encompasses all the

"You should remember that I didn't train in bujutsu *for fun. I trained for necessity—to learn how to survive. Fear is not bad if you understand where it comes from. As President Roosevelt of America said, 'The only thing we have to fear is fear itself.'"*

Karate Masters

"Our culture, our discipline, our moral values and traditions make us what we are. If for the sake of our student's fee we were to throw all of this away, our students would have the right to tell us that we have proven ourselves false because we had shown by our actions that we do not believe in our own birthright."

facets of the production from the director to the scriptwriter to the music. Martial arts are the same. There are numerous elements which make up the total art.

Q: What about those who look at the art as a method of fighting only?
A: Self-defense used to be the essence of the arts, but that is in the past. I think that if a student wants just that and nothing else, then he can simply buy a gun or a knife. At least he will have much greater kill-power than a black belt. To reach a *shodan* rank takes years of training and dedication. Yet even with all these achievements, a shodan is still no match for a gun. The black belt hasn't been born, no matter what his rank, who can block a bullet or jump away from one. This is why a martial arts expert must be an impeccable example of integrity. Is that not what Western man wishes more than anything else—the ability to trust his fellow man? Our culture, our discipline, our moral values and traditions make us what we are. If for the sake of our student's fee we were to throw all of this away, our students would have the right to tell us that we have proven ourselves false because we had shown by our actions that we do not believe in our own birthright.

Q: Do you think modern trends should be adopted by karate masters to spread the art?
A: They should. Advertising, for instance, is one such trend. If it is done tastefully then it won't demean the martial arts. There is nothing intrinsically wrong with advertisements, as long as good taste is observed. The martial arts should be treated with respect, but they must deserve respect before they can demand it.

Q: What is your opinion about the future of karate-do?
A: Many elements should be considered if we are to seek the proper path for the arts. It takes many years to develop and promote high-standard teachers. A black belt alone doesn't indicate that the practitioner is an instructor. However, I consider everyone a potential teacher in many ways. The future of the arts looks very promising and everything will be alright as long as the students and instructors don't forget what the essence of karate is. That's my message for the future generations—don't forget what the true essence of our art is.

Q: How do you look at yourself after all your years of training and dedication to kobudo and karate?
A: The martial arts are a miniature of life itself—a model to live by. They involve all of the elements of living. What you have learned in the arts, through practice and understanding, you can hopefully apply in day-to-day living. My life has been wonderful, and one of the reasons for my happiness has been the relatively untroubled course of Okinawa arts compared to other arts. I would like practitioners to remember that martial arts exercises help people to remain agile, no matter what their age. I have to say that I am a lucky man who is very grateful that his life in the arts has been pleasant. I wish everyone could have the feeling of peace, friendship and brotherhood for all mankind that I have found in the martial arts. O

"The future of the arts looks very promising and everything will be alright as long as the students and instructors don't forget what the essence of karate is. That's my message for the future generations—don't forget what the true essence of our art is."

Val Mijailovic

Knowledge Does Not Belong to Me

He is not only physically imposing, but HE IS also a giant in spirit and martial arts ability. Val Mijailovic is the kind of fighter that if you got jumped in a dark alley with him, you'd be very glad he was on your side. A direct student of Tak Kubota, Mijailovic is as powerful with his words as he is with his fists. With a natural talent for the finer points of the art, he stresses that attitude is the major factor to be successful in the way of true karate-do.

As one of the "old guardS" and pioneers in American karate, Mijailovic has clear opinions of what the art is—and also what it is not! His opinions have been known to raise a few eyebrows in the karate world. But he gained the right to express his opinions the hard and traditional way, tempering his words with blood, sweat and tears on the dojo floor. As a competitor, he has gathered many of the most important trophies the karate circles, including the first IKA World Cup title.

After many years of dedication, still loyal to his sensei and the ethical code of the warrior, Mijailovic devotes much of his current time to the martial arts. With many top students under his wing, he works hard to preserve the traditional values of budo with endless passion. "You have to have tradition," he says. "Without tradition, you have no foundation; and without foundation everything is lost."

Q: How long have you been practicing the martial arts?
A: Since 1970. I started in judo with Mr. Bob Ota at the Hollywood YMCA. At the same time, my brother, Dragan, was training with Soke Takayuki Kubota of the *International Karate Association*. I didn't have the money to join Soke Kubota's classes so I used to go and watch my brother train. Soke recognized my passion for karate and offered to let me clean the dojo twice a week in exchange for training. I trained six days a week. After 18 months, I received my black belt. The norm was five to six years for a black belt in those days, but since I competed often, Soke decided to promote me sooner. The styles of martial arts I have trained in are *judo* with Sensei Bob Ota,

Karate Masters

"Being dragged across the floor like a mop was the way you learned. And if you showed pain or complained about your injury, you were a dead duck. The first thing that they did was to attack any injury. So you learned not to show pain and to never complain."

iaido with Sensei George Domon, *aikido* in college and *gosoku-ryu* with Soke Tak Kubota.

Q: Who were your first teachers?
A: My early teachers in karate were the first generation students of Soke Kubota. At that time, Sensei Isamu Manako was teaching the beginning classes. Later I was taught by Senseis John Gelson, Harvey Ubanks, Ron McCauslan, George Bird, Ben Otake and Soke Kubota. Things were a bit different in those days. "Tougher" is a mild description. Being dragged across the floor like a mop was the way you learned. And if you showed pain or complained about your injury, you were a dead duck. The first thing that they did was to attack any injury. So you learned not to show pain and to never complain.

Q: How did the students respond to traditional Japanese training methods?
A: To us it was a world of myth and magic. When one spoke of the martial arts, people stopped and listened. If you said I am training in judo, karate or kung-fu, people asked who you were training with and wanted to know all about the arts. There were only a few schools on the West Coast. The dojo were very small and only one company sold uniforms. I remember when I got promoted, I had to wait six months for my black belt to arrive from Japan. Some people learn extremely fast, but I was a slow learner. I remember Sensei John Gelson saying to one of the black belts that it's OK that I learned slowly. His theory was that if I learn slowly then I will not forget. I was born and raised on a farm in Serbia, and so physically I was strong. I used to spend lots of time in the fields tending sheep and cattle, so I was always running, jumping, climbing trees and so on. I feel this really helped me in training. Also, I was in judo prior to karate, so I feel that judo training made a big difference to my balance and flow.

Q: Do you have any particularly memorable karate experiences that inspired you?
A: I was fighting in a JKA tournament, and we were in the finals. In those days, we used what was called the "Brazilian system," so we had been fighting all day and into the night. I was a young black belt. In the finals, I a fought a Japanese fighter much older than me. We fought two overtimes, and they gave us a rest before the final overtime. I was doing great in the previous rounds—he would score a point, then I would score a point, and so on. During the rest period, one of my friends came by and said, "Hey, Val! You're doing a great job with that *godan* from Japan." The last overtime began, and I lost within 15 seconds. From that day on, I told myself that titles mean nothing in the ring. As one of my teachers, Sensei George Bird, used to say: "Hey, man, I don't see any license plates on you!"

Q: What are your most important teaching points?
A: I teach at the IKA Headquarters dojo in Glendale, California, and hopefully will be for many years to come. One of the most important points I teach is to empower and encourage the students to learn how to correct themselves. Many instructors teach their techniques over and over again, and the student does not grow because he is not allowed to create. That may be the way you were taught, and maybe that is the way you teach, but that is not the only way. A front kick can be done 100 ways and each way will be right and within the form. Your way is the best way for you. Because I am 150 pounds heavier than you, perhaps your kicking style won't work with my body structure—but if it works for you, that is all that matters. Have a little fun and let the students experiment, then point out their weaknesses. For beginners, teach them the concept of acknowledging their mistakes and not dwelling on them. Our central nervous system learns by forming new neural pathways, and if students mentally punish themselves each time they make a mistake, then those pathways are not formed and what they just tried to learn is forgotten. Explain this to your students. By acknowledging the mistake and going on, the student will subconsciously correct that mistake. Teach your students to appreciate the gift

"Many instructors teach their techniques over and over again, and the student does not grow because he is not allowed to create. That may be the way you were taught, and maybe that is the way you teach, but that is not the only way. Have a little fun and let the student experiment, then point out his weaknesses."

Karate Masters

"Change is constant and on-going. The ability to adapt to our environment is the most important aspect of training. Our environment requires us to change and thus survive. In competition, one needs to flow and adapt to all changes instantly. There are times when one must be hard and fast, and other times loose and flexible. It all depends on the circumstances of the match."

of movement. Explain techniques metaphorically. People learn in different ways so use different analogies. It is how you say it. If you love what you say, and it is pure, then the students will accept and love it, too. There is nothing more beautiful, powerful or energizing than a dojo full of students moving in harmony. Every step and every breath becomes one and the same. The energy of this combined life force in one place and one time is pure, forgiving, and non-judgmental—a beautiful concept of who we are and what we can achieve. How fortunate we are to be the teachers. Respect and honor your students and they will become you and beyond.

Q: Do you think there are still pure karate styles?
A: Like, life the martial arts, is about growing and evolving. Evolution brings change and change is for the better. Shotokan is a living art; therefore, it must change in order to exist. Shotokan, shito-ryu and the other arts are our foundation. Like our parents, they teach us the basic values of life. Once we understand who we are, then we can choose where we go. But that journey is ours to make. If the foundation is strong, it will support our ventures. Sometimes we go to far and we fall, but our foundation will always be there.

Change is constant and on-going. The ability to adapt to our environment is the most important aspect of training. Our environment requires us to change and survive. In competition, one needs to flow and adapt to all changes instantly. There are times when one must be hard and fast, and other times loose and flexible. It all depends on the circumstances of the match. My training changes according to what I feel are my weaknesses. If I feel that my right punch is dominant, I will train with my left until symmetry of speed and power is achieved. If I enter a tournament and I know I can score with a right front kick, then I will challenge myself to score with a *kizame* instead of the front kick. I always enjoyed surprising myself. Our subconscious is so fantastic; it is there waiting for an assignment. Personally, I respect all different *ryu* because in the very end they are all pursuing the same goal.

Student training will have a greater number of possibilities and tactics depending on the style, but when someone puts down another style or claims that their style is the best, then I have no respect for this behavior. Recently I saw a news piece on someone in Beverly Hills who opened a school teaching movie stars how to defend themselves in case of kidnapping. This ignorant 25-year-old said: "The ancient martial arts are not suitable for the modern times, so I have developed these fighting techniques for today's world." What can you say to this nonsense? The world is full of monkeys, and I guess money talks.

Q: What is your opinion of full-contact karate and other events such as the UFC?
A: Full-contact karate and kickboxing are all in the family. They have earned their own right and respect. I honor all that are devoted to their art. We all have the same dreams of self-improvement. During the early 1970s, there was a clash between the traditionalists and the younger martial art forms. Full-contact karate and kickboxing are derivatives of the original forms. The frustration of many people at the time was that they wanted to show the full potential of traditional arts so they tried to come as close to reality as possible by full-contact competition. But there was that one obstacle—the rules. With any rules it becomes impossible to truly test oneself.

The Ultimate Fighting Championship is what it is. It is nothing new except the name. In the past, it was done in alleys and underground gambling places. It has been going on for thousands of years. The only difference is that now we see it on TV and fighters get more money. Our society is a violent one, and the general public likes to see destruction. Rooms full of testosterone and beer on Saturday nights will be supporting the UFC for a long time to come. In my opinion, it is not right or wrong; it just comes down to personal choice.

Free-fighting conditions our instincts. By free-fighting for long periods of time, one develops an instinctive state whereby the thinking or planning is

"I always enjoyed surprising myself. Our subconscious is so fantastic; it is there waiting for an assignment. Personally, I respect all different ryu because in the very end they are all pursuing the same goal."

Karate Masters

"Free-fighting conditions our instincts. By free-fighting for long periods of time, one develops an instinctive state whereby the thinking or planning is eliminated, and we react instead of plan. It is my opinion that this state of existence during a competition will prevail. The 'no-mind' attitude always worked for me."

eliminated and we react instead of plan. It is my opinion that this state of existence during a competition will prevail. My theory is to clear the mind and leave the ego at home. The "no-mind" attitude always worked for me. Allow your body to react on its own to the situation—your body knows what to do, that is why we train. Your body has memory stored in every muscle of the body and telling it what to do only takes precious time away from the battle.

Q: Do you feel there are fundamental differences between Japanese, American and European karate practitioners?
A: As far as the physical capabilities, the answer is no. The difference lies in the intent and commitment of what you are doing. One of the most difficult things to teach a student is the intent and commitment during a match. Once the competitor commits to a technique, there is no turning back. For example, if he commits to a front kick, it is like breaking a brick. If a person questions whether he can break a brick, then chances are he will not break it. If the intent is pure, then the possibility becomes a reality.

As far as the physical training, the Western world is equal to the Japanese one. However, in understanding the purpose of training, Westerners are still far from the Japanese. Many people think it is extremely important to go to Japan to learn the art of karate-do. Well, it is always good to travel and experience what the world has to offer. I don't think it is necessary, but I do recommend it. I spent a little time in Japan back in 1977, and it was a great journey. What stayed with me was the culture and its strong foundation in tradition.

Q: Karate nowadays is often referred to as a sport. Do you agree with this definition?
A: There are many faces of karate, and sport is one of them. A bow and arrow can be used to kill or for an Olympic competition. It all depends on what the intent is. It is important for the student to understand what he is training for. Tournament training is totally different than self-defense training. For example, a tournament fighter needs to know how to present his

techniques so that the judges will see them and call the points.

Q: Do you feel that you still have further to go in your studies?
A: Training has always been a passion for me. I look forward to what life has to offer. As I grow older, things become clearer. Much like the farmer gets to know his land, I get to sense changes in my training. The best way that I can describe it is like being on autopilot. So much sensory input has been absorbed by the mind, body and spirit throughout the years of training that at this point all these realms have merged as one. When sparring, you begin to see movement in its simplest form. One of my early instructors said, "What I have forgotten, you will never know." That tells us of the changes that we encounter in the arts. As far as I am concerned, studying martial arts is an on-going evolution and evolution has no end. Therefore, one cannot complete the learning.

"Training has always been a passion for me. I look forward to what life has to offer. As I grow older, things become clearer. Much like the farmer gets to know his land, I get to sense changes in my training. As far as I am concerned, studying martial arts is an on-going evolution and evolution has no end. Therefore one cannot complete the learning."

Q: Do you think it helps to train with weapons?
A: On my first day of iado, Sensei Domon put a live blade in my hands. He said, "This is your sword, and be careful because it is very sharp." It was my first and only lesson on the responsibility of knowledge. After a few weeks of instruction, he put a blindfold on me. From that point on, I spent most of my training blindfolded. By training with weapons, we develop focus and concentration. I often use the example of a sword when teaching. If a student doesn't understand a movement, I tell him to imagine a sword in his hands and then execute the technique. It helps the student to overcome his mental block.

Q: How important is the use of the makiwara?
A: The makiwara has many benefits, but if it is done incorrectly, it can cause many health problems. I used to punch the makiwara for many years, and it got to the point that my hands were screeching when I made a fist. Now I feel that there is no need to do anything excessive. A lot of the training in

Karate Masters

"As a free-sparring competitor, I think kata is very important. Kata gives us the means of remembering and paying tribute to our teachers. It gives us the tool for testing ourselves. Kata tunes and refines our energy flow and it allows us to unite energetically and spiritually. I love to practice kata almost as much as free sparring."

the old days included 1,000 kicks, 1,000 punches, 1,000 elbows. In reality, all we did is wear out our joints and loosen our ligaments.

Q: What is the most important element of karate-do: self-defense, sport or tradition?
A: The most important thing is to teach a student to teach himself. We can teach the student the basic forms and all that we know, but each person is different and each person's body functions and behaves differently. The length and strength of each muscle in our bodies is different, and the same technique cannot be executed by everyone the same way. Everyone develops his own style, including the different elements of self-defense and sport, within the basic forms and tradition. As a free-sparring competitor, I think kata is very important. Kata gives us the means of remembering and paying tribute to our teachers. It gives us the tool for testing ourselves. Kata tunes and refines our energy flow, and it allows us to unite energetically and spiritually. I love to practice kata almost as much as free sparring.

Q: What do you consider to be the major changes in karate since you began training?
A: The change is mainly in the tournament competitions or what is called sport karate. Putting gloves on just takes so much away from the true karate-do. It is the empty-hand that we practice. When gear and safety equipment is put on the competitor, he will take chances that are normally not considered. It is a different ballgame when you have your mouthpiece in. The intent is different and restricted, but I take it as part of the natural evolution of the things.

The important point here is to educate the students so they know what is sport and what is budo.

Q: With whom would you like to have trained with, regardless if he is dead or alive?
A: Many of my sensei have already passed away. I often wish that I had film or video footage of them so the memories could be in someplace else other than my mind. When I teach, I always mention their names when teaching their techniques. That is my way of honoring them and giving them the proper credit they deserve. In the early 1970s, we used to travel around the country and train in different dojo. Thus, we experienced many forms of Japanese martial arts. Of course, it would be an honor to train with the founders of the arts, but we do see their faces through our teachers.

Q: What would you say to someone who is interested in learning karate-do?
A: Begin with ease. Do not hurry; it will always be there for you. By starting slow, you will learn faster. Stretch well before each class and take the time to stretch after the class. Appreciate your abilities, be grateful and honor yourself. Don't forget to have fun. Be humble, listen well and absorb all that you can from as many teachers as you can—they all have something for you. Do not judge others by their abilities. Respect others as yourself and they will respect you, and be responsible about your ranking. My current concern is about too many people with insufficient knowledge teaching out there. That's very bad for the art. There is a greater number of students leaving the dojo after a few months of training than ever before—and most of the time it is because of the instructor. Very often the instructors get burned out by teaching too many classes, or they put themselves on such an ego trip that the student always feels inferior. The Western student doesn't like that. We like to be treated fairly, and instructors need to learn how to earn the student's respect, not shove it down their throats.

"Appreciate your abilities, be grateful and honor yourself. Don't forget to have fun. Be humble, listen well and absorb all that you can from as many teachers as you can; they all have something for you. Do not judge others by their abilities. Respect others as yourself and they will respect you—and be responsible about your ranking."

Karate Masters

"I teach all that I know. Knowledge does not belong to me. We will grow through the challenge of our students. Personally, there is nothing more rewarding than to see my students grow and surpass me. You can never know karate; it is like medicine—you can only practice it."

Q: What keeps you motivated after all these years?
A: The dojo keeps me motivated. It is a forgiving, non-judgmental place. It unifies, and is a pool of energy that constantly replenishes me. It embraces all that is good and promotes learning and understanding of the physical, mental and spiritual aspects of humanity. I teach all that I know. Knowledge does not belong to me. We will grow through the challenge of our students. Personally, there is nothing more rewarding than to see my students grow and surpass me. Many people ask the question, "You must have some secret techniques that you don't teach?" I always tell them, "No, I don't." I have techniques that are to be taught at the right time, when I feel that the student is mature enough to accept the responsibilities that come with that knowledge. In my life, I have many worlds—as we all do—work, family, friends, hobbies, et cetera. Karate is a part of my existence. It lives in all my worlds. I do not dwell over it, nor do I prioritize it. I enjoy it as I do my work and my family. It is a never-ending challenge like life itself. You can never know karate; it is like medicine—you can only practice it.

Q: Do you think bunkai is important?
A; Bunkai helps the student understand the kata. It teaches us timing, balance and reaction. It is unfortunate that the modern karate is moving away from bunkai.

Q: What is the philosophical basis for your karate training?
A: Since my childhood, I was intrigued by the human body and its real potential. Growing up on the farm I had to do many chores. Constantly chasing or being chased by dogs, rams, bulls—and kicked and whipped by the tails of cows and horses. So a kid learns to jump, duck, run and predict danger at an early stage of life. One of the things that we used to enjoy was climbing to the top of a tree, grabbing the end of a branch and then pushing

ourselves away from the tree. As we were falling, we broke our fall by grabbing the next branch and so on, all the way down. Another great challenge was to run as fast as we could over the river rocks. On weekends we spent all our time hunting with our father. When we came to America, there was not much to do. Martial arts filled that void.

As I began training in judo, I was introduced to the Eastern philosophy, and I found it intriguing. I didn't have any friends, and I needed to work so Sensei Ota took me on as his helper doing gardening. As we worked and drove house to house, he hold me the stories of his training. He was a 65-year-old man, very calm and he always had a smile on his face. No black belt in his dojo could budge him, let alone throw him. He would stand loose in the middle of the mat and black belts would try—one after another—to throw him ... all with no success. One night he took three of us to a Japanese theater and told us that we were going to see a movie called "*The Seven Samurai.*" I couldn't keep up with the titles because of my poor English, so I watched the movie and began to understand why Sensei Ota could do all those things in judo. I began to understand that it was the combination of cause, intent, mind, body and spirit that made him complete.

"*My philosophical basis for training comes from my teachers. As I train each technique, I try to better the previous one. Even though I am standing in the same stance and executing the same technique, each time I learn more from the one I just did. The better I do the move, the better I want to do it.*"

All of the above was confirmed to me once again by Soke Kubota. His strength comes from heart and compassion. He is a 165-pound man who would often fight 280-pound policemen and firemen. All you see and hear is a glob of arms and legs flying up in the air. Six-foot man-mountains went tumbling across the dojo floor until only Soke Kubota was left standing, and he would say, "Little ouch is OK!" I have seen this for the past 40 years, and I still see it today.

So my philosophical basis for training comes from my teachers. As I train each technique, I try to better the previous one. Even though I am standing in the same stance and executing the same technique, each time I learn more from the one I just did. The better I do the move, the better I

Karate Masters

"Each day is an eternity to me, and I would not change one moment of my past. There is so much to see and experience in this plane of existence. By saying I am the best, I would only insult my teachers and their teachers. There is no best."

want to do it. This attitude gives me the infinite possibilities concept that I strive for.

Q: How much training should a senior karate man do to improve?
A: Regardless of how much you do now, it is never enough. You just have to do your best and all you possibly can. Soke Kubota gets up at 4 a.m. and trains until 6 a.m. Then he has breakfast and goes to the dojo. He begins teaching at 8 a.m. and goes until noon. Then he trains by himself after lunch for another few hours. His children's classes begin at 5 p.m, and he teaches until 8 p.m. This has been going on for 60 years. And he still manages to write books, develop new kata and act in movies.

Q: What is the most important quality that defines a karate master?
A: Humilit.

Q: What is your opinion about incorporating other supplementary training methods into karate?
A: I always liked the natural way of training. Running, sit-ups, and push-ups. During high school, I tried weightlifting, but it did not work for me. When I lift weights, my body tightens too much, and it slows me down. Fortunately, I was born with a large bone structure. I always had more then enough strength for martial arts—the challenge was not to abuse it.

Q: What are the most important attributes of a good student?
A: Good work ethic and the ability to listen. Just show up and give the 100 percent!

Q: There is very little written about you in magazines. Why do you not thrive on publicity?
A: I guess it all comes down to what is important in one's life. Each day is an eternity to me, and I would not change one moment of my past. There is so much to see and experience in this plane of existence. By saying I am the

best, I would only insult my teachers and their teachers. There is no best. One may become a winner of the tournament and celebrate that day, but after that day is over the cycle of life is such that the champion soon becomes the ex-champion. I have never sought publicity or fame because I would have had to say things like "I am or I was." Saying, "I am," releases a beast that is called your ego . It is always hungry and it cares for no one but itself.

Q: Have you felt fear in your karate training?
A: In the early stages of martial arts training I experienced fear. Once I gained the understanding of where and why fear existed in me, then I filtered fear out and only kept what I needed from it. That is a pure form of concentration. The true spiritual aspect of karate-do is training. We do not have to sit and define it. By just doing, it becomes spiritual—overcoming fear is part of this growing process.

Q: What are your thoughts on the future of karate-do?
A: When I look to the art of karate-do today, I see a lot of changes. It is not necessarily lacking something, but just that it is different. It is milder, but it needed to be that way. In the old days, many people could not take the physical demands of karate. It is understandable because many people liked the idea of training but could not devote the time that was asked of them. Many people quit karate for a number of years because life took them to new adventures. But very often those same students come back 5 or 10 years later and stayed. Karate-do has come a long way and branched out to many forms—it has become a permanent entity in our society. It is associated with discipline and respect by the people of the world. Young people who are martial artists are respected and treated favorably by the business community. All this is good and it will stay good—because that is karate-do's nature. O

"The true spiritual aspect of karate-do is training. We do not have to sit and define it. By just doing, it becomes spiritual—overcoming fear is part of this growing process. In the old days, many people could not take the physical demands of karate. It is understandable because many people liked the idea of training but could not devote the time that was asked of them."

Yoshinao Nanbu

Walking His Own Path

ONE OF THE MOST GIFTED AND TALENTED KARATE PRACTITIONERS OF HIS TIME, SENSEI NANBU DECIDED TO BREAK FROM THOSE WHO CAME BEFORE HIM. WALKING HIS OWN PATH, HE DEVELOPED ORIGINAL KARATE METHODS AND STYLES THAT ARE A TRUE REFLECTION OF HIS PERSONAL BUDO JOURNEY. HE IS A TRUE WORLDWIDE ICON OF JAPANESE KARATE. A PIONEER BY ANY MEASURE, THIS OUTSTANDING KARATE-KA WAS BORN IN 1943 IN KOBE, JAPAN. HE MOVED TO FRANCE AS A YOUNG MAN TO BREAK INTERNATIONAL BARRIERS AND SHOW THE EUROPEANS THE TRUE ART OF KARATE. RECOGNIZED BY THE LATE TANI SENSEI AS "ONE OF THE MOST GIFTED AND TALENTED PRACTITIONERS OF HIS TIME," SENSEI NANBU DECIDED TO BREAK AWAY FROM THE RESTRICTIONS OF THE PAST AND DEVELOP HIS OWN KARATE METHOD. HIS OPEN MIND AND FLEXIBLE SENTIMENTS ABOUT OTHER ARTS ALLOWED HIM TO INCORPORATE PRINCIPLES AND CONCEPTS NEVER USED IN KARATE-DO BEFORE. THIS ADAPTABLE ATTITUDE REVOLUTIONIZED THE APPROACH TO THE TEACHING OF KARATE. TODAY HE IS RECOGNIZED AROUND THE WORLD AS ONE OF THE FOREMOST AUTHORITIES IN THE ART OF JAPANESE KARATE. A TRUE WARRIOR OF BUDO, SENSEI NANBU HAS CONQUERED EVERY CHALLENGE HE HAS EVER FACED.

Q: How did you get involved in the budo arts?
A: My family has always been involved in budo. My great grandfather was a great *yokozuna*, the most prestigious title in sumo circles. My uncle, Mr. Togashi, was a 9th-degree black belt in judo, and my other uncle, Mr. Yano, a master in the Japanese fencing art of kendo. My father was a 5th-degree black belt in judo and an expert in the weaponry art of *naginata*. I was already a shodan at 19 when I entered the University of Osaka. It was there where I met Tani Sensei, at that time a 9th dan in shito-ryu and one of the stylistic leaders in the world. Master Tani developed the method called *shukokai*, which is a personal approach to the shito-ryu style he learned under Kenwa Mabuni.

Q: How was the training at that time?
A: Extremely tough. Very hard and physically demanding. Every day we had to do 1,000 front kicks with *kiai* and punch the *makiwara* thousands of

Karate Masters

"Every day we had to do 1,000 front kicks with kiai and punch the makiwara thousands of times, not even stopping when our knuckles were bleeding. There was no way out. No excuses to quit."

times, not even stopping when our knuckles were bleeding. There was no way out. No excuses to quit. I was rapidly promoted to captain of the team. In 1963, I became the All-Japan University champion. This was a very difficult title to achieve then. At that moment, there was a total of 1,250 competitors. I remember my opponent in the final match had his *gi* torn apart from my front kicks! Due to this victory, I was awarded the very special Medallion of "Grand Merite," a coveted national recognition presented by Mr. Ohama, the president of the greatest student association in Japan.

Q: When did you decide to travel to Europe?
A: Mr. Henry Pleé invited me to go to France and teach the art in Europe. I was very excited! I was on my way to the journey of my life. I left the university and went to France in 1964. I began teaching for Monsieur Henry Pleé at his school in Montagne Saint-Genevieve. It was there I saw many new things for the first time in my life and these opened my point of view as an individual.

Q: You competed in the championships held in France and Europe at that time. A Japanese instructor living in Europe and competing against the Westerners was very unusual. How did it feel?
A: It was an exceptional thing, but I really wanted to test myself, and I promised Sensei Pleé that I was going to compete. I didn't have any problem with that. I know that it is very unusual to see a Japanese sensei enter a competition and fight against those who supposedly know less karate, but I never considered myself better than any other human being so I did not have a problem being a Japanese karate instructor in Europe and competing against Europeans. I didn't want people to respect me simply because I was Japanese and supposedly knew more than Westerners about karate. I wanted to earn respect and so I put myself to test. Only good things came out of that. The European karate community respected me highly and supported me greatly in anything I did.

I kept my Japanese and traditional approach to competition, though. My spirit said, "I have no right to lose a match." I was carrying a sword with me to all competitions to remind me that I should die if I lost a match. I won almost all of the major titles at that time and gained a lot of respect from all French and European karate-ka. In the final match of the International Cup (forerunner of the European Championships), I faced and defeated the great Domique Valera, who was occasionally a student of mine! It was a great match, and I have a lot of respect for him. I kicked him very hard in the stomach with a *mae-geri*, and Dominque didn't even blink! Then he kicked me back really hard in my stomach. I kept a poker face. No sign of pain. Later on, in the locker room, I opened my gi, and my stomach was black and blue. I looked at him and said, "Really good kick." Valera opened his gi and his stomach was also all bruised and he said: "Not bad, not bad at all." Domique Valera was an exceptional karate-ka—very talented. All I have is great respect for him.

"I have always been an individual in constant progression. In 1972, and after years of researching, fighting and training, I realized that I had many ideas about what I was doing. My martial arts journey has always been in constant evolution. The same year I decided to create the sankukai style."

Q: When did you quit competition?
A: It was in 1966. A little bit later I went back to Japan and Tani Sensei proposed that I become the official representative of *shukokai* for Europe and Africa. I accepted the offer and put myself into the shukokai shito-ryu style of karate in these two continents. Around the same time, and during my visits to Japan, I had the opportunity to train with several other people who opened my eyes to different conceptual approaches to martial art techniques and philosophies. It was very rewarding experience for me, not only as a martial artist, but as a human being, as well.

Q: What happened after that?
A: I have always been an individual in constant progression. In 1972, and after years of researching, fighting and training, I realized that I had many ideas about what I was doing. My martial arts journey has always been in constant evolution. The same year I decided to create the *sankukai* style. Of course, Tani Sensei wasn't happy about it and declined to see me again. I never meant to offend or hurt anyone, but I had to be true to myself and follow my own path in life, regardless of what other's people interest may be. Sankukai was a very natural evolution of the shito-ryu method I was practicing already. That step in

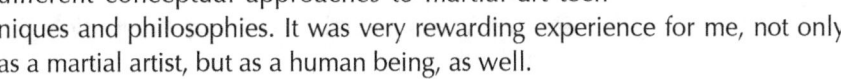

"After all these years living and teaching in the Western world, I have learned to look and feel in a very different way. I find myself in a balanced spot, where I don't see good or bad in the Western or Eastern society or culture. Both have good and bad things, and the citizens are a reflection of these attitudes. We are no more than the product of our societies, but I truly believe that a thinking individual can go beyond barriers and cultural boundaries to really find the truth and the essence of his existence."

my life was not a way of saying, "I want to break free and do my own thing." It was a natural progression in my budo journey and something I couldn't deny. If I had denied that evolution, I would have been denying my own existence. Unfortunately, some people didn't see it that way.

Sankukai was a great and almost immediate success, probably because of my established reputation in Europe. People loved it and karate-ka from all over the world realized how suitable that style was for competition. In 1973, I did 11 tours to teach the art. The lateral footwork (*tai-sabaki*) was the main principle in the fighting techniques. Using the opponent's force and momentum to counter his action is a wiser approach than using force against force as other karate-do styles use. In 1976, and due to the great acceptance of the style, I established the official World Sankukai Association to regulate the style in 43 countries. The same year we held the World Cup in Nice, France, and the World Championships in Monte Carlo, Monaco.

Q: When did you first publicly demonstrate what you describe as "nanbudo"?
A: It was in 1978, when we were holding the 2nd Sankukai World Championships, that I decided to demonstrate something that I had worked on for many years without mentioning to anyone. I showed nanbudo to the world—*The Way of Nanbu*. Once again, it was a natural thing in my progression as a martial artist.

Q: You retired for more than a year in the south of France, in Cap d'Ail, Monaco. How did this retirement affect your perception of the art and the direction of your research?
A: I was extremely happy with the success of sankukai around the world. If money was my reason to do things, I could have stuck to sankukai because it was working perfectly, but once again, my goal is different. Being isolated for more than a year, Mother Nature became my teacher. I observed how nature works and tried to adapt those principles to the art of nabudo. The beginnings of nanbudo were very difficult because most all my sankukai students and

affiliates around the world didn't follow me into the new expression of the art. In 1978, when I decided to drop sankukai, I was shocked and couldn't understand why they weren't following me.

I was not sure of the future, due to the fact that the majority of my students weren't at my same level of development—both physically and spiritually. This is understandable. I accepted that, but I was not going to allow personal interest to prevent me from growing as a human being. Today, after starting the same process again, the art of nanbudo is recognized worldwide and practiced in more than 50 countries.

Q: What is nanbudo?
A: Nanbudo is not a synthesis of different martial art styles and it is not an eclectic approach to budo either. It is a complete art. At first sight, due to the physical techniques and elements involved, people may think it comprises karate, aikido, tai chi, zen, and some other elements. But the art of nabudo goes beyond that simplistic definition. Similar to a professional sports car designer who calculates the wind and speed to come up with a more aerodynamic shape for a new car, I have developed a mechanical way to use the human body in a wiser and safer way. The wind is still strong so the design is still evolving, like nature itself.

Q: What is your opinion of the competition aspects of karate-do?
A: It depends on the individual. The bottom line is that if you know how to use it properly, the art of karate-do is a school for the formation of human character. Competition is simply a game that emulates the element of surviving in life. It keeps it real and in proper perspective.

Q: How do the *nanbu-taisho* exercises affect a student's health?
A: While learning and practicing these exercises, there are considerable benefits to health, largely due to the strengthening on the internal musculature and increased blood circulation. It is particularly beneficial to the functioning of the heart, but there have also been improvements in some of my students in cases of asthma and other illness. For this reason, many people of all ages take up nanbu-taisho just for their health, and some instructors teach it for health only. There is more to nanbudo than just a fighting.

The martial applications themselves are swift, subtle and very lethal. They are fully effective but cannot be learned or used effectively until a considerable groundwork of exercises and form have been laid down. In nanbudo, as in any other martial art, the fighter is only as good as he makes himself. Success will depend on the amount of effort personally expended.

Some people make good fighters and some people do not. My method is similar to other martial arts—it contains the knowledge, the methods and the skills, some unusual, for fighting—but the rest depends on the student and on the student's patience, endurance and personality in confronting and dealing with violence. Possibly the only aspect in which nanbudo differs from most other martial arts is that everyone can reach his own level of strength and self-defense ability without getting hurt.

Q: What is your opinion about individuals developing their own martial art style?
A: I know people who were white belts 10 years ago and now they have their own styles and they are 10th-degree black belts or whatever rank they've given themselves. It takes more than that to develop a new approach to the ancient arts. There is a price that has to be paid and some dues, too. The eclectic approach is very convenient for those who don't want to pay their dues. Definitely, this is not what I did when I created nanbudo. Everybody knows where I came from, what I did, what I accomplished as a young karateka and the years I deeply studied the arts before expressing my own perception of the principles of budo.

Q: Can you imagine life without karate?
A: That's not possible. Karate and budo are not just aspects of my life but very major parts of it. Learning karate has to become a way of life. I have shaped my life toward learning karate and budo. From this, one learns to marshal one's time in other areas—greater benefits come without the individual realizing what is happening inside. Budo is a vehicle for a deep transformation inside the human spirit. Don't get me wrong; nothing is free and an individual has to work hard towards that goal.

Q: Do you see differences between Westerners and Japanese when it comes to the art of nanbudo?
A: To me, all individuals are the same. It is true, though, that I have found that Westerners are much better trainees in my system than are the Japanese—they seem to better understand what each movement means. They are naturally curious and are continually asking questions. Why? I don't know. I guess it is part of the exuberance of the Western character! After all these years living and teaching in the Western world, I have learned to look and feel in a very different way. I find myself in a balanced spot, in which I don't see good or bad in the Western or Eastern society or culture. Both have good and bad things, and the citizens are a reflection of these

attitudes. We are no more than the product of our societies, but I truly believe that a thinking individual can go beyond barriers and cultural boundaries to really find the truth and the essence of his existence.

Q: Are you a traditionalist?
A: That is a good question considering all the barriers I broken in my past and how much I have evolved since I began training karate! If by traditionalist you mean someone who is teaching the same techniques he learned 35 years ago, then I am not a traditionalist, because everybody knows that the physical techniques I teach today are extremely different than those I used to teach when I was doing shito-ryu or sankukai. As far as the moral and ethical values of budo, I definitely want to preserve those, so to that extent you may say that I am a traditionalist. To be honest, I don't know why people think that being a traditionalist is something wrong. Morality and ethics are something very important in order to have a strong society. Creativity is not an excuse for blind rebelliousness. Disagreement for disagreement's sake is not being creative. Unfortunately, there are a lot of karate-ka with that attitude nowadays. The great Taisen Deshimaru wrote: "Life's problems are different for each of us, and each of us needs a different way of solving them. Therefore, each of us has to create his own method. If you imitate, you'll be wrong. You have to create yourself." The martial art are not different from life.

"I was not sure of the future, due to the fact that the majority of my students weren't at my same level of development—both physically and spiritually. This is understandable. I accepted that, but I was not going to allow personal interest to prevent me from growing as a human being."

Q: Where does the budo spirit lie?
A: Karate-do, nanbudo and all of the martial arts in general are something that can only spring from within. Because of that, you should inspect yourself as you would a weapon and notice your strong points and weaknesses. This internal journey will make you a better human being. There is something I like to call your "sphere of influence." As human beings, it is within this sphere of influence that you can be more efficient as an individual. You simply don't want to go beyond the boundaries of this sphere because all of your true power and energy will be inefficient. O

Masters' Techniques

Nanbu Sensei faces his opponent (1). He blocks the attack by moving to the side and using his left hand to redirect the energy (2). He then counter-attacks with his right hand to the face (3), moves to his right (4), sweeps his opponent (5), and finishes him with a punch to the face (6).

Both fighters face each other with left leads (1). Nanbu Sensei deflects the front kick attack to the outside (2), and spins around (3), sweeps his opponent's supporting leg (4), and finishes him with a kick to the face (5).

Nanbu Sensei faces his opponent (1). He deflects the front kick attack with his right hand (2), and spins 360 degrees to place a ushiro ura-mawashi geri to the back of his opponent's head (3).

Yuishi Negishi

A Modern Samurai

BORN IN TOGICHI, JAPAN, ON DECEMBER 7, 1940, SENSEI NEGISHI STARTED HIS KARATE TRAINING AT AGE 15 UNDER THE GREAT SHITO-RYU TEACHER MANZO IWATA, A DIRECT DISCIPLE OF FOUNDER KENWA MABUNI. HE WAS EDUCATED IN A FAMILY IN WHICH THE CODE OF SAMURAI GOVERNED THE HOUSE AND STRICT DISCIPLE WAS ENFORCED. GRADUATING IN ECONOMICS FROM TOYO UNIVERSITY, HE BECAME THE CAPTAIN OF THE UNIVERSITY KARATE TEAM IN 1964 AND THE HEAD COACH THE YEAR AFTER. NEGISHI ALSO STUDIED MYATA-RYU BATTO-JUTSU DIRECTLY FROM HIS GRANDFATHER, KAZUZYO HASEGAWA. CURRENTLY, HE IS THE PRESIDENT OF NIPPON BUDO SOSEI-KAI SHITO-RYU AND THE LEADER OF THE TRADITIONAL SCHOOL OF JAPANESE TAI-JITSU, NIPPON SHINKYOKU-RYU, WHERE HE IS THE FOUNDER'S 10TH GENERATION DIRECT DESCENDANT. ALTHOUGH HE TEACHES BOTH ARTS AS SEPARATE ENTITIES, HIS DYNAMIC APPROACH HAS CREATED AN EFFECTIVE MIXTURE OF HARD KARATE POWER AND SOFT TAI-JITSU TECHNIQUES.

Q: How has karate evolved since you began training?
A: The art has evolved significantly, especially in the last 20 years or so. This evolution has affected the technical aspects of karate. For instance, when I began my training, the conception of fighting distance was quite different. We used to train short techniques such as *kizami-tsuki* or *mae-ashi geri* because they were better for real fighting. Nowadays, since the emphasis on karate's sportive aspects is bigger, the fighting distance is wider and most techniques are delivered by the rear hand and leg. This is a subtle change, but it affects the way the art is taught in many schools around the world. Karate should be taught as a complete martial art, which allows individuals who feel so inclined, to compete, practice and train techniques that are suitable for sport competition.

Q: Are these changes good or bad?
A: As I said before, it depends on the goals of the student. If you're thinking only about a physical activity and not about self defense, then it's fine. But if your mind is focused on real self-defense, the sportive aspect of the karate

Karate Masters

"Evolution is inevitable, but the direction this evolution takes depends on the final goal of each practitioner. As long as you know where you are going, it's fine. Just don't get upset when you find you're a karate champion who can't defend himself in a real fight."

won't help you much. In fact, it can be negative for your mental approach to real self-defense. Evolution is inevitable, but the direction this evolution takes depends on the final goal of each practitioner. As long as you know where you are going, it's fine. Just don't get upset when you find you're a karate champion who can't defend yourself in a real fight.

Q: Why are there so many different karate styles today?
A: All of these variations depend on the instructor's perception of how to perform a certain movement and how to apply it in combat. It's very often taken as fact that when an instructor is young he teaches very differently than when he is old. This simple factor has caused misunderstanding not only in karate, but in the martial arts in general. A teacher's perspective changes with time and his overall perception of the art varies according to that. In most cases, however, the essence and principles are the same, but the physical way of applying the concepts changes. The understanding about the functionality of the physical movement changes; therefore, the way of teaching it changes also. A karate-ka doesn't practice the art the same at age 25 years as he does at age 55. If he is an instructor, then you can be sure that his age will affect the way he teaches a technique he learned 30 years ago. It's called "maturity."

Q: Are some styles better than others?
A: All karate is good. The best advice I can give is to focus on the art that you can best use. There are some karate styles that are more suitable for certain kinds of physical configuration. In the long term, this can make a difference in the external appearance of your technique. For instance, goju-ryu is a style of karate-do that suits a short body. You can be 6 feet 3 and be

a great goju-ryu exponent, but from the external point of view, goju-ryu is a style that looks better on short people. But if you are tall and big and you really enjoy goju-ryu, you shouldn't avoid this art simply because it doesn't fit your body type. The bottom line is to train in the style you feel most comfortable doing. Enjoy your training and keep practicing, even if many things don't make sense in the beginning. Time brings understanding in the art of karate—you need time to mature and see things that are not visible in the first years of training. You need patience to progress and to understand the deeper principles of the art. By sweating in your *gi* every day, you'll be closer to the union of the body and spirit. That's when you will see what the art is really about.

"The bottom line is to train in the style you feel most comfortable doing. Enjoy your training and keep practicing, even if many things don't make sense in the beginning. Time brings understanding in the art of karate—you need time in order to mature and see things that are not visible in the first years of training."

Q: How much personal influence should an instructor incorporate into his teaching?
A: Everything! The teacher is a vehicle to preserve the art. The way the teacher sees the art, the way the teacher feels the art, and the way the teacher expresses the art is the only reference that the student has. Every single karate-do instructor in the world influences and changes the art in some way according to his personality and point of view. That's a logical thing. There is nothing wrong with that. The art is nothing but the expression of the artist, and in this case the art of karate is a vehicle used by the karate-ka to express himself. Duplicating what you have been taught without thinking and analyzing what you're doing is just to follow blindly—that's not the right attitude of budo. You are supposed to use the art to elevate and grow, but you should not follow without thinking for yourself. In the true expression of any art form, a copy has no worth, only originals have value.

Q: Are you against the growing movement of sport karate?
A: Not really. Sport is a small part of karate. It can be used wisely to develop positive qualities in young practitioners, but if the teacher focuses too much on sport, students will be missing the whole picture. Training has to be bal-

Karate Masters

"Karate should come first, then if you have extra time to dedicate to these other training aspects, the better for you. Don't substitute your technical karate training for running or lifting weights because you will be making a mistake. You must first develop a strong technical foundation before you consider spending time in other physical conditioning aspects."

anced. Real fighting is very different from point fighting or sport competition, not only in physical techniques, but also how both situations are approached mentally. Sport karate can only be practiced for a short time, but the martial art of karate can be practiced for your whole life.

Q: What is your opinion of supplemental training like running and weight lifting?
A: Anything you can do to improve your health and strengthen your body for karate is good. Having a good training to improve your wind, using weights to develop muscles, and practicing yoga to improve flexibility is something I recommend to all practitioners. The problem comes when a student gets caught up in physical training at the expense of the time he trains in karate. Don't fool yourself. Running a marathon, lifting weights or practicing yoga one hour a day won't improve your karate. It won't make your *gyaku-tsuki* faster or your kata more precise. Karate should come first. If you have extra time to dedicate to these other training aspects, the better for you. Don't substitute your technical karate training for running or lifting weights because you will be making a mistake. You must first develop a strong technical foundation before you consider spending time in other physical conditioning aspects. When you reach the rank of *shodan* or *nidan*, then perhaps you can go and develop purely physical areas such as strength, but not at the expense of substituting your karate classes for weight training sessions. A strong karate technique has nothing to do with the way your body looks. Physical appearance has nothing to do with real karate.

Q: Why did the old masters change the original karate techniques so much?
A: It's hard to answer that question. Master Funakoshi used to practice karate forms with a high center of gravity and short hand movements, much like shito-ryu. Then Master Nakayama came along next and changed the positions and developed a different form of karate. He pushed the art of karate as a form of physical education, and I guess he decided to modify certain technical aspects to better serve his new goal.

Q: Do you think *kobudo* training helps the karate practitioner?
A: I think so. The old *bushi* arts involved weapons training, not only empty-hand techniques. They were different elements of warrior training and education. Later on, all of these different aspects were separated; but in the beginning, a warrior was a "complete package." Training with traditional weapons helps students to develop important physical attributes that will improve their empty-hand techniques. In the process of learning how to use a weapon, the student uses the body in a very different way compared to the simpler empty-hand movements. The body works differently when you are using a *bo* than when you are performing *gyaku-tsuki*. The body rotation maybe be essentially the same, but the timing of the hip turning has to match the speed of the weapon in order to get *kime* in the right moment. If hitting with the bo takes more time than hitting with your fist, the synchronization of your body torque will have to be adjusted to that particular speed. Once you drop the weapon and go back to empty-hand, you'll find that the body moves more in sync with the technique. It's something very difficult to explain in words without being too technical. But those who train in both arts—kobudo and karate—will definitely understand what I'm trying to say.

"Training with traditional weapons helps students to develop important physical attributes that will improve their empty-hand techniques. In the process of learning how to use a weapon, the student uses the body in a very different way compared to the simpler empty-hand movements. The body works differently when you are using a bo than when you are performing gyaku-tsuki."

Karate Masters

"Zen training is paramount for karate-do development. The spiritual aspect is very important when you are practicing Japanese karate. Not paying attention to spiritual and mental development will limit your progress and evolution as a karate-ka. This is not only true for karate-do but for all styles of martial arts as well."

Q: The legendary goju-ryu karate master, Gogen Yamaguchi, said that for a total understanding of his style students should embrace yoga and shinto. Are there any special spiritual elements that need to be studied in shito-ryu karate?

A: Zen training is paramount for karate-do development. The spiritual aspect is very important when you are practicing Japanese karate. You need both to have the complete art. If you only focus on the physical techniques, there will be many aspects you'll overlook in your personal journey toward mastery. Not paying attention to spiritual and mental development will limit your progress and evolution as a karate-ka. This is not only true for karate-do, but for all styles of martial arts as well. You need to find a balance between your body and mind. The body is trained through demanding karate sessions of *kihon*, *kata* and *kumite,* but the mind should be trained equally to counterbalance the physical side—this is only achieved through serious and dedicated Zen training.

Q: Do you think the media is responsible for the public perception of martial arts?
A: Karate and martial arts are the result of many years of training, research and evolution. They contain cultivation and refinement, but unfortunately, instead of trying to preserve the heritage that our ancestors preserved for us, magazines and promoters have looked for the easiest and fastest ways to make money and have moved away from the basic principles of budo. Movies also share the blame in this. Young practitioners think that the martial arts are all about Bruce Lee screaming and yelling with *nunchaku* flying all over the place. This is not real budo, and I don't believe this kind of attitude is good for future generations.

"Young practitioners think that martial arts are all about Bruce Lee screaming and yelling with nunchaku flying all over the place. This is not real budo, and I don't believe this kind of attitude is good for future generations."

In a few years, the kids that were educated under this modern philosophy will open their own schools and become teachers. What do you think they are going to teach? If you don't educate youth in the way of budo, don't expect real martial arts to survive—maybe the new approaches of full-contact fighting—but not true budo. If there is a lack of proper education, the martial arts will suffer in the future.

Q: Is it necessary to travel to Japan to learn karate?
A: Karate is a great art and its sportive aspects will help many young people to achieve what they want in life. Japanese aren't necessarily better than Caucasians, but they definitely understand more about the traditions of budo. If you want to go to Japan to experience the culture and learn the traditions of budo, then do it because you won't get that anywhere else. But if you are only interested in the physical side of the art, just find a good teacher and follow his guidance. These days, it is common knowledge that the majority of the great Japanese teachers are living outside of Japan.

Karate Masters

"The analysis of the different karate techniques found in kata is very important. You need to understand that bunkai is structured in different levels of application, with varying difficulty. The first step is when you apply the physical movement from kata directly, without changing the movements. This very basic application opens the student's mind to how karate uses the technical mechanics for physical movements."

Q: Can a practitioner's physique make a difference in his kata or kumite?

A: It's true that a medium-sized person will make a kata "look better," but this has nothing to do with the true kata performance of a budo practitioner. The physical appearance may affect a kata competition by influencing the judges, but it doesn't mean anything to a karate-do kata practitioner. In kumite, a practitioner with long limbs will have a certain advantage against someone who is shorter. But the shorter karate-ka may be more dangerous in a real fight. For karate competition, your physique may be a determining factor, but for karate-do as part of budo, definitely not.

Q: How important is *bunkai* in the study of kata?

A: Kata is an integral part of the art of karate. In fact, karate can't be totally understood without a thorough study of kata. The analysis of the different karate techniques found in kata is very important. You need to understand that bunkai is structured in different levels of application, with varying difficulty. The first step is when you apply the physical movement from kata directly, without changing the movements. This very basic application opens the student's mind to how karate uses the technical mechanics for physical movements. The next step is to incorporate the principles found in that particular technique and apply a more creative approach without totally breaking away from the kata movement. This phase allows the student's creativity to come out. Finally, and only after you totally understand the intrinsic principles of that particular movement, you can enter into what we can call a "non-classical" phase. In this phase, you use the principles of the technique but in a totally free format. You have already learned the principle, and now your application of the original movement doesn't look like that kata movement anymore. The principle is there—the main concept of the movement found in the kata is still there—but your external application is different. That is when you can say you have truly *transcended* kata. Reaching this level of skill and understanding requires many years of dedicated training and study.

Q: What is your advice to future karate generations?
A: I'm not planning on leaving anytime soon! Kidding aside, it is very important that all the top karate teachers in the world understand that the future of the art is in their hands. Whatever they put in their students' hearts is what will drive the art of karate in the future. Students should always remember that karate-do is not simply a sport; there is a sportive aspect, but karate is not *just* a sport. Karate-do is budo and as such it has to be internalized. Budo is for the rest of your life and it transcends trophies and medals. Budo is about life. If students remember this simple fact everything else will fall into place because budo teaches you how to practice and lead your life. Once you understand budo, the rest is easy. The tricky part is for teachers to make sure the students really understand budo, so the important values are preserved for future generations. Preserving physical techniques is not a big deal, but preserving the right attitude takes a dedicated effort. This is our responsibility as leaders of karate. O

"Students should always remember that karate-do is not simply a sport; there is a sportive aspect, but karate is not just a sport. Karate-do is budo and as such it has to be internalized. Budo is for the rest of your life and it transcends trophies and medals. Budo is about life."

Seiji Nishimura

A Critical Reflection

SEIJI NISHIMURA HAS A COMPILED A COMPETITION RECORD THAT MOST PEOPLE WOULD ENVY. BORN ON JUNE 9, 1956, IN KUMAMOTO, JAPAN, SENSEI NISHIMURA'S IMPRESSIVE RESUME IS THE PRODUCT OF MANY YEARS OF HARD AND DEDICATED TRAINING. AS A STUDENT OF COMMERCIAL SCIENCES AT THE UNIVERSITY OF FUKUOKA, NISHIMURA DECIDED TO IMMERSE HIMSELF INTO THE WORLD OF SPORT KARATE. FOR MORE THAN A DECADE, HE WON VIRTUALLY EVERY MAJOR NATIONAL AND INTERNATIONAL TOURNAMENT THAT HE ENTERED. HE CURRENTLY SERVES AS A NATIONAL COACH FOR THE JAPAN KARATE-DO FEDERATION AND WORKS AS A PROFESSOR AT FUKUOKA UNIVERSITY.

AS ONE OF THE MOST WELL-KNOWN REPRESENTATIVES AND LEADERS OF THE *WADO* STYLE OF KARATE, NISHIMURA BALANCES HIS TRAINING BETWEEN *KATA* AND *KUMITE* AND LEADS HIS STUDENTS INTO A DEEPER UNDERSTANDING OF THE SPIRITUAL ASPECTS OF BUDO. "TRUE KARATE-DO," HE SAYS, "IS NOT STRICTLY FOR TECHNIQUE BUT FOR DEVELOPING YOUR MIND. KARATE IS FOR LIFE. IT IS A WAY OF LIFE, A WAY OF THINKING."

NISHIMURA HIMSELF IS CLEARLY A PRODUCT OF HARD, RELENTLESS TRAINING. HIS CAT-LIKE MOVEMENTS ARE FAST AND SMOOTH, BUT WITH THE POWER OF A THUNDERING RACEHORSE. HIS TECHNIQUE IS IMPECCABLE AND HIS COMBAT TIMING IS EXTREMELY PRECISE—QUALITIES THAT A FIGHTER ONLY DISPLAYS AFTER MANY YEARS OF EXPERIENCE, SELF-DISCIPLINE AND CRITICAL REFLECTION.

Q: When did you start to train in the martial arts?
A: I started training in karate at a very young age. In high school, my teacher was Kazuya Hirai. I also trained a little bit in judo, which I consider to be a great art. Then at the university I trained with Shizuo Yahiro of the *goju-ryu* style. And later, after graduation, I became student of wado-kai teacher Toru Arakawa. They all gave me different things that I have incorporated into my training. Today, I am a wado-kai man, but I definitely have influences from the other styles I have practiced. I truly believe they made my karate richer and more versatile.

Karate Masters

"The wado style is very subtle in the way it uses energy. You don't crash into the opponent; you use a lot of tai-sabaki *to redirect your opponent's energy and find the right position. It uses soft techniques as compared to other harder styles."*

Q: What are the specific strong points of wado-ryu?
A: The wado style is very subtle in the way it uses energy. You don't crash into the opponent; you use a lot of *tai-sabaki* to redirect your opponent's energy and find the right position. I truly believe that wado is a very good karate style for competition due to its mobility and practical approach to fighting. It uses soft techniques as compared to other harder styles.

Q: With all of the technical changes during the past few years, do you think there are still *pure* styles in karate?
A: Different styles use different approaches to the same situation. They give the student options and that is really good. Every karate-do style is simply the personal perception of an individual's idea of how to do things. You must be careful and not jump from one style to another, but it is definitely good to be able to use different approaches to combat. Every style has a personality and this only brings more interesting techniques to the overall art.

Q: How has your personal expression of karate developed over the years?
A: Every new day is an opportunity to research new things and improve what you have been doing previously. Your expression of the art changes naturally as you grow older and hopefully wiser. You keep getting more knowledge about different aspects of the art and other related matters. It is only when you keep training and working hard that your true self comes out in what you are doing. It is this constant dedication to the tasks at hand that brings maturity and stability to your life.

Q: What does kata represent to the art of karate-do?
A: A kata is a work of art, just like a painting by an old master. When you look at the painting, you try to see it in the light that the artist painted it. You study it and find the meaning the artist was trying to convey through

the medium of oil and canvas. Kata is simply a moving work of art. It was a means of communication for artists who lived thousand of years ago. The message is there and is very clear. You don't have to intellectualize it or sit in front of it and mediate. All you have to do is perform the movements in order to understand the message. You feel what those people wanted to tell you. Kata is very important because it makes you develop awareness. When you do a kata with a group of people, you have to sense the other individuals. If someone is out of line, you have to be aware of this; otherwise, you will crash into him. In other words, every movement has to be together and your timing similar. Not everyone moves at the same time, and you have to remember that. Each kata must be done as if your opponent were real. In kata, you do not memorize your movements. Instead, you focus on the imaginary opponent's attack. You can always do beautiful kata, but if you don't put concentration into it, kata will be dead. Kata must be alive. It is 50 percent physical and 50 percent mental. Without that 100 percent effort you are bound to have dead karate.

"Kata is simply a moving work of art. It was a means of communication for artists who lived thousand of years ago. The message is there and is very clear. You don't have to intellectualize it or sit in front of it and mediate. All you have to do is perform the movements in order to understand the message. You feel what those people wanted to tell you. Kata is very important because it makes you develop awareness."

Q: Why do some people feel kata movements are not useful at all?
A: Well, if one of your movements isn't very strong, don't blame it on the movement. Simply because you don't understand a kata doesn't mean there is something wrong with it. If you change a kata before your understanding reaches the level the kata is on, you'll be defeating the purpose of the kata. It's like that painting by one of the old masters. If you go up to that canvas with a brush loaded with black paint and paint right through it, it destroys

Karate Masters

"In karate-do, as in any other martial art, the fighter is only as good as he makes himself. Success depends on the amount of effort put in and on the individual personality. Some people make good fighters and some people do not."

the means of communicating with that artist.

The flip side of the coin is that kata has to be taken for what it is today and not for what it might have been before. Long ago, kata was practiced as a series of self-defense situations against an imaginary opponent, but if you interpret kata like that nowadays, I think your progress will stop there. You must try to find a balance between these two different aspects. Contrary to what may appear at first sight, they are not opposite. It simply takes years of study to strike that perfect balance.

Q: Some people advocate training left-handed kata. Do you?
A: It can be very useful considering the fact that in a fighting situation things will not run as smoothly as in tournament competition. It is true that kata emphasizes more one side than the other, so it is important to compensate for that. It is not difficult to teach a beginner this training method, but to a black belt who already has set himself on a right-handed basis, it is much harder.

In competition, the southpaw has an advantage over the right-hander because a left-hander will be constantly competing against right-handed opponents. Chances are few that a right-hander will be fighting a southpaw. This is probably why it is interesting to train kata in the opposite direction. It helps to balance the body and the practitioner's skills.

Q: Do you think martial arts movies are positive for karate-do?
A: I'm afraid the violence shown in some of the martial arts movies today creates the wrong impression. Personally, I would like to see filmmakers emphasize the philosophical side more than the physical part of the arts. This would bring more understanding and sensitivity into people's mind.

Q: Do you think there are differences in martial arts inside and outside of Japan?

A: Yes, definitely. What is going-on in Japan isn't the same as what is going-on in Europe or America. From the Westerner's perspective, the Japanese are an anachronism. We are conservative by nature. We want to protect the Japanese historical culture of martial arts. Traditionally, we have no interest in changing them. We have no interest in polishing the arts to make them better. This is the traditional Japanese way and this approach lasted for many years. In the Western world, things are different. Due to the external influences for improvement, things are changing even in Japan.

Q: Is karate-do budo or sport?

A: Competition in karate is simply a sport. Nothing more, nothing less. But karate-do is budo, and budo is something that you can take with you for the rest of your life. Karate doesn't end when your competition years are over. It lasts until you die. If you approach karate like it was only a sport, you are missing the point.

"In competition, the southpaw has an advantage over the right-hander because a left-hander will be constantly competing against right-handed opponents. Chances are few that a right-hander will be fighting a southpaw. This is probably why it is interesting to train kata in the opposite direction. It helps to balance the body and the practitioner's skills."

Historically, everybody knows the art of karate-do was developed for pure self-defense. The idea of training was to take the human body and turn it into a lethal weapon. You had to develop your fists, feet, elbows, knees, et cetera to the point they became deadly tools of survival. Nowadays, our society is very different than when karate was created. Developing your body with pure self-defense in mind is not the main goal in modern training. We have gone a long way from bujutsu to budo, and some values have changed. It is part of a civilized evolution. In the past, you used your techniques to kill people and

Karate Masters

"In the budo arts, the difference between one whose mind wanders and one who is attentive is much more apparent than in any other style. Not only will the inattentive one get low marks, but he is more likely to have his bones broken when a free-fighting situation occurs. A person must always confront his fears head on; otherwise fear will overwhelm him."

survive an attack; nowadays you use the punches and kicks to improve yourself as a human being.

Q: What is the most important quality for a student to possess?
A: An attentive mind. In the budo arts, the difference between one whose mind wanders and one who is attentive is much more apparent than in any other style. Not only will the inattentive one get low marks, but he is more likely to have his bones broken when a free-fighting situation occurs. A person must always confront his fears head on; otherwise, fear will overwhelm him.

Q: Modern instructors seem to have abandoned some of the old ethics and principles of karate-do. How do you feel about this?
A: I truly believe that those instructors who give into the demands for modernization are in reality cutting off their noses despite their faces. Without principles, the martial arts become no more than murderous forms of personal combat. If a student really wanted just that, and nothing else, he could buy a knife or a gun and have greater kill-power than the deadliest black belt.

Q: Are you a traditionalist?
A: If that term describes someone who keeps doing the same techniques as his ancestors, then I am not a traditionalist. This is because the physical techniques I teach today are different than those I used to learn. But I do consider myself a traditionalist in the sense that I uphold the meaningful and valuable tradition that our previous masters and teachers cultivated and

developed. This includes respect for yourself and for others, self-discipline and self-control. All these aspects are part of the traditional arts, and I strongly advocate them. On the other hand, I am not afraid of the flow of time and of making changes without losing my center. Blind traditionalism lacks vitality and life. Traditionalism, to remain valuable, must be dynamic and open.

Q: Do you think that there is any style of martial art better than the rest?
A: No particular style of martial art is inherently better than any other. As far as effectiveness, any art will do the work of self-defense if you train hard and maintain a humble attitude. Individuals are the ones who make a style work, not the other way around. The person is always more important than the style he practices. What everybody must understand is that there are some styles that may fit better to some individuals than to others. You need to find what martial art fits you best. The problem is that you may feel attracted to a style that doesn't totally fit your body and mental approach. The most important thing is to find a style that you enjoy practicing and dedicate yourself to it. You will only progress if you enjoy what you are doing.

"I truly believe that those instructors who give into the demands for modernization are in reality cutting off their noses despite their faces. Without principles, the martial arts become no more than murderous forms of personal combat."

Q: How important is discipline?
A: Very important. Discipline sometimes frightens people, so it has to be put into a framework in which it can be seen as non-threatening and positive. It is a healthy discipline coupled with love and respect. There are many people out there looking for attention. And people seeking attention need discipline. Unfortunately, they sometimes do things wrong so they can get this attention. When I was young, I knew that to set higher goals I would need

Karate Masters

"The person is always more important than the style he practices. What everybody must understand is that there are some styles that may fit better to some individuals than to others. You need to find what martial art fits you best. The problem is that you may feel attracted to a style that doesn't totally fit your body and mental approach."

more discipline. I encourage the students who come to my classes to set goals for themselves. If these are unrealistic, I try to help them set realistic goals. When they succeed, I try to reward them as a positive reinforcement to continue.

Q: How do you see the current political state of the art?
A: Politics are bad news for all martial arts styles. Many great practitioners, with enormous potential, leave the arts simply because they are tired of politics. They have been burned so badly by the politics that they have given up the idea that one day people will unify, standardize and regulate in an harmonious fashion to promote the art. We have gone through some pain of growth and development, but it is paying off. The hard part is really over. What we need are good people who are intent on making karate even more accepted.

Q: Are students more mature than when you started to teach?
A: I think we are getting a more serious student who is thinking about his mental and spiritual development. It seems as though people are searching for something and they are finding it in the karate schools. I'm finding that the students who come into my schools now are better quality students than those years ago. They are more serious about their personal development and growth. They are not motivated by the physical dynamics of breaking boards or by weapons and competition. I think what is motivating them is the calmness that they are trying to attain ... the peacefulness, physical cultivation and mental cultivation. I think that's great.

Q: What do you think about the idea of karate turning into a sport?
A: To me, karate should never turn into just a sport because it can offer much more than any sport. For instance, it not only teaches you to develop your mind, but also your character. Certainly, sports can do this to a degree, but karate, by itself, can do more to develop a person.

Q: Why does a lack of control in competitions seem to be causing more injuries?
A: Because there are many instructors sending students to compete with low technical and control skills. In karate competition, you are going to get hit. Elite competitors hit hard to the body but have great control to the face. Of course, sometimes accidents happen but those are the exceptions. To punch a man in the face is one of the easiest things to do in karate, it requires no training whatsoever. A person with no training is capable of bowing in at the beginning of the match and punching another competitor right in the face, no matter how much training the second fighter has had. Karate is about the skill to control your techniques. If you wish, you can control the power; if not, you unleash it!

"Many great practitioners, with enormous potential, leave the arts simply because they are tired of politics. They have been burned so badly by the politics that they have given up the idea that one day people will unify, standardize and regulate in an harmonious fashion to promote the art."

Q: Is heavy bag training important for karate competition?
A: Power comes from different sources, but mostly from body mechanics. It is true that training with pieces of equipment such as the heavy bag will help you to develop power in your techniques, but you can spend five hours punching and kicking the bag and still lack the power we are talking about. The reason is very simple—power in karate should be developed through a consistent and dedicated approach to technique. First you have to endlessly

Karate Masters

"Elite competitors hit hard to the body but have great control to the face. To punch a man in the face is one of the easiest things to do in karate. It requires no training whatsoever. Karate is about the skill to control your techniques. If you wish you can control the power; if not, you unleash it!"

repeat the basic technique in order to make it a reflex action. Only by constant repetition will proper body mechanics be developed. Only when your body mechanics are close to perfect should you gradually begin to incorporate the heavy bag. Too much heavy bag training will make your technique sloppy, so be careful. Try to add more power without jeopardizing your technique. I have seen a lot of practitioners who had a very clean technique become extremely sloppy as soon as they started to punch the heavy bag.

Q: Nowadays more people open schools and become teachers in record time. What's your opinion?
A: To become a *sensei* is not something that can be done in 10 years. It takes more time than that. To teach karate doesn't mean you are a *sensei*. There are many teachers but not many sensei. The sensei's work transcends his dojo. Through precept and example he inspires his students and close associates to aspire to greater heights as individuals. He is in a very unique position to achieve dignity for himself, his students and the discipline he represents. He must be willing to subordinate personal prejudices, vested interests, financial gain and self-aggrandizement. He must accept total commitment to the art and continuously work for its betterment. The sensei who has achieved human dignity is respected and not feared. He is recognized and accepted not as a martial arts expert, but as a man of dignity dedicated to the task of human betterment through the utilization of his talents. If a teacher displays these qualities, then he is a true sensei. If not, he is simply an instructor of fighting.

Q: How important is learning self-control at an early age?
A: It is important the young people learn how to control their lives—to stay calm and enjoy life without going wild. The right attitude and behavior will bring the right things to you. Don't get involved with the wrong people who will bring bad things into your daily life. Stay away from those individuals

and focus on studying and training in the martial arts.

Q: Do you have to go to Japan and train there to fully understand karate?
A: If possible, it is interesting to visit Japan, not simply for the technical training—that you can get anywhere—but for the cultural and educative aspects of *budo*. Visiting and training in Japan is something that I strongly recommend to all karate-do practitioners. The experience and the atmosphere will stay with you forever. It is an experience that money can't buy.

Q: Does the self-defense aspect of karate require a separate kind of training?
A: It is important to train in karate for self-defense and not think that because you are a champion in karate competition that you can protect yourself. In tournaments, all those techniques which you perform for points are not actual combat skills. True karate-do is not strictly for technique. It is also for developing your mind, because a person learning technique without the mind is not good in combat. Karate is for life. It is a way of life and a way of thinking. I use it and practice it everyday. It has to be used for when you find yourself in times of crisis. Karate teaches you to concentrate and think calmly under stress and strain.

"To teach karate doesn't mean you are a sensei. There are many teachers but not many sensei. The sensei's work transcends his dojo. Through precept and example he inspires his students and close associates to aspire to greater heights as individuals. He is in a very unique position to achieve dignity for himself, his students and the discipline he represents."

Q: What is your opinion of breaking boards?
A: Breaking four or five boards ... what will you do with this? You can learn kicking and punching and maybe never have a reason to use it in daily life. What is important in karate practice are the moral characteristics you get from it—endurance, perseverance, courage, self-esteem, self-confidence, self-control and humility. Breaking boards has nothing to do with budo.

Karate Masters

"You can learn kicking and punching and maybe never have a reason to use it in daily life. What is important in karate practice are the moral characteristics you get from it—endurance, perseverance, courage, self-esteem, self-confidence, self-control and humility. Breaking boards has nothing to do with budo."

Q: How should a karate practitioner approach a self-defense situation?
A: The main thing to keep in mind when you consider any self-defense altercation is to keep it as basic as you can. Such simple things as grabbing hair or using finger-joint locks are very effective. If a guy grabs me by the sleeve or lapel and tries to punch me, I'm not about to try and block his hand and go through a lot of fancy hand work. I'll just stop him cold with a good kick or punch. That's where real self-defense is at, not all that flowery non-sense you see in many martial arts schools.

Q: How can you put tournament experience to work in a streetfight?
A: Fighting is more than 50 percent physical conditioning. Whoever is in better shape, stronger and more flexible is likely to be the winner. This holds true for tournaments, and it is also a fact on the streets. About 25 percent of your fighting ability lies in your technique, not so much how many different things you know, but how well you do the basic techniques like the frontkick, sidekick and reverse punch. If you can do a few of these things well, that's all you'll need in an actual encounter.

The last 25 percent is how much mental strength you've really got. I don't care how cool you are in the gym—it's another story to be able to handle yourself on the street. That's where you either have guts or you don't. Nobody can teach you how to stand up against fear; it is something you have to work on yourself. A good instructor can instill the principles of karate and the proper fighting attitude, but you have to do the rest.

The other quality you must discover is good common sense. Avoiding a fight, even if it means backing down or walking a few steps out of your way, is a lot wiser and a lot healthier for everyone. It takes guts to do that, too. Sometimes a simple apology, even though the recipient is not worthy of it, is best in the end. After you have practiced karate long enough, you will realize the value of being able to control yourself in any and all situations.

Q: What is the most important attribute in karate competition?
A: Speed of movement. Speed is one of the most elusive qualities a karate champion possesses. If you are faster than your opponent, you are going to score no matter what. The problem arises when you try to punch faster and faster but nobody tells you how to do it.

"Nobody can teach you how to stand up against fear—it is something you have to work on yourself. A good instructor can instill the principles of karate and the proper fighting attitude, but you have to do the rest."

Q: What is the best way to develop speed?
A: Constant repetition of the movement. This imposes coordination patterns on your subconscious. You need to correct your basic techniques from the very beginning and repeat them over and over. You have to learn to relax your body—particularly your shoulder for punches —because that's the only way to move faster. Think that your muscles are arranged around the joints in groups moving it in opposite directions. Movement is achieved by contraction of one group combined with relaxation of the opposite group. Relaxation is the key factor to move faster in karate. Interestingly enough,

Karate Masters

"Movement is achieved by contraction of one group combined with relaxation of the opposite group. Relaxation is the key factor to move faster in karate. Interestingly enough, speed depends as much as on the degree of relaxation as on the degree of contraction. The main causes of excessive tension are the natural reactions of fear and excitement."

speed depends as much as on the degree of relaxation as on the degree of contraction. The main cause of excessive tension are the natural reactions of fear and excitement.

Q: How can a karate practitioner relax his body to trigger a physical action with the utmost speed?
A: He needs to relax his mind and empty his mind of any interference. The conscious mind interferes by deliberately planning the next move in advance. The real moves are a reflex. A reflex is a reaction which does not have to be thought about. For a karate practitioner, this is a trained reaction. This is the main reason why you want to repeat the basic techniques over and over. The more basic, simple and direct the technique is, the faster the reaction will be.

Q: What is the philosophical basis for your karate training?
A: I would recommend doing a lot of mental training. The mind navigates the body so you have to learn how to develop your mind in order to make it work for your karate. It is very important to understand how the mind works and how much it can influence your daily life.

Q: Have there been times when you felt fear in your karate training?

A: In the beginning, I have to say that I felt fear many times in my karate training—many, many times. The training was hard and tough and fear was something natural. Fortunately, I learned how to control that fear and transform it into a source of power to overcome obstacles and reach my goals. Fear is not bad as long as you know how to control it and use it positively.

Q: What is the ultimate personal goal of karate-do?

A: The true karate-ka should be searching for his true self. It is not about the crowd in front of him. True karate has nothing to do with all that fanfare existing in tournaments. There is always something new to learn and experience, but it's up to the student to seek and learn for himself. The real value of acquiring an ability in anything, especially karate-do, is always trying to do better than you did yesterday, and do even better than that tomorrow. If you face that challenge honestly and meet with any success at all, you will discover and appreciate everything that the art of karate has to offer. I mentioned before that you must know how to control the mind, but I also have to say that you need to know how to stop the mind from controlling you. Don't let it to control your actions because sometimes it can be very tricky. As you grow old, don't let your mind remind you that you are getting old. Keep training and moving forward toward your goals. Work hard for your dreams and never give up. O

"True karate has nothing to do with all that fanfare existing in tournaments. There is always something new to learn and experience, but it's up to the student to seek and learn for himself. The real value of acquiring an ability in anything, especially karate-do, is always trying to do better than you did yesterday, and do even better than that tomorrow."

Tsutomu Ohshima

Strict Eyes

SINCE 1955, WHEN HE ARRIVED IN THE UNITED STATES OF AMERICA, MR. OHSHIMA HAS TRIED TO KEEP HIS VERSION OF SHOTOKAN KARATE THE WAY IT WAS ORIGINALLY TAUGHT BY HIS TEACHER, FUNAKOSHI SENSEI. OHSHIMA NEVER ACCEPTED A HIGHER RANK THAN A 5TH-DAN BECAUSE THAT WAS THE HIGHEST RANK HIS TEACHER EVER GAVE. MR. OHSHIMA ACKNOWLEDGES THAT THE BOMBS IN HIROSHIMA AND NAGASAKI—THE BIRTHPLACES OF HIS MOTHER AND FATHER RESPECTIVELY—ARE A VERY IMPORTANT ELEMENT TO UNDERSTANDING WHO HE IS TODAY. HE STUDIED UNDER FUNAKOSHI SENSEI WHILE ATTENDING WASEDA UNIVERSITY IN TOKYO AND WAS SELECTED BY FUNAKOSHI HIMSELF TO BE THE CAPTAIN OF THE UNIVERSITY KARATE CLUB. IN 1955, OHSHIMA LEFT JAPAN TO LIVE IN LOS ANGELES. HE FORMED SHOTOKAN *KARATE OF AMERICA* AND HAS MAINTAINED IT AS THE MOST TRADITIONAL BRANCH OF JAPANESE KARATE IN THE WORLD. IT'S MORE PURE, MANY WOULD SAY, THAN JAPAN'S OWN *JAPAN KARATE ASSOCIATION*, WHICH WAS FORMED AT ABOUT THE SAME TIME. IN 1962, HE WENT TO FRANCE TO TEACH, INVITED BY MR. HENRY PLÉE, AND DEVELOPED THE FOUNDATION FOR THE ART OF KARATE IN EUROPE. HE CANNOT UNDERSTAND WHY JOURNALISTS SEEM UNABLE TO CONVERSE WITH HIM AT A CERTAIN LEVEL OF DIRECT KNOWLEDGE AND DISREGARD THE ACTUAL WORDS HE SPEAKS. HE REMAINS POSITIVE THAT HIS IMAGE IN PRINT WILL ULTIMATELY BE THE SAME AS THE IMAGE HIS STUDENTS HAVE OF HIM. THIS IS TSUTOMU OHSHIMA, AN ACCESSIBLE HUMAN BEING AND A GEM OF BUDO.

Q: How would you describe Funakoshi Sensei when you started training?
A: I remember he was teaching at Waseda University. At that time, he was already an old man, and we had to carry him up the stairs to the dojo and then back down again after class. I believe he was in his 80s.

Q: Is there any special anecdote you remember?
A: There are many, but these would be only anecdotes and probably wouldn't have a long-term benefit for anybody but for those whom were there. But there are some stories that helped me to understand Funakoshi Sensei better. For instance, at a certain point in time, the students were confused about the proper way to perform a side-kick. Master Funakoshi, when showing the tech-

Karate Masters

"Before the war, the Japanese were very proud of our traditions and cultural beliefs. Not only in the martial arts but also society in general. As for fighting, we believed that our samurai were the best fighting men in the world, but the atomic bomb changed many things."

niques, would only make a small, low motion with his foot. This movement was very similar to a front snap-kick except that his was body facing to the side. Many of us thought that the reason why he was doing the kick that way was because he was an old man and couldn't perform it otherwise. So we kind of changed it a little bit and executed the side-kick with a more powerful movement, as well as fancier and higher. I did the technique this way for many years. One day I started to feel pain in my back. Then Obata Sensei, the first captain of the Keio University Karate Club, came to the United States.

Q: What happened then?
A: I explained the back pain and mentioned that it really hurt when I was doing this kick. He looked at me and said, "I think there is something wrong with the side up motion that you are using you to perform the kick. If you do it this way, it is very bad for your lower back. That's not the proper way to do it. Didn't you see how Funakoshi Sensei did it?" I was shocked. Master Funakoshi was showing us the proper way to do it all along, but I didn't understand that until many years after.

Q: How did Japan change after the World War, and how did these changes affect budo and Japanese society?
A: Before the war, the Japanese were very proud of our traditions and cultural beliefs. Not only in the martial arts but also society in general. As for fighting, we believed that our samurai were the best fighting men in the world, but the atomic bomb changed many things. Japanese society was shocked, and we were to believe that foreign technologies were stronger. So after the war, we lost respect for what we had and the new generations accepted a more materialistic attitude. They began to copy Western ways of behaving and thinking. I saw that after the war. My countrymen no longer respected their own culture, and immediately I felt that there was something that had to be saved. My grandfather was a samurai, and you

Ohshima

"My friends and I were training very hard every single day. We thought many times that we all were going to die. That was the mentality."

can say what you want about the old samurai. Maybe they were cruel; maybe they were missing something that we consider important today ... I don't know. But I can tell you this: They were honest, truthful and courageous. They were willing to face themselves, they could overcome their fears and they did not have to ride from anyone. This is a mental development from which modern society needs to learn.

Q: How do you remember those dramatic days?
A: We knew the day was coming. My friends and I were training very hard every single day. We thought many times that we all were going to die. That was the mentality. So courageously, we prepared ourselves for the moment. We were all ready to die.

Q: When you came to the United States of America, how did people react to your training?
A: During the 1950s, right after WW II, the Japanese thought that going to America was best. I came to the U.S. and soon questioned why people who had the opportunity of playing all these games—football, baseball, basketball—wanted to learn the martial arts from me. They knew they weren't going to learn another sport from me. At that time, some of my friends told me that we should try to change karate into a sport to make it more appealing to the masses! But I never wanted to do that because tradition and the

Karate Masters

"The United States of America and the Western world have tremendous potential power. All human societies have. Our enemy is not some other place. Our enemy is in our own minds. We always have to project improvement for ourselves."

ethics of budo would be lost and practice would have no other meaning than trying to beat someone else. My idea was to show the American people through karate-do that our culture was not stupid or a second-class thing and that it was a serious and intellectual activity. In 1955, people didn't really know what to expect from karate classes. They viewed them as a hobby, something to give them a sense of what Japanese culture was all about. I don't think they realized that karate is a serious business and not something to be taken lightly. The United States of America and the Western world have tremendous potential power. All human societies have. Our enemy is not some other place. Our enemy is in our own minds. We always have to project improvement for ourselves. This is what all these great people throughout history have taught. This is what the martial arts teach. This is what the Bible teaches.

Q: How would you summarize the philosophy of karate-do?

A: Well, I can summarize my own opinion, but I cannot speak for my masters or my seniors because they may have a different opinion. To me, it's important to try to face yourself directly, strictly and honestly. That [philosophy] has had a very strong impact on my life. At one point, I thought that I was OK. When I started to look at myself through different eyes, I realized that I'm full of weakness and cowardice. That gave me more reasons to push myself. So, what is the karate philosophy? As I previously said, I think it is when you face yourself and are honest. For example, during one of our seven-day special training sessions, there were some movements that I could not do. The best way to handle that is try harder next time. That is when and how I learned how to bring up the best in myself.

When you are young, you are full of energy. Of course, I wanted to be strong, and I did not want to cheat. Anyway, I jumped into special training. The first practice was OK. The second practice was OK. The third practice was OK. After five or six days, however, I was exhausted and had lost my concentration. I thought to myself, "What is this?" For a few seconds, I did not like that. If I look back on my life, I did the special training about 100 times. During those times, I think I did a good job during the special training two or three times. I think. Maybe I forgot. But most of the time, probably 99 percent, I could not push from the bottom to top.

Q: Tell us about your special training.
A: We have had about 100 of these special sessions and some of those have occurred here in the United States. During this training, all we do is practice, eat and sleep. These are the most important events for any karate students because they push themselves to their limit. Some of them have described this training as "the most demanding and strenuous mental and physical experience of their lives." Right now we do this for a minimum of eight times [per year], and they last 3 1/2 days. The training includes things like practicing at midnight, executing 1,000 techniques and/or holding a horse stance for 90 minutes. It is not easy, and that is why we call it special training. It's not ordinary, easy practice.

"People think that someone is a loser because nobody follows him or because nobody recognizes him. The general public does not always care about quality or depth. They want to take the easy way out and go with the flashy things."

People think that someone is a loser because nobody follows him or because nobody recognizes him. For example, I have always tried real hard and done everything straight, but that [type of lifestyle] is not always interesting to other people. That can be disappointing and frustrating. The general public does not always care about quality or depth. They want to take the easy way out and go with the flashy things. And that's OK. For me, however, I want someone to remember me in 200 years. Of course, I will not be here. But when people talk about me, I want them to say that this guy was OK. He did a good job. He tried somehow. I realize, of course, that 99 percent of the people are not going to care about the human mind or show any interest. Again, that is alright. That does not hurt me. I am not looking to be popular. I just want to try my best.

Q: Were you expecting that Westerners would accept these extremely hard and demanding training sessions?
A: In the beginning, many Japanese instructors thought that American students would quit if they were forced to do the special training. They thought the Americans students wouldn't be able to handle such training because they're too materialistic. When I started the special training in 1959, it was very experimental. People did have trouble adapting to the physical disci-

Karate Masters

"When I started the special training in 1959, it was very experimental. People did have trouble adapting to the physical discipline. But all the tough guys wanted to take on this crazy Japanese guy and prove that they weren't chicken."

pline. But all the tough guys wanted to take on this crazy Japanese guy and prove that they weren't chicken. I challenged them to show me how strong they were, and they ended up adjusting very well to the demands of the training.

Special training is beautiful because the intense mental attitude of the students makes for a good atmosphere. Everybody tries so hard and works so hard. No one is perfect, and we all make mistakes. But no one who gets through the training has failed on any level. I always say at the end of special training that the students can quit karate the following day, and it wouldn't take away anything from what they have accomplished.

Q: Do people try to leave once they see what they got themselves into?
A: The answer is yes. Some of them do, usually after one day or two. They see the possibility of getting hurt, and they feel the exhaustion in the bodies due to the strenuous physical training. Bruises heal, but mental scars don't. You have to give 100 percent because the idea of all this is to forge a new power in yourself, a new mental level. The ability to fight is really the lowest achievement of karate.

Ohshima

Q: How important is confidence to a karate practitioner?
A: Let me give you my definition of confidence. First, a humble person often comes across the same as a person who has an inferiority complex, [but that doesn't mean he has the complex]. Second, a person with confidence has no need to hurt anyone. Why? Because he has confidence. Next, if a person without any confidence gets a position of power, money or strength, he will become cruel, mean and bad. On the other hand, if a person with confidence and humility gets the same position, he will not be this way. These philosophies do not apply just to the martial arts. There is actually no connection. I am not a moralist or even a crazy person. OK. Now, let's think about a period of time from the ancient days until today. If a selfish, mean, nasty guy survived [some ordeal], everyone would look up to him. He would be [considered] a winner. The martial arts show, however, that that type of mentality is a weakness. What kind of human being is a real winner? A genuine human being. It's very clear. If a genuine human being cannot be a winner, I would have quit a long time ago.

"Bruises heal, but mental scars don't. You have to give 100 percent because the idea of all this is to forge a new power in yourself, a new mental level. The ability to fight is really the lowest achievement of karate."

Q: What do you mean when you say that you must face yourself with strict eyes?
A: When someone else does something wrong, we don't forgive him. However, when we do something wrong, it's OK and we expect others to forgive us. That is ugly, stupid, immature or a sign of a weakness of the human mind. So, when I talk about facing yourself with strict eyes, I'm talking about making yourself stronger every day. Can you do this without being selfish and without forgiving someone every day? You can't. Of course, we try, and so do I. But I am not successful every day. It's important, however, that we try really hard.

Q: What is the purpose of meditation before and after class?
A: Zen meditation was important to the samurai about 800 years ago. They called it the martial arts of moving Zen. When we get excited, we move around, but we hope that our mentality is clean and calm. We want to feel

Karate Masters

"Special training is beautiful because the intense mental attitude of the students makes for a good atmosphere. Everybody tries so hard and works so hard. No one is perfect, and we all make mistakes. But no one who gets through the training has failed on any level."

the same thing before and after. After WW II, about 1945, I went to Japan. The people were struggling, and many were trying to cut off the traditional mentality, such as Zen. Many said that was junk.

Q: What does it mean to achieve a black belt?
A: To my students, reaching a black belt is something priceless. It is not a trivial thing. It is not a badge only of physical accomplishment, but a sign that a person has achieved a certain mental level. These people have learned to face themselves, and that carries over to the rest of their lives. I wouldn't be teaching this art if I thought that it was only about punching and kicking. After I left Waseda University, I could have gotten any kind of good job. I didn't have to teach karate, but karate is much more than fighting.

Q: Do you think practitioners should only focus their attention on karate practice?
A: And become a failure like me? I hope not! I don't encourage this approach at all. They should have other things in their lives to have a balanced existence.

Ohshima

Q: During your training sessions, you refer repeatedly to the importance of penetrating an opponent and you emphasize the importance of breathing properly. Why?
A: Actually, you should first penetrate your opponent with your mind and technique will follow. Of course, deep breathing and the subconscious mind also play a role in this. These all go together simultaneously so you can penetrate an opponent. If your mind doesn't want to go and your body does, it will never work. If you do not have confidence, you will not have luck against any opponent, even if he is weak, sick or dying. It's important to face stronger, tougher opponents comfortably or they will destroy you.

If you stop [breathing] for a couple of minutes, you will die. Seriously, breathing is important in any field, not just in the martial arts. It's important for musicians, athletes, carpenters, etc. It's funny that breathing is the same character in Japanese as secret points. That makes me really proud of my country as a culture. They understood that.

"Zen meditation was important to the samurai about 800 years ago. They called it the martial arts of moving Zen."

Q: How do you develop confidence?
A: If I could express in a few words and you could understand right away, I would be a multimillionaire. Seriously, you have to train yourself continuously. It doesn't work with just words, and it doesn't happen overnight. You cannot change that easily.

Q: Mr. Ohshima, you mentioned once that those who have a higher position should sacrifice themselves for the benefit of others. Would you please elaborate on that concept?
A: There are many kinds of individuals on the earth and they all have the right to live equally, but the truth is that not all are equal. Some are mature, and some are immature. Education plays an important part on how an individual will be when grows up. Usually, when we get older, we become more selfish and greedy, with no time or energy for others. It is important to have a good educational system that doesn't spoil the young generation.

Karate Masters

"To my students, reaching a black belt is something priceless. It is not a trivial thing. It is not a badge only of physical accomplishment, but a sign that a person has achieved a certain mental level."

Everybody wants to lead, but a leader has to be a first-class human being. He can stand by himself and work hard, but he cannot do everything for himself. He has to do things for others. In the martial arts, we are racing toward [a situation in which we will see] who can be the strictest with himself. The martial arts contribute to human society in this way. We are racing toward who can be the strictest with himself and honest with himself. This was the original idea in the martial arts. Unfortunately, many people don't get this message. In the old times, this was the most important idea in budo ... reach a higher level and become a strong human being. But strong doesn't mean big arms; it means who can be a more strict human being with himself. That is the idea of the martial arts, and that is the essence of Budo.

Q: Do you need a lot of techniques to be successful?
A: It depends on your definition of successful. Do you want to move your hands 100 times in one minute? Do you want to face your opponent and just look at him so he cannot attack you? If one of those is the goal you want to reach, I do not know. I am not a poor technician, so I do not know. I do not depend on one technique.

My black belts know that what they are learning is not for appearance or just for the use of competition or self-defense, but for their own spirit and soul ... for their lives. They have learned to recognize their own imperfections and ugliness. They can be proud of it, because it is not an easy task. In the world, there are good people and dishonest people. What is important is that good people don't give up to the crooked people. One little stone in a big lake makes a ripple that spreads out very far, and that's what we try to do in the martial arts. What is the essence of this? To end the ugliness and selfishness in the world, we have to cut out our own ugliness and selfishness first.

A successful individual in our modern society is someone who has a lot of money and properties. "He is a successful person," they say when the see a millionaire. But what they don't realize is that there is no connection between the material things that person has and his mental maturity. There are many immature and lucky "successful" people in the world. In terms of success in the Western world, I am not successful at all. But I am successful in my terms because I have good members and good friends who trust me very much. So I am quite happy. I never have any troubles of my own, nor do my members who have been practicing seriously for many years. Everything I have belongs to my students. It is not mine, regardless of how expensive the things surrounding me may be. My students gave them to me.

"Everybody wants to lead, but a leader has to be a first-class human being. He can stand by himself and work hard, but he cannot do everything for himself. He has to do things for others."

Q: How important is it to have an open mind when practicing the arts of budo?
A: Look at me. I'm an old man who is 70 years old. An opponent could destroy me within a few minutes. I know in my mind, however, that I've got to face this guy, and it could be a fight for my life. What I feel is strong, and I will go into it [the encounter] with an open mind. I feel that way. I will forget my age; I will forget that my body has a herniated disc and I will forget that my legs will not move like they once did. I do not know how to resolve this, but I'm ready to make the best of it right now. I will make my fists right now and maybe the technique will follow. For me, it is like that.

Q: What does penetrating with fullness mean?
A: When you are sick, you experience emptiness. Emptiness occurs when you are old, especially compared to the fullness of younger people. There is also emptiness in your body and mind when you exhale. This movement is formed on emptiness. Everybody, every day, breathes when they are at their strongest. When you cannot move or do anything, that is emptiness. When you cannot think or move or do anything, that is emptiness. So, I was talking earlier about a small lady who has to defend herself against a big guy. That is why the fullness penetrates emptiness. She has a chance to survive.

Karate Masters

"In the world, there are good people and dishonest people. What is important is that good people don't give up to the crooked people. One little stone in a big lake makes a ripple that spreads out very far, and that's what we try to do in the martial arts."

Q: What targets do karate-ka look for on an opponent?
A: You are asking me to answer that question as a karate-ka, but we never think of that. On the other hand, everyone has a target for his life, and I am certainly trying to provide the way that will enable him or her to accomplish a beautiful life. When we die, we hope that we have had a wonderful life with few tears or sadness. We should appreciate everything we have until the last minute. To me, that is my call and my target, and I am sure I will be there.

Q: Many styles have dozens of kata and some practitioners even create their own. What is you opinion of this?
A: Let's say that one teacher creates a kata. Years later, 20 of his students create another 20 new forms; by the next generation, there are more than 1,000 kata! This makes no sense. How can I change what I was taught by Funakoshi Sensei? I don't think he ever considered what he taught as some kind of style or school. The fundamental element of shotokan is that we try to be strict with ourselves because there is no limit to what we can accomplish. We must be straight and honest with ourselves. This is the tradition of Funakoshi Gichin.

Q: Master Funakoshi only taught a limited number of forms, correct?
A: Yes. Before he went to Tokyo from Okinawa, Funakoshi Sensei visited and trained with many masters to learn their forms. I assume that maybe he learned 60 or 80 kata, but I believe that he probably didn't spent many hours on each of them. The idea, as Funakoshi Sensei showed in the later years of his life, is that it is nonsense to memorize dozens of kata. It is ridiculous. He never told me this, but his teachings were in that direction. In the Western world, the people think that if you know 60 kata, you are better than the practitioner who knows only 30. And that is wrong. This exemplifies a process of accumulation in which the truth is that true budo and true karate are just the opposite. It is about simplification. We have to simplify, simplify and simplify what we do. Quality in our acts, not quantity. Quality

Ohshima

"Karate is a crystal of the human spirit and its heritage is a gem I intend to preserve. We are all trying to get out from underneath our stupidity, blindness, weakness and cowardice. We must open our heart to the right way to act."

in our kata, not quantity of forms. If you know 20 kata, then make 10 better. If you only know 10, make five extremely good. Even five is too many for a true budo-ka. Put yourself into the kata. Make the form 10,000 times. Then, when you think you have grasped the essence, go back and repeat it another 50,000 times. Only when you reach the threshold of repeating a kata 150,000 times can you start to think that the kata is yours.

Q: How does repetition bring maturity to kata?
A: Kata is not simply the memorization of a series of movements. I'm a very creative person. I could have created 100 new kata, but what and why? Kata training is the opposite of that. Kata is for the spirit, for your own maturity. If you digest kata, you become one.

Q: What does it means "to become one"?
A: Both your unconscious and conscious are directly connected to your physical movement. If those two move with your body, they idealistically will take a long time. The idea is to become one with what you do, with the kata, with the physical movement. You express your best with all of your energy. That is the direction of the true karate. And kata training is for that. To invent a new kata to impress a bunch of people is not karate … it is being a Hollywood star.

Karate Masters

"If you do not have confidence, you will not have luck against any opponent, even if he is weak, sick or dying. It's important to face stronger, tougher opponents comfortably or they will destroy you."

Q: During your early days, is it true that you cleaned the dojo yourself?

A: Yes, I did and it is something of which I am proud. Many people don't understand this. Cleaning is not a low-class act. All my students used to watch me doing it, and I never asked them to do it. In fact, some students used to joke and say things like, "Mr. Ohshima, you like cleaning, uh?" I used to say, "Yes, I do!"

When you clean the place where you train, you are showing appreciation and respect to the place that gives you a chance to practice. Don't forget that polishing the floor is in fact the art of polishing your own mind. I thought some day my students would understand. Some did, some didn't, but that's life. Interestingly enough, after over two years, most of the students were cleaning with me! First, the black belts did, and then the rest of the students realized that if the black belts were doing it, they better do it, too. Nobody asked them to do it; we don't have slaves in this country. The top guy has to work harder so other people will follow him. Somebody who can't demonstrate shouldn't be respected in his position just because of the size of his arms. Younger generations have to learn. But these young people should see that the person at the top is pushing them for them and not for him. Karate is a crystal of the human spirit and its heritage is a gem I intend to preserve. We are all trying to get out from underneath our stupidity, blindness, weakness and cowardice. We must open our heart to the right way to act.

Q: Do you think karate philosophy is some kind of religious belief as some have described?

A: I am a modern man about religion, and I have doubts. I don't believe that I need some messenger, a preacher. Maybe I'm a little bit critical. Karate is a way of life, maybe a little lower than what we understand as "religion," but it can used to achieve a higher level of mentality. Even if they are not intellectually motivated for pursuing religious or philosophical ways, they can find spiritual attainment through training hard in traditional karate. Karate tradition and practice are cultural gems. Many aspects of the art are aesthetically pleasing ... the cleanliness, the purity of form, the power of the body performing a technique, the respect between students and teacher, et cetera. The movements found in karate are more than one man's idea of how to fight. They are the product of a long cross-cultural evolution. They [movements] are more than the most efficient control of the human body. They are part of a spiritual path that is based on physical reality.

"In terms of success in the Western world, I am not successful at all. But I am successful in my terms because I have good members and good friends who trust me very much. So I am quite happy."

Q: What are the differences between budo and religion?
A: With religion, you always deal with abstraction. It is easy to lose your way, to become proud or confused. In the arts of budo, there is the experience of the total moment. When you are waiting on an opponent or waiting for an attack, your mind is empty, your body is awake and totally relaxed, and you experience something that can't be put in words, simply because it has nothing to do with words. It is experience. During meditation, you come into contact with a feeling that is much more than just a cultural treasure and more than just an ability to fight. Of course, the martial arts are very related to Shintoism, so I'm very fond of that study. I have been strongly influenced by Zen, and every night, no matter where I go, no matter how late I stay out, I never miss my sitting in meditation.

Q: How do you see yourself in the future?
A: I'm not sure, [but I do know that] I want to live comfortably without money. That's enough for me. I make my best and my members make their best. And though I won't have a chance to see it, it makes me happy to think that maybe after 200 years somebody will still be practicing karate here where I have taught. O

Yoshiharu Osaka

Karate's Perfect Form

Osaka Sensei was born in Fukuoka, Kyushu in 1947. He won the JKA Kata World title nine times and became the world champion in both kata and kumite. With a gentle disposition, his calmness hides his great passion, energy and dedication to the promotion of the art. Considered by many as having "perfect form" in the style of JKA shotokan, Yoshiharu Osaka traveled extensively under the tutelage of the late Nayakama Sensei. Osaka not only provided assistance for him during seminars, he also helped with the demonstrations. What looks simple and graceful when he performs is extremely difficult for we mere mortals. He is a very reserved man when talking about other instructors or styles. His qualities as an instructor are second to none and for many he is one of the best teachers in the world. He has a great ability to make students feel confident about their potential, making them understand without harshness or embarrassment. I have known Osaka Sensei since I was a teenager providing assistance for his seminars in Europe. Currently the technical director of the JKA Honbu Dojo, Osaka sensei represents more than what many people understand today in karate circles. His depth of technical knowledge is as big as his strong spirit and delicate kindness. A true warrior, a true samurai. A treasure that the world of karate should be most proud.

Q: When did you start training in karate-do?
A: It was in 1963. In 1966, I entered Takushoku University and trained there for more than four years. Eventually, I was asked to join the JKA instructor's course.

Q: How was the training at the University?
A: Very hard. The atmosphere was very competitive and that made everything more difficult and tougher than any other place. I really enjoyed my time there because there was a sense of honor in winning trophies and tournaments for your university.

Karate Masters

"Westerners usually try to think about how and why and then [they] do. The Japanese are taught to do [things] first and get used to the physical movements. The thinking about how and why comes later."

Q: Sensei, are there differences between Japanese and Western practitioners? If so, how do they affect physical techniques?

A: Once you have been taught the correct body mechanics and physical elements of a technique, you'll see that those are relevant to how the human body moves and they have nothing to do with the color of your skin or your genetics. But to answer your question, yes, there are some differences. Some are physical and others are cultural, and those are obvious for everybody to understand. Westerners usually try to think about how and why and then [they] do. The Japanese are taught to do [things] first and get used to the physical movements. The thinking about how and why comes later. For some reason, the Japanese approach makes things stay longer with the practitioner because his [the practitioner's] first experience is physical and not intellectual. There are some other differences that can't be seen at first and require a deeper look to detect. For instance, Western karate-ka are very good at performing kata, but you can see weaknesses in the way they use their ankles and hips when going from one stance to another. Another aspect is that the Japanese focus on the transitional phases of the movements in kata. Western practitioners tend to think in terms of completed movements, but they have to pay more attention to what is happening between the end of one movement and the end of the next. Let me explain this a little better, please. Let's take a *shuto-uke* in *kokutsu-dachi* as movement one and *oi-tsuki* as movement two in any given sequence. Western students normally tend to forget how the hip, the muscles in the legs, the tension in the back, the relaxation in the shoulders, and the spring action of the ankles should act during the transition between action one and two. The final point of the movement is not as important as the transitional phases between them. The only way to correct this is focusing is in strong *kihon* practice. This is the only way to truly develop these transitional phases ... not the repetitive action of the kata without paying attention to the details.

Osaka

Q: You always mention that the details are the key. What do you mean?

A: For instance, everybody knows how to do a *gyaku-tsuki,* but what is truly important to know is how to use the body parts in a sequence in which the previous segment of the body pushes the next and the next does the same thing with the following. The ankle moves, then the knee, then the thigh, then the hip, then the trunk, the shoulder, the elbow, et cetera. If we pull the hip before we bring it into play with the ankle and the leg, the logical sequence of the action will be lost and the power of the movement will lack total potential. The order of the sequence and how every segment of the body come into play are the keys to really bringing the best possible potential out of a practitioner's body. Correct technique is the result of a natural movement. If the technique is correctly practiced, the actions are harmonious, relaxed and powerful. The problem arises when people don't learn the right way and then go and teach incorrectly.

"Correct technique is the result of a natural movement. If the technique is correctly practiced, the actions are harmonious, relaxed and powerful."

Q: You are an expert in kata and have been a world champion for many years. What is your perspective of kata training?

A: Kata should be kept as the original form that was developed. Kata represent the history of our art, and we can't change it as we please. Of course, the practitioner's style will affect the final result, [and you also have to consider that] the correct speed and timing in the movements—as well as the proper application of strength and muscle contraction and expansion—will change the outside part of the form. The practitioner will put his own flavor [into it], but he shouldn't alter the form to suit himself. Perfection in kata is something impossible to attain, but it is the goal we all should try to reach. It is an impossible goal, but that's why it is a life experience. The real challenge is in every time we do the movement and in every single time we repeat the kata. There is no goal in kata training. The goal is the training itself.

Karate Masters

"Kata should be kept as the original form that was developed. Kata represent the history of our art, and we can't change it as we please."

Q: Sensei, if you train in a traditional dojo with wooden floors, can that affect your performance in competition if the competition area features a mat?

A: If you don't train and get used to the particular surface, it may ruin your kata ... yes. If you are planning to compete in kata division, I would recommend that you train on the same kind of surface you are going to compete on. Just get used to it. If you don't compete, you don't have to worry about this. Just train diligently in the dojo, regardless of the surface.

Q: Compared to other schools like goju-ryu or shito-ryu, it seems that the JKA does not pay as much attention to the bunkai of the kata. Why?

A: In order to understand kata, it is important that the practitioners understand the process and evolution of that particular form. The old masters used kata as a way of passing their knowledge and personal experiences to future generations. This is the main reason why a kata may have many variations. Bunkai is important in JKA shotokan, but there are some principles and ideas we all should remember. Traditional bunkai of the traditional kata, developed by our ancestors, is based on attacking methods used at the time they lived. We are now in the 21st century and even the ways individuals attack you in the streets have changed. They have new technologies to abuse decent citizens. It is important to understand that we need to bring new perspective to old solutions for modern problems. Nakayama Sensei used kata as a training method for achieving technical perfection and bringing all the necessary attributes to the body of the practitioner. When looking at bunkai, we need to study the principles and try to apply them in a realistic environment. Self-defense does not always have to do with physical techniques. The study of bunkai, even if you will never use it in a self-defense situation, will help you to understand the techniques in kata. For the purpose of understanding the form, knowing the bunkai is extremely important. I personally believe that the old masters wanted us to participate in kata by using their knowledge as a sounding board for us to develop and research new and different possibilities that adapt to our time. We need to study and develop methods for applications based on our own bodies and levels of understanding. I believe that it is here when we can find a link between kata and the personal expression in kumite. Knowing all shotokan kata without having the proper understanding and feeling for each form is useless. Personal expression of the art must be emphasized here.

Q: What do you mean by that?
A: In budo, expression of an art can be interpreted as strength by some people, and at the same time, elegance by another. In essence, a genuine art such as karate will never be created until the artist is able to train his mind and body constantly and is able to acquire essential vigor to reach a stage of personal expression. In order to reach this stage, he must continually apply research and discipline.

"Perfection in kata is something impossible to attain, but it is the goal we all should try to reach. It is an impossible goal, but that's why it is a life experience. The real challenge is in every time we do the movement and in every single time we repeat the kata."

Q: Do you consider kata an important part of karate training?
A: Definitely. All the strategies and techniques that a karate-ka needs for self-defense and fighting are contained in fundamental kata. It is important to differentiate between practicing kata and studying kata. At an advanced level, we need to investigate, research and probe the techniques we use.

Nakayama Sensei always said that *heian* kata makes the execution of advanced kata techniques very simple. I still think that way. Technical precision is critical. Focus on the intention of the movement and learn the proper timing, tempo and rhythm of the form. Keep maximum concentration while training and the correct attitude throughout the kata. The positive benefits of its [kata] training and practice are unquestionable.

Karate Masters

"We are now in the 21st century and even the ways individuals attack you in the streets have changed. They have new technologies to abuse decent citizens. It is important to understand that we need to bring new perspective to old solutions for modern problems."

Q: What is your opinion of makiwara training?
A: Makiwara training is necessary for real karate. If you want to develop strong techniques, you need to train with the makiwara. Unfortunately, many people don't understand that its value is not based on developing calluses on your hands. Instead, the value is technique, focus and proper kime. There is nothing like it to develop a strong body and a strong will.

Q: Why have we seen technical changes in the JKA during its history?
A: Karate techniques have not changed, but they have developed, which is different. The developments and modification of the techniques have been the product of a very intensive study. The only reason why these were done was to create a more efficient karate technique. They were not done for the idiosyncrasy of one particular individual. Unfortunately, I have seen basic karate techniques changed by some individual because of his inability to perform the [technique] correctly. [Of course], maybe he has been taught wrong, too. JKA karate tries to make the body stronger and the techniques more powerful. It is based on physics and principles of body mechanics. Shotokan is a system that is based on the expansion of the body and using the natural power of it to perform the techniques. The movements are big most of the time, and this can be used later in time to improve health and other physical benefits, too.

Q: Karate or karate-do?
A: For me, there is only one, and this is karate-do. But I'll try to answer your question. If you understand the art as karate-do, you'll practice it as a way of life. The training, the philosophy and the ethical values of the art will be present in all facets of your life. The dojo will be no different than your work

place because the training is not only physical. On the contrary, if you see what you practice as karate, your training will be strictly physical and this will be pretty much as if you practice baseball, tennis or basketball. It is interesting to note that when someone approaches the practice of karate simply as a sport, this person will stop training as soon as another activity captures his attention. In karate, the idea is to beat others in competition or a fight. In karate-do, the goal is to overcome your own limitations and become one in spirit and body. It is important that the principle of *shingi-ittai* or mind and technique are together.

Q: How was the training under Nakayama Sensei?
A: I was fortunate to have trained under one of the most knowledgeable instructors in the history of karate. He always emphasized the importance of the basics. We did a lot of kihon, regardless of our rank and position.

"We need to study and develop methods for applications based on our own bodies and levels of understanding. I believe that it is here when we can find a link between kata and the personal expression in kumite."

Q: You traveled with Nakayama Sensei for many years, and he said you were an example of technical perfection.
A: I am proud of his words, and all I can say is that I have always tried my best. I don't consider my karate to be perfect in any way. If fact, I think I'm very far from it. Many of my seniors are much better than me. Nakayama Sensei was a very kind man and maybe he said those words in an attempt to make me train harder because he saw many mistakes in my technique. I would like to say here that every karate practitioner must follow the principles of the technique and even if the outside "mold" doesn't look beautiful, his karate can be perfect because perfection is based on the proper use of the body and mechanical principles—not on the way the body looks.

Karate Masters

"In essence, a genuine art such as karate will never be created until the artist is able to train his mind and body constantly and is able to acquire essential vigor to reach a stage of personal expression. In order to reach this stage, he must continually apply research and discipline."

Q: How do you see the influence of the sportive element in the art of karate?
A: I truly don't think sport competition has to interfere in the development of true karate-do. Competition is a part of the training and can be helpful if it is properly used. It is a phase of the art that teaches things that we can't learn in the dojo. It requires a different mental discipline and a different kind of self-control. This is the main reason why Nakayama Sensei began the competitions. But in karate-do we emphasize the complete process, the continued effort of becoming a better budoka. Competition has its place in karate, but its place is not in the regular basic training. Sometimes I get too worried because the emphasis these days is too much on tournaments and championships rather than in developing the important principles and ethics of karate as a way of life.

Q: What are the main differences you see between WKF and JKA competition?
A: In the JKA, we learn to not make a mistake because you will lose if you do. Our approach to competition is based on budo ... one strong attack, only one chance. This makes the matches less attractive for the spectators. On the other side, WKF rules allow more techniques, the competitor plays differently and there are more opportunities of recovering from going down in the score. If your opponent gets a point, you can always get it back. The style is lighter and maybe faster. Timing is important, but it is paramount in the JKA. There is more mental strategy involved. If you don't perfectly time the attack and the defense, you lose the match. Strength and concentration can be more relevant. I don't want to say what style is better. This is something that any practitioner needs to find out for himself. I personally like the idea of a karate practitioner establishing his base on the principle of the *ikken-hissatsu*, which is so important in the art. Olympic recognition for karate seems to be very important these days, but I'm concerned because I have seen judo lose control of the art when entered in the Olympics. It lost

the principles of the founder, Jigoro Kano. Karate must keep its essence as a martial art and budo.

Q: How does budo apply to the art of karate-do?
A: The goal of budo is to develop the practitioner as a warrior and as a human being. Some people think of a budo-ka as a warrior, and this is not correct in budo, although it was correct in the old bujutsu because a practitioner needed to have extensive knowledge of fighting because he was facing enemies in the battlefield. Budo involves more than fighting, and in fact, learning fighting arts is not the main goal in budo practice. The idea of budo, as Nayakama Sensei described it, is "to gain deep knowledge of the [our] chosen art to perfect our character and see clearly in our own nature and existence." And karate-do can help you to do that.

Q: What we should do when we "hit the wall" in our training?
A: We all hit the wall sooner or later. Sometimes karate may be boring, but the true benefits are there for those who continue training. Sometimes we can get bored, but we need to keep going and training. Keep your training simple and focus until you feel better. In karate as in life, you must be capable of working through adversity and overcoming your weaknesses. Some people reach *shodan*, keep training and become *godan* and then they stop training! They go back to shodan because they didn't keep working and training. We must train all the time. Even if it is just a little. Students must train harder at higher levels. Not train less. Nakayama Sensei said that "karate is attained one step at a time and so is life. Train every day and try your best, and the truth will come to you."

Q: Should training change as the practitioner ages?
A: Of course! Karate has to be a reflection of who you are. And nobody is the same at 20 as he is at 50. Karate matures with age, and your karate must reflect your personal maturity as a human being. The natural body instinct slows down with age, but you have to keep training to revert this process back as much as you can. Train to develop focus and muscle control. These elements will be present during all of your years of karate, regardless of your age. Funakoshi Sensei always mentioned that karate should be used for perfection of character. The intelligent practitioner will change and adapt his training to his age. Specific injuries will affect how you'll train and practice when you get older. You must always practice physically and mentally. It must always be both ways.

Karate Masters

"In karate, the idea is to beat others in competition or a fight. In karate-do, the goal is to overcome your own limitations and become one in spirit and body."

Q: How has your perception of karate changed from the time you were a competitor to now that you don't compete?

A: I had a great teacher in Nakayama Sensei, so I always practice karate-do as though I were still competing when I was young. When you are training for competition, you learn how to score and how to defeat the opponent. When you quit competition, the meaning of being strong reaches another level. You try to become strong and powerful to use your body properly for karate-do. You study your body and find out that going back to the basics is the secret. Karate technique will keep improving no matter what. And I hope future generations understand what they are doing so they can develop new technologies for training and [new] ways of using the body to perform karate better.

Q: Did you train with weapons in the JKA?

A: Karate is the art of the empty hand. We don't include weaponry training at the JKA, but it is true that Funakoshi Sensei practiced several weapons like the *sai, tonfa, bo,* et cetera. Later on he focused more in karate-jutsu and followed the example of other similar forms of budo. However, training in kobudo is something that anyone can do as a personal thing and for individual research. I believe weaponry training may be good for the student if he has the time and interest.

Q: What advice would you give karate practitioners for their personal training?

A: Proper mental training and understanding what you are doing is paramount to developing the right attitude so the essence of karate-do is not lost. Always focus on proper technique and make sure you understand what you are doing. Repeat the basics over and over. Repetition is the key. Try to feel and develop the proper control of your muscles when performing the technique. Concentrate on correct form and the natural movement. Correct the mistakes and add speed and power little by little. Then work on timing. The body must be built with proper training and this takes time, so don't expect results over night. Don't try to do too much too soon because there will be a loss of technique, and you'll never reach your true potential. Grow little by little and progressively. Training hard is the secret, but you must train hard within the structure of a correct and progressive training plan. Never stand still in karate. Always try to improve step by step. Finally, don't just train; you also have to think when you train.

Q: Sensei, you always try to develop new and better ways to execute karate techniques. Do you pass these discoveries on to the students?
A: That's a good question! Every discovery I make during my research is through personal experience. Students must learn how to see these elements in my technique when I'm teaching and copy them until they have a sense for them. Then, they should adapt these concepts to themselves and develop their own style of delivery of the technical principle.

Q: Do you mean that you keep them secret for yourself and the student must steal them from you?
A: That's a nice way of saying it.

Q: Osaka Sensei, do you have any final thoughts?
A: Be honest and sincere in your training. Use your maximum effort when you train and learn to understand your body and how it changes with age. Karate is based on hard training and sacrifice, but there is also joy and fun. Don't try to do anything that your brain doesn't understand, but understanding things that your body can't perform may be detrimental for a true karate practitioner. If you are a teacher, teach with love and a sense of warmth. Always try to help your students but make sure, as I said before, that you understand yourself. In karate, we say that you have to know yourself, your body and your mind before you can actually help others. Nakayama Sensei, before he died, was worried that karate practitioners were only in training for competition reasons and always thought that getting Olympic recognition shouldn't be our primary goal. He wanted us to understand the true way of martial arts and this is the way I'm following. O

"The idea of Budo, as Nayakama Sensei described it, is 'to gain deep knowledge of the [our] chosen art to perfect our character and see clearly in our own nature and existence.'"

Eihachi Ota

A Man of Ethics

EIHACHI OTA'S SOFT-SPOKEN AND QUIET DEMEANOR IS REMINISCENT OF THE TRADITIONAL SOCIAL VALUES OF OKINAWA. BORN IN NAHA CITY, THE CAPITAL OF OKINAWA, HE BEGAN HIS MARTIAL ARTS TRAINING AT THE EARLY AGE OF 12. AFTER RECEIVING COMPLIMENTS FOR HIS DEDICATION TO THE ART, GRANDMASTER SHOSHIN NAGAMINE INVITED HIM TO TRAIN IN HIS PRIVATE DOJO. EVEN THOUGH HE ENDED UP TRAINING MORE UNDER MASTER MASAO SHIMA, THIS WAS SIMPLY BECAUSE SENSEI SHIMA'S DOJO WAS CLOSER TO HIS HOME. OTA'S LIFELONG PASSION FOR KARATE FINALLY PAID OFF WHEN HE BECAME ACKNOWLEDGED AS ONE OF THE TOP STUDENTS IN THE SCHOOL AND ON OKINAWA.

IN 1969, SENSEI OTA MOVED TO THE UNITED STATES. DESPITE BEING THOUSAND OF MILES AWAY FROM HIS ROOTS, HE KEPT TRAINING IN THE ART HE STUDIED IN HIS HOMELAND. HE SEES KARATE-DO NOT AS SPORT BUT AS A WAY OF LIFE, AND EXPECTS HIS STUDENTS TO ALSO ACCEPT THE ART AS PART OF *BUDO*, AND NOT SIMPLY AS A PHYSICAL ACTIVITY. IN 1973, SENSEI OTA OPENED HIS FIRST DOJO AND HASN'T STOPPED TEACHING SINCE.

AN EXPERT IN THE OKINAWA WEAPONRY ART OF *KOBUDO*, SENSEI OTA EMPHASIZES THE RESPONSIBILITY THAT LEARNING THE USE OF THESE DANGEROUS WEAPONS REQUIRES. HIS LIFE IS BASED ON THE ETHICS OF BUDO, AND HE IS A PERFECT EXAMPLE OF A HUMBLE KARATE-DO MASTER. HE IS MORE INTERESTED IN LIVING A QUIET LIFE AND SHARING KARATE WITH HIS STUDENTS THAN GAINING FAME AND RECOGNITION IN A MODERN WORLD WHERE THE FUNDAMENTAL PRINCIPLES OF ETHICS AND HONOR ARE BEING FORGOTTEN.

Q: How long have you been practicing the martial arts?
A: Since junior high school, which is more than 40 years. The only two methods I ever trained in are *shorin-ryu* karate-do and *yamani-ryu* kobudo. I never felt the need to train and practice any other martial art style. These two methods gave me what I was looking for, and I've been happy training diligently in them. Probably the fact that I had great teachers like Grandmaster Shoshin Nagamine (*Hanshi*, 10th dan and founder of *Matsubayashi* shorin-ryu), Master Seigi Nakamura (*Hanshi*, 9th dan),

Karate Masters

"When I began training at the Shima Dojo, I would show up early to practice on my own. When Nohara realized that I was doing extra practice, it sparked a competition, and he also started to come early. After a while, we both would come hours before class to out-do each other. Eventually, we started to train together."

Master Masao Shima (*Hanshi*, 9th dan), Master Chokei Kishaba (*Hanshi*, 9th dan) and Master Kensai Taba (*Hanshi*, 9th Dan) has a lot to do with the fact I didn't need any other masters. It's hard for me to accept that after having the privilege of training and learning from these men that I need to shop around a little more. When I was a young person and began training at the Nagamine Dojo, I often wondered what it was like for him training when he was my age. Grandmaster Nagamine's instructors—Chotoku Kyan and Choki Motobu—are legendary figures in the history of karate. I was curious about training with these legendary figures as well.

Q: What was your early training like?
A: I trained at Master Shima's dojo, which was in a different district from the *honbu* in Okinawa. The Shima Dojo was regarded and respected as one of the strongest and toughest dojo in Okinawa because a lot of emphasis was placed on *kumite*. Moreover, the nickname for Master Shima was "The Devil," because he was very strict and his classes were grueling. The senior student was Koichiro Nohara. When I began training at the Shima Dojo, I would show up early to practice on my own. When Nohara realized that I was doing extra practice, it sparked a competition, and he also started to come early. After a while, we both would come hours before class to out-do each other. Eventually, we started to train together. When I left to go to school in Japan, some people said that it affected the spirit of the dojo because that competitive spirit was missing; I don't really think so because there were many other great students there, but it was a great compliment.

Q: When you came to the United States, how did Westerners respond to traditional karate training?
A: To me, karate training is something very individual and personal. I have had many students respond well to traditional training and enjoy the

process, but I realize it is not for everyone. I think this is even true of many practitioners in Okinawa and Japan as well. I have always been passionate about the arts and trained as hard as I could. I believe that when anyone feels this way about something and is passionate, he tends to excel. Sometimes when a practitioner is a gifted athlete, he actually achieves less because he does not have the work ethic or persistence. The right attitude is more important to a student than the natural ability to kick and punch.

Q: How has your karate changed over the years?
A: All karate styles have the same basics —the blocks, punches, kicks and stances. What is unique or different between styles is the delivery system for the particular body motions. I try to base my technique and footwork on what I feel works in a combat situation and from my own personal experiences of what works for me. This ultimately affects the way techniques are delivered and can modify the philosophy and strategy behind the physical execution of the techniques. As a practitioner spends more time training, it is natural that the techniques and delivery systems evolve ... if for no other reason than age, injuries, physical condition, et cetera. This will affect the way a practitioner executes and thinks about kata as well.

"I have always been passionate about the arts and trained as hard as I could. I believe that when anyone feels this way about something and is passionate, he tends to excel. Sometimes when a practitioner is a gifted athlete, he actually achieves less because he does not have the work ethic or persistence."

Q: Do you think there are still *pure* karate styles?
A: Karate always evolves. It evolved before, during and after Funakoshi's establishment of shotokan; it evolved even during Funakoshi's lifetime. So the question is really, "Was there ever pure karate?" I do not believe that the style is the most important thing. I believe it is the individual and how he learns and develops character through diligent training. It is interesting to me that in Okinawa stylized barriers do not exist as much. We always trained and practiced together, regardless of style. But this almost never happens in Japan or the United States. Perhaps this has more to do with cultural differences than with different schools.

Karate Masters

"To mix styles just to mix them is not necessary or beneficial from my point of view. I do not believe that one style is superior to another. Instead, it is the individual who makes the difference. Mixing styles will not help a practitioner achieve what hard work and dedication can."

To mix styles just to mix them is not necessary or beneficial from my point of view. I do not believe that one style is superior to another. It is the individual who makes the difference. Mixing styles will not help a practitioner achieve what hard work and dedication can. However, training together with practitioners from different schools and styles can be very beneficial and a great learning experience. A lot of things changed with the introduction of full-contact karate and kickboxing. I think everything is helpful if you know how to use it and learn from your experiences. In my school, I have to find a common curriculum for class that works for everyone. Therefore, things like *makiwara* training and full-contact sparring are practiced outside regular class and are a matter of individual choice. I find that it is a matter of personal choice; some like the physical fitness aspect of karate while others like self-defense. The important thing is that people achieve their personal goals and enjoy training in a mutually respectful way. It is very hard to define "purity" in martial arts these days. So many elements are being combined together in every art that is difficult to call any system "pure."

Q: Are there are any fundamental differences between Eastern and Western karate practitioners?
A: Every culture has its own unique aspects. The training approach varies even between Japan and Okinawa, so it is hard to make comparisons between different countries, let alone different cultures. To me, it is a matter of individual effort. It is the person who dictates success in karate, not the style or geography. Today, many people look at karate as a sport, but I think it is dangerous to generalize. I believe there are many schools, even within the same style, that emphasize the sportive aspects while others emphasize tradi-

tional training and the long-term development of character and spirit. In the very end, everything boils down to the attitude between the instructor and the student. Going to Okinawa or Japan to learn the art is no longer necessary these days. Trips overseas can be very beneficial and students are always welcome to join me when I travel to Okinawa. However, it is not necessary in order to achieve the highest levels of proficiency. Hard work and discipline are far more important to a student's long-term success in the martial arts than trophies and athletic talent.

Q: Do you feel that you have further to go in your studies?
A: Without question. As a person ages, he must find new ways to practice karate based on his current situation. Learning is a process that never stops. As soon as I reach a goal, I immediately have a new one to work towards. I train outside of class at least two hours a day. I am still actively teaching between four or five days a week, not including seminars and clinics. I travel all over the world to teach at dojo that are part of my organization. To me, the most important thing to develop is respect. If I do not show respect to students, it breaks down the teaching process. Conversely, if students do not show respect back, it interferes with the learning process. Learning how to build this relationship is critical. It sounds like an obvious thing, but it is far more difficult to do than most think. Just look around and you'll see that the world of martial arts is sorely lacking this basic principle of respect.

"As a person ages, he must find new ways to practice karate based on his current situation. Learning is a process that never stops. As soon as I reach a goal, I immediately have a new one to work towards. I train outside of class at least two hours a day. I am still actively teaching between four or five days a week, not including seminars and clinics."

Karate Masters

"The most important thing is that the training allows the student to develop discipline, character and respect. If this is achieved by emphasizing self-defense versus kata or kumite, then the ultimate goal is being reached. An instructor must teach with a view to the students' abilities."

Q: Do you think it helps students physically to train with weapons?
A: Without question, *kobudo* builds the body in ways that empty-hand training can never do. It also demands a greater degree of mental concentration because the weapons are very dangerous to the student wielding the weapon—especially sharp weapons like the *kama*.

Q: What's your opinion of makiwara training?
A: Makiwara training is critical to developing *ikken-hissatsu* or one-punch stopping power. There are two ways to punch the makiwara. The first is like a normal punching motion in which the fist is retracted immediately after contact has been made. This is repeated continuously until you are unable to continue. Striking the post in this way allows the makiwara post to vibrate unimpeded, demonstrating the force of the blow. The movement of the makiwara dramatically increases the difficulty of striking the target in the right place with the correct part of the hands. If the timing is not perfect, injury may result. The second method of striking the makiwara is to leave the punch extended, maintaining contact with the makiwara and allowing your fist to absorb the vibration. This strategy forces the practitioner to hold the fist tight for a longer period of time, which develops muscle control at the moment of impact. This type of training uses a different rhythm and cadence than the first. Together, both techniques develop the foundation for ikken-hissatsu.

Q: What is most important in karate training: self-defense, sport or tradition?
A: To me, all elements are important, but the most important thing is that the training allows the student to develop discipline, character and respect. If this is achieved by emphasizing self-defense versus kata or kumite, then the ultimate goal is being reached. An instructor must teach with a view to

the students' abilities. But as one progresses and advances, additional training is critical. Usually this kind of training is difficult to do in a large class setting, particularly if the majority of students are less experienced.

Q: What's the proper training ratio between kata and kumite?
A: In kata, there are no surprises; the movements and sequences are the same all the time. The important aspect is that the practitioner develops what we call "internal timing." This means to coordinate the joints and hips with the delivery of the techniques. If a practitioner throws a punch and connects, but does not have the lower body and hips and breathing properly coordinated, the technique might not be effective in combat. Kumite develops what we call "external timing." The practitioner must adjust to changing circumstances and learn to master distance and space. The bottom line is that both are critical for success in a self-defense situation. If a practitioner ignores either part of the training, he will put himself at a disadvantage.

Q: Do you think it is necessary to engage in free-fighting to achieve good fighting skills in the street?
A: Yes. As I mentioned earlier, free-fighting or *kumite* develops what we call "external timing," a critical skill for combat—it is an integral part of the whole karate-do picture. But going out there and getting into fights in order to find out if a techniques works or not is very stupid and definitely not acceptable for a budo practitioner.

Q: How important is *bunkai* in understanding kata and the art of karate-do?
A: Extremely important. Without understanding bunkai, practitioners are missing the deeper meaning behind the techniques. Many applications of the techniques found in kata are not obvious to the eye and it takes a deep

"Without understanding bunkai, practitioners are missing the deeper meaning behind the techniques. Many applications of the techniques found in kata are not obvious to the eye and it takes a deep study and understanding of the principles and concepts behind the movement to be able to find a more advanced way of using the art."

Karate Masters

"Collectively, I feel very fortunate and lucky to have met so many nice people and shared with them the great memories I have. All these memories are a strong part of what karate means to me. I stay motivated because of the profound influence and effect karate has in my life. To me, the most important thing is how much the diligent study and training has changed me as a person."

study and understanding of the principles and concepts behind the movement in order to be able to find a more advanced way of using the art. Sometimes students simply touch the surface of bunkai. You have to go deep if you really want to find the real way to apply karate in a real situation.

Q: After all your years of training and experience, explain the meaning of karate.
A: Karate is about discovering yourself and internalizing all the qualities required to become a good human being—character development, respect, discipline, ethics and dedication. I have kept training because of the many great memories and have met so many great people during the 40 years of my training. Collectively, I feel very fortunate and lucky to have met so many nice people and shared with them the great memories I have. All these memories are a strong part of what karate means to me. I stay motivated because of the profound influence and effect karate has in my life. To me, the most important thing is how much the diligent study and training has changed me as a person. I feel karate has changed my life dramatically ... and for the better. This is what I hope others will realize after they have studied for a period of time. When a practitioner realizes these benefits, hopefully the process of study will become a lifelong pursuit. As a lifelong commitment, the practice of karate-do can change your life for good. To me, the benefits of karate far outweigh the commitment of time and effort.

Q: How much training should a senior karate-ka be doing to personally improve?
A: This is an individual thing. But in general, the more time spent, the more progress that will be made. A senior practitioner must devote time to keep his basic techniques strong and sharp, but at the same time, he must allo-

cate time to improve and keep moving forward. You can't always practice what you were taught 30 years ago. You need to dedicate time to practice and master the more advanced techniques and principles if you want to grow in the art—but never at expense of not training your basics.

Q: What advice would you give to students on the question of supplementary training such as weight lifting?
A: I think any kind of physical activity is good if helps to maintain your body in good shape. You have to be careful to combine activities that bring benefits to your karate training and not prevent you from improving in the art. I love to run, and I try and do the Los Angeles marathon every year. I also lift weights but not necessarily like a bodybuilder. I use the weight training to build speed, strength and endurance specifically for karate techniques. So basically, I think the student should look for activities that will compliment his karate classes. Unfortunately, many people think that because they can run longer, lift more and stretch deeper their karate will improve. That is not necessarily correct. Dedicate time for your karate first and then use whatever extra time you may for these supplementary training.

"I use the weight training to build speed, strength and endurance specifically for karate techniques. So basically, I think the student should look for activities that will compliment his karate classes. Unfortunately, many people think that because they can run longer, lift more, and stretch deeper their karate will improve. That is not necessarily correct."

Q: What are the most important attributes of a student?
A: Again, I think it is an issue of establishing and building mutual respect between the teacher and student. This includes diligence, perseverance, discipline, humility, courage and respect. A student must be dedicated, hard working and serious minded. I try to lead my students by example, and I think I train harder than anyone. This gives my students the chance to stand next to me and follow. I think if more teachers followed this practice, both they and their students would develop mutual respect and go further in the

Karate Masters

"I try to develop an attitude of respect, which means not being judgmental of others. My students follow me and my way of doing things. But I realize that my way may not work for everyone, and I have to accept this. This is part of showing respect."

study of the art. Certainly, this is the traditional way of martial arts. I think that students often do not have the right perspective. You asked me earlier about whether or not I feel I still have more to learn and what motivates me to continue my training. To me, learning is a continual and ongoing process and I think that if students viewed their training in this way, fewer students would quit after only a couple of years.

Q: There is very little written about you in magazines. You obviously do not thrive on publicity like some martial artists. Why?
A: Karate training is a personal thing and a personal choice I have made. This choice and decision is not really a matter of public inspection. On the other hand, as I get older, sharing my knowledge and experience with other practitioners has become more important to me. I try to develop an attitude of respect, which means not being judgmental of others. My students follow me and my way of doing things, but I realize that my way may not work for everyone, and I have to accept this. This is part of showing respect.

Karate instructors belonging to the old generations should do more in public to promote the art. We should use interviews, magazines, books and video to continue the legacy that was passed onto us by our teachers. Staying isolated in our dojo without making ourselves accessible is a big mistake. This is part of the essence of karate—the humbleness. We need to be humble by making ourselves accessible. Isolation is not good for anyone and some karate masters isolate themselves so they can show they are like little gods. Unfortunately, there is always a group of people who fall for that stupid attitude.

Q: Have you felt fear in your training?
A: Fear is a part of all human beings and exists inside us all. Training can teach a student how to deal with this fear; please note that I use the word

"deal." You cannot totally eliminate the element of fear because is a feeling all human beings have, but you can learn how to control it, channel it and use it in a positive way if you find yourself in a difficult situation. Learning how to use fear to our own benefit is the key. Saying that you don't feel fear because you are tough is not a very smart thing to do.

Q: What are your thoughts on the future of karate-do?
A: Karate has changed my life 100 percent. Karate is more than a way to defend oneself or improve physical conditioning. It is a way of life and a way of improving one's life. Sometimes even being a naturally gifted athlete can be an impediment to a practitioner's development, because those students may not have to work as hard as others in order to achieve the same level of proficiency. There is something about the discipline and determination that is forged through years of hard training and striving to become the best you can that gives a practitioner more insight into the spirit of karate than showmanship or gymnastic ability ever could. I practice karate because I become a better person as a result, and I teach karate because I believe my students learn to become better people through hard training. It's not that my classes aren't physically demanding—just ask my students—but the ultimate goal is something far beyond exercise. Karate may offer different things for different people depending on their age, interests and level of ability, but I have no doubt that practitioners of all ages and levels can benefit from this training … sometimes in ways they might never have anticipated. Karate will always evolve, but we should never forget our lineage and history. So go ahead and grow, but always remember where your roots are. O

"Karate may offer different things for different people depending on their age, interests, and level of ability, but I have no doubt that practitioners of all ages and levels can benefit from this training—sometimes in ways they might never have anticipated."

Mas Oyama

The Divine Fist

HE WAS THE REIGNING KING OF ALL THE LEADING FIGURES IN THE KARATE WORLD AND THE *KANCHO* FOR THE *KYOKUSHINKAI* STYLE FOR MORE THAN 50 YEARS. HIS ACHIEVEMENT IN THE ART HAS BEEN EQUALED BY FEW AND SURPASSED BY NONE. OYAMA SENSEI HAS AUTHORIZED MORE THAN 20 BOOKS ON THE ART OF KARATE AND HIS OWN LIFE, WORKS THAT HAVE BEEN PRINTED IN MORE THAN 23 DIFFERENT LANGUAGES. BESIDE SMASHING BRICKS, WOOD AND STONES, MAS OYAMA TOOK THE CHALLENGE A LITTLE FURTHER AND PITTED HIS STRENGTH AGAINST BULLS WEIGHING AS MUCH AS 1,000 POUNDS. HIS TECHNIQUE WAS TO KNOCK THEM INTO A DAZE BY PUNCHING THEM BETWEEN THE EYES WITH A DEVASTATING *GYAKU-TSUKI*. OYAMA'S BULL-KILLING MADE HIM AN UNMEDIATED HERO NOT ONLY IN JAPAN BUT ALSO EVERYWHERE IN THE WORLD. MANY OF HIS PERSONAL STUDENTS INCLUDED INTERNATIONAL CELEBRITIES FROM JORDAN'S KING HUSSEIN TO ACTOR AND ACADEMY AWARD WINNER SEAN CONNERY. OYAMA DIRECTED HIS WORLD ORGANIZATION WITH UNENDING ENERGY AND DEDICATION FROM HIS HEADQUARTERS IN TOKYO. HE BECAME ONE OF THOSE FEW PEOPLE WHO LEAVE A MARK IN THE WORLD FOR ALL THE GENERATIONS TO COME. AFTER HIS DEATH, MANY OF HIS DIRECT STUDENTS WENT ON THEIR OWN AND DEVELOPED NEW APPROACHES TO THE ART HE DEVELOPED. MASUTATSU OYAMA WAS FOR MANY THE REAL KARATE FIGHTER—A LEGEND WITH NO EQUAL.

Q: Sensei, would you tell us a little bit about your beginnings in the martial arts?
A: I was born in South Korea in 1923 and received my first introduction to the martial arts at the age of nine from a Korean farmer who came to work for my father. In 1937, I went to Japan to attend a boy's military school and study aircraft engineering. The truth is that after I finished school I had no intention of following that career. Karate was all I could think of and it was then I decided to study *goju-ryu* and *shotokan*. Although I was doing very good, I was not completely happy with what I had and decided to develop my own way of doing karate. I then created my own style that I called "kyokushinkai." In 1952, I made my first trip to the United States of America with Kokichi Endo, a judo master. I gave 270 exhibitions and appeared on

Karate Masters

"Nei-chu So was a Korean teacher who I truly consider the highest authority in the goju style of karate. He was a devotee of the Nichiren Sect of Buddhism and it was he who advised me to retire from the world for a period of time to train my mind and body in solitude."

television seven times. My ability to break whiskey bottles with my empty hands surprised the Americans, and they gave me the nickname "The Divine Fist." Later on, I returned a couple of times to open schools in Chicago, California and New York. I have worked very hard for many decades to promote the art of karate and expand the kyokushinkai style. I wrote more than 20 books on karate and its philosophy and demonstrated the art all around the world.

Q: You studied shotokan under Funakoshi Gichin and goju-ryu under Nei-chu So. What were the main differences between these two great men?
A: Everybody knows Master Funakoshi. I had the great pleasure of training at his dojo, but his emphasis was more on philosophy and ethical principles than on fighting so I decided to part ways with him. I truly respect him very much. He was a great man. Nei-chu So was a Korean teacher who I truly consider the highest authority in the goju style of karate. He was a devotee of the Nichiren Sect of Buddhism and it was he who advised me to retire from the world for a period of time to train my mind and body in solitude.

Q: Did you also train with Gogen "The Cat" Yamaguchi?
A: Yes, we trained together for a while. We shared many ideas and knowledge. Our approaches were also a little different, but we had a great time together.

Q: How was your retreat in solitude?
A: My first time was in 1946, when I isolated myself in a temple on Mount Minobu. Then, shortly after the war, I decided to retire in seclusion on Mount

"Training in the day was intensive and required tremendous concentration. As a result, for a long time, I forgot about the importance of finding a release. For this reason, I was usually in good form during the day and despondent at night."

Kiyozumi in the Chiba prefecture. I went there with another karate-ka, but it soon got too much for my partner, and he decided to leave. I was left by myself, which was the best thing that could have happened to me. I lived in a small shack, with no electricity, running water or newspapers. Once a month I saw a human being, my friend Kayama, who brought me food.

Q: What kind of training did you do there?
A: Everything from thousands of punches and kicks to meditation and chanting from Buddhism scriptures. As a result of that type of training I became a man of strong build and gained great confidence in myself. I felt refreshed and reborn. Training in the day was intensive and required tremendous concentration. As a result, for a long time, I forgot about the importance of finding a release. For this reason, I was usually in good form during the day and despondent at night. But towards the end of my stay at the mountains, I got glimpses of what is meant by both "release" and the "thoughtless state." I

Karate Masters

"A true fighter cannot know the true gravity of martial arts until he has experienced it. I am probably the only post-war Japanese karate teacher leader to have undergone actual dangerous combat and, as a result, I have been criticized by so-called peaceful karate men. I think a true martial arts teacher must encounter and overcome true danger."

gradually became capable of deepening mental unification until I moved from concentration to release and then to the thoughtless state of liberation, where I was able to foresee an opponent's motions and react to them at once without thinking.

Q: When did you start to teach karate to the public?
A: It was around seven or eight years after I began practicing the arts. My first school was opened in 1946 in Suginami, Tokyo, but the real start and beginnings of the kyokushinkai style didn't happen until approximately 1956.

Q: Your style of fighting is known for being one of the most effective Japanese karate styles. How did you develop this method and what is its main emphasis?
A: *Kyoku* means "the final meaning of life" and *shin* means "truth and heart." I developed the idea after realizing that even after 30 years of practice we are still students. In my classes, the most important aspect is the first 10 minutes when we meditate. Through Zen meditation the students concentrate on empty-mind or what is called in Japanese "mushin," which involves losing one's identity. The idea is clearing the mind so the student only concentrates on the training, allowing him to perform much better karate.

Q: Is it true that you invite fighters from Thailand to train and fight against your students?
A: Yes, it is true. Thai boxers are extremely good fighters, probably the best fighters in the world, so I invite them to fight against us. We have defeated many of them. The tempo and timing of Thai boxing is slower than kyokushinkai. We have faster technique and faster combinations. Karate is not an imitation; it is an original art. Now that we are talking about fighting let me say something here; the proper way to use your skills is to do it for the sake of the society you belong to and not for your own sake. Perhaps I

should be embarrassed to have risked life and limb in endeavors of no greater importance, but at the time, given my intense ardor for karate and the world reputation of the Japanese people, I had no choice but to fight. And I believe that any man determined to follow the way of martial arts ought to have experiences of this kind. A true fighter cannot know the true gravity of martial arts until he has experienced it. I am probably the only post-,war Japanese karate teacher leader to have undergone actual dangerous combat and, as a result, I have been criticized by so-called peaceful karate men. Obtaining these experiences involves the danger of injury and even deformity, but there are things that cannot be mastered on the basis of theory alone. I think a true martial arts teacher must encounter and overcome true danger.

"A sound mind in a sound body, as the famous maxim of the Greeks goes. And 2,000 years later students of the martial arts are still after the same thing. The physical training of the modern-day practitioners of the art of karate is a living legacy from this illustrious past."

Q: What about the *tameshiwari* or "breaking" aspect of the style?
A: Breaking in my style is a way of testing our progress. It takes a lot of concentration and inner power because you can't only use your arm or leg. The power comes from the *hara,* and it takes a minimum of 10 years to develop the correct technique to use *hara* in breaking. Testing your full power against another human being is way too dangerous but against material like bricks or wood it is OK and much safer.

Q: You have written many books on karate. Do you really think karate can be learned by reading a book?
A: No. If the person has no previous experience, then the answer is no. There is no way an individual can learn the techniques, ethics and right attitude of karate without the guidance of an authentic instructor. But if the per-

Karate Masters

"Failure to be creative because of the traditional views hinders the performance of respective practitioners. To keep up with the results demanded, traditional views like morality have to change with the times. Traditionalism in some ways destroy creativeness. However, it is this creativeness which increases the proficiency of any physical talent."

son has previous training, then he can pick up things from the books that will help him in his karate journey.

Q: What is the final goal of practicing the martial arts?
A: The martial arts are arts that transmit more to the student than a ritualistic set of movements and postures or physical attitudes of attack and defense. The arts seek to unify and stimulate fruitful interaction between the physical and the mental, seeking perfection of man through fusing the dualities of mind and body into a smooth, strong, finely-tuned instrument. The ancient Greeks were after the same thing. A sound mind in a sound body, as the famous maxim of the Greeks goes. And 2,000 years later students of the martial arts are still after the same thing. The physical training of the modern-day practitioners of the art of karate is a living legacy from this illustrious past. The physical aspects of the art are both rich and spectacular, but to be effective these powerful weapons must be under control. So as the focus and strength of kicks and punches is developed, the student also develops a mental focus and strength tha will direct his activities.

Q: What are the main physical characteristics of a well-trained karate-ka?
A: The essence of powerful and graceful movement and action in karate is balance, control and coordinated effort. The body learns to immediately and accurately respond to the physical demands of the situation. We condition the body to react properly and automatically when faced with certain events. Likewise, our mental control increases and mental and physical attributes strengthen and toughen each other.

Q: And the ethical and moral aspects?
A: The practitioner learns to display quiet courtesy and respect for the worth of individuals. This inherent spirit of the martial arts can help bridge the superficial gaps that often occur among the members of mankind. The discipline teaches the modern student to regard differences in age, class and race in the proper perspective, realizing them for what they are ... unessential variables of the human condition. The qualities engendered by martial arts are exactly those which our modern society so desperately needs. The deplorable lack of respect today for individual rights, authority and the integrity of the individual are a result of a disorder which can be found almost everywhere in the modern world. Through the proper application of the spirit of the ancient practitioners of the martial arts, we can begin to counterbalance this disorder. The pursuit of a trained and balanced mind and body is as important today as it has ever been throughout history.

Q: Are you a traditionalist?
A: Tradition is based on a chain-of-command relationship. Each entity of this chain

"The traditionalist thinks that weight training is the concept of slow reactions. Tradition in karate teaches that weights slow the practitioner down. This is also a fallacy. It is the mental processes which are responsible for a slowness in technique, not physical processes."

never questions the previous one because of the injection of morality from its predecessor. Consequently, over a period of some time, the product becomes quite stereotyped. Failure to be creative because of the traditional views hinders the performance of respective practitioners. To keep up with the results demanded, traditional views like morality have to change with the times. Traditionalism, in some ways, destroy creativeness. However, it is this creativeness which increases the proficiency of any physical talent. For instance, the traditionalist points out that superior technique will always beat power and size. This is a fallacious for two reasons. First of all, the more muscle that can be brought into focus on a specified technique is obviously going to make that technique stronger. Secondly, a lightweight

Karate Masters

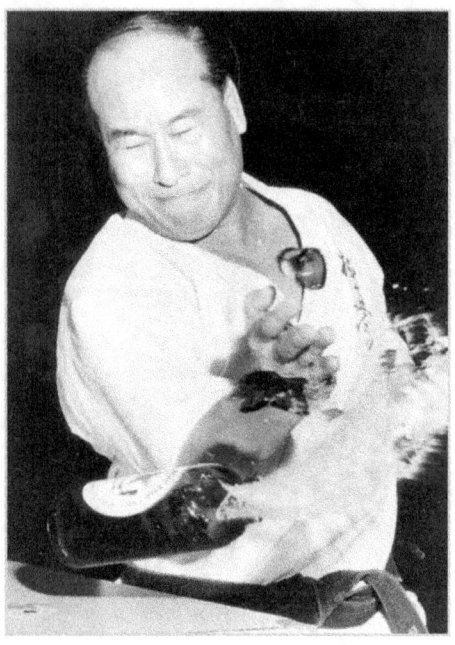

"When a teacher is teaching kumite and kata without teaching some of its philosophy and history, he is teaching in ignorance. I realize this is a harsh thing to say, but it must be said. Ignorance and poor management in karate can be dealt with through reading and talking and listening to those who know."

prize fighter has never beaten the heavyweight champion of the world. Why? Because he does not have the size and the power for a contact, street, non-mystical situation; power and size will always claim the winner.

Q: Do you think weight training is good for the karate-do practitioner?
A: Weight training can add colossal results to performance, especially from a power standpoint. The traditionalist thinks that weight training is the concept of slow reactions. Tradition in karate teaches that weights slow the practitioner down. This is also a fallacy. It is the mental processes which are responsible for a slowness in technique, not physical processes. In order to be effective, you have to be quick. However, in order to be quick, you must learn how to relax. Relaxation is the key, and it is the only key to being explosive. If a karate-ka tries to punch like he would push a weight, obviously the results are going to be synonymous with traditionalism. Instead of tensing through the whole movement—like in weight training—the karate-ka has to learn how to tense only at the end of the completed technique. Again, this is a mental process. A strong, big and fast karate-ka is an infallible combination.

Q: Why do you think people don't understand this?
A: Ignorance prevails anytime the facts are not present. The world was thought to be flat at one time. Taking a bath daily was considered unhealthy several years back. Centuries ago the earth was believed to be the center of the universe. Though all of these statements were held as truths in their own special time in history, man proved them wrong. As relevant facts made their appearance, the unknown became known. The mystical beliefs became non-mystical beliefs. Thus, man's ignorance was no longer supported by his beliefs but was erased by scientific facts. It is out of this realm of ignorance that most karate-ka view weight training. They lack the knowledge of the

physics of the movements. They fail in their attempt to see how working certain muscle groups through proper weight training can improve a comprehensive discipline. The key word under investigation is "proper." Each discipline requires a different approach to achieve its respective optimal results. Therefore, for a karate-ka to increase his power through a weight program, he must work the muscles that will be engaged in the various hand and leg techniques. A thorough knowledge of the physics of the movements is imperative.

Q: What is your opinion of how some instructors behave with the students?
A: Within the martial arts, sensei who influence thousands of students often don't know what they are talking about, although they can show you many trophies they have won. Their crime is not their ignorance; in many ways we are all ignorant of more things than we could ever grasp in one lifetime. The crime is that their egos will not permit them to admit their ignorance to themselves so that they can seek truth. We can go one worse when we meet the sensei who is completely unaware of his ego-ignorance problem. The ego problem appears to be one in which a man's self-esteem has grown so big that he sees himself like a little God. He may clean sewers during the day, but at night he can shove a man against a wall, thereby establishing that he is the better of the two. He has power over other men. Any teacher is aware of the fact that he can be a strong influence on his students. If he is a good influence, all the better. At this point, we could say that we should leave the matter alone; if he is a good instructor, that's all that counts. Well, sadly enough that's not true. When a teacher is teaching *kumite* and *kata* without teaching some of its philosophy and history, he is teaching in ignorance. I realize this is a harsh thing to say, but it must be said. Ignorance and poor management in karate can be dealt with through reading and talking and listening to those who know. We must all

"The spiritual aspect of karate is something from the spirit, and it has nothing to do with breaking somebody's teeth. That is merely the physical level—a step up the ladder, but that's not the end. And this is what I feel most people are missing ... an attitude in mind and body in the true spirit of the martial arts."

help to throw some light into the karate world so everybody can understand properly and act accordingly.

Q: You mentioned once that ignorance is something you can't stand.
A: There is nothing wrong with not knowing, but if you don't even seek the knowledge, if you don't even bend to find out what the truth is ... I can't understand it. I feel very strong about what I do. I feel I am very devoted, and I feel I really understand what I am doing. I don't put anyone down. There are different levels in karate. There is a physical level, a mental level and a spiritual level. Some people say there is only a physical level, simply because they only work the body. But then you pick up magazines and they talk of the spiritual aspect of karate ... and it seems to me that they are floundering around trying to find out who really knows this. They can't really come out and say, "Well, the spiritual aspects of karate are this and this, or such and such." It's a pity. If he is up to the mental level, he will really understand the physical and mental. But if he is not up to the spiritual level, or the mind, then he can never understand...he can't go past that, so he can't speak about it. The spiritual aspect of karate is something from the spirit and it has nothing to do with breaking somebody's teeth. That is merely the physical level—a step up the ladder, but that's not the end. And this is what I feel most people are missing; an attitude in mind and body in the true spirit of the martial arts.

Q: So karate is more of a personal journey?
A: Right. True karate is so you can develop yourself, your mind and your body. It is a study and grow. The true karate-ka builds a rapport and brings out certain understandings from human beings for each other. We know how hard the physical body can be driven, and we know that we can fight very strongly. But it is not there to defeat one another or another opponent. We learn karate in a very pure way. To study karate to become great fighters is a lesser goal, but it doesn't mean we can't try to be good fighters. There is more to karate than just fighting. It's bad for a man to live with the thought of hurting others. We don't think like that. If this thing happens, it's a natural conclusion. You train your body to become better, stronger. But if you devote your life to something, it has to be something beautiful.

Q: Do you believe in training in many styles?
A: Not really. Many people take this technique from this style and that one from that other method, but I don't think this is the right approach, especially in the period when the student is still developing the fundamental

techniques of the art. You must study your style for many years, and if you take from another style, it must be within the laws of that particular style. The mental aspect of karate is shown in the understanding of the style, in mastering of the body itself. In other words, to be able to come in to train hard even when you feel tired. With every exercise, to feel that you are over your body, is mastering your body. This is something very difficult to achieve when you are jumping from one style to another.

Q: Oyama Sensei, is there anything else you'd like to add?
A: Kicks and punches, dodges, attacks and defenses are the physical framework of our art. But by themselves they are really just so much flesh and bones. They need a soul, and the soul of our art lies much deeper than just the physical. It lies in the mental discipline for which each individual must strive. If I could, I would like to live the rest of my life as a hermit on some secluded mountain where I could train, eat and sleep when I want, without having any responsibilities or obligations. But because of the big development of the art, I can't do this. I'm planning to do it but only after all of my projects have been accomplished. Then don't be surprised if I disappear some day. O

"Many people take this technique from this style and that one from that other method, but I don't think this is the right approach, especially in the period when the student is still developing the fundamental techniques of the art. The mental aspect of karate is shown in the understanding of the style, in mastering of the body itself."

Shigeru Oyama

In the Footsteps of the Master

SHIGERU OYAMA WAS BORN IN 1936 IN TOKYO. HE STARTED HIS MARTIAL ARTS CAREER WHEN HE WAS ONLY 9 YEARS OLD AND WAS TO BECOME ONE OF MAS OYAMA'S CLOSEST AND TOP STUDENTS. IN 1965, SHIGERU OYAMA CAME TO UNITED STATES TO BE THE USA KYOKUSHINKAI CHIEF INSTRUCTOR, BUT NOT BEFORE PASSING THE BRUTAL 100-MAN KUMITE TEST. WITH LITTLE ENGLISH AND LESS MONEY, SHIGERU OYAMA WAS OFF TO HIS NEW ADVENTURE. FOR MORE THAN FOUR DECADES SHIGERU OYAMA TOURED THE WORLD, GIVING DEMONSTRATIONS AND PROMOTING THE ART TAUGHT TO HIM BY *KANCHO* OYAMA. IN 1981, DUE TO HIS INCREASING PERSONAL POPULARITY, WHICH HE FELT SHOWED DISRESPECT TO MAS OYAMA, HE BROKE AWAY FROM HIS TEACHER AND WENT HIS SEPARATE WAY. IN 1985, HE FORMED THE *WORLD OYAMA KARATE ORGANIZATION* WHICH QUICKLY EXPANDED WORLDWIDE. SHIGERU OYAMA NEVER ALLOWED POLITICS TO ENTER INTO HIS KARATE AND STILL PRIVATELY KEPT IN TOUCH WITH MAS OYAMA AFTER THEIR SPLIT. UPON THE DEATH OF HIS TEACHER, TO THE SURPRISE OF MANY, HE WENT TO MAS OYAMA'S FUNERAL TO SHOW RESPECT AND HONOR TO THE MAN WHO HAD GIVEN HIM SO MUCH IN LIFE.

Q: When did you begin karate training?
A: I started when I was 9 years old. Mas Oyama was living at my home because he and my father were very good friends. He would teach in my backyard since my father had a very big garden. Mas Oyama's teacher at that time was a *goju-ryu* teacher named Nei-chu So. Nei Chu was also a Korean from Oyama's own province, and he would come to our backyard and teach karate. Mas Oyama was about 21 years old and already a fourth dan from training under Gichin Funakoshi. Mas Oyama didn't have any money to start a dojo so he taught about 80 people in my backyard. I began by watching him and then became formally involved in training.

Q: What was the relationship between Mas Oyama and your family?
A: It was after World War II and Mas Oyama only had a little money. The goju-ryu master was also living at my house. They would both teach karate at my home. My father was a very wealthy man, so Mas Oyama began to

Karate Masters

"Mas Oyama paid for my high school and college tuition. I was Mas Oyama's uchi-deshi. He was like a second father to me. When we were at a clinic, we would do free fighting. I would always have to do the fighting to prove that his style of karate was the best."

work for my father. My brother Yasuhiko and I became friends with Mas Oyama. Mas Oyama paid for my high school and college tuition. I was Mas Oyama's *uchi-deshi*. He was like a second father to me. We traveled the world together for 20 years, and I never lost face for Mas Oyama. When we were at a clinic, we would do free fighting. I would always have to do the fighting to prove that his style of karate was the best.

Q: How was the training in those days?
A: Well, like I said, I began by just watching. He used to do *sanchin kata* with loud *ibuki* breathing. Of course, I had no idea of what he was doing—not at all. Basically, he was training himself. I guess that was the main reason he started to teach at a later stage. He was more concerned with his own development. When he started teaching, we were basically copying his movements. He never taught the way we teach today. I guess the whole atmosphere was very interesting. You had white belts with five years of training and white belts with one month of training, but until you saw them perform, you just couldn't tell. I was white belt for almost five years until I received my black belt. A little bit later Kancho Oyama came up with the belt system: white, brown and black. The training wasn't as glamorous as people think today.

Q: Did he focus on kata or kumite?
A: He liked fighting. For him, *kumite* and *kihon* were the most important things. It's true we used to do kata for more than a half hour, but our classes were three or four hours long. Kata was not a big part of it. A lot of empha-

"I think the United States has the potential to develop the best martial artists in the world. Most of the world's best instructors have come here."

sis was placed on conditioning drills and exercises to strengthen our bodies and spirits. It is very interesting for me to note how my young days went so fast. I wanted to fight and all of a sudden—bang! I was 30 years old.

Q: Did Kancho Oyama invite other schools to train?
A: Yes, he did. In fact, our school was known for hard contact in kumite, so we had visitors and guests from others school. Some were goju, shotokan, Chinese kenpo, wado-ryu, et cetera. He loved to fight. In fact, he would fight with each and every one of the students at class. If 30 students came to train, he would do kumite with all 30. If 100 students came to practice, he fought all 100. He was not afraid of anyone. He fought black belts from all styles. It didn't matter to him who they were.

Q: It is said Mas Oyama studied Thai boxing in order to change the traditional karate he previously studied. Is this true?
A: That's not really true. Mas Oyama didn't study Thai boxing, but he watched the way the Thai boxers trained and fought. He found Thai boxing to be very efficient, and he began to train with hard contact. When you train

Karate Masters

"Many details in technique change once you decide to train with contact. We don't believe in the point-sparring system. For us, what really works is knockdown tournaments, and the reason for this is simple—self-defense is contact—the street is contact."

with contact you have to change the way the technique is done—balance is different, momentum is different, and body control is different. Many details in technique change once you decide to train with contact. We don't believe in the point-sparring system. For us, what really works is knockdown tournaments, and the reason for this is simple—self-defense is contact—the street is contact.

Q: Did you train in other martial arts systems besides kyokushinkai karate?
A: Yes, I did. I studied weaponry, but I don't think traditional weapons are practical for street defense these days. I still teach them, though. As far as empty-hand methods, I studied kendo, iaido and judo. But I went back to the roots of my karate style because, although I think these arts have good things, I don't think they have much to teach us about fighting.

Q: Can you explain the 100-man kumite?
A: Mas Oyama created the 100-man kumite. This was a test of your stamina, strength, endurance and fighting spirit. I was going to the United States to open the USA Kyokushinkai Headquarters for Mas Oyama. Mas Oyama told me before I went to America that I had to face the one-hundred-man Kumite test. At that time, I was the chief instructor of the kyokushinkai *honbu* dojo in Tokyo. I taught from 10 a.m. to noon, 4-6 p.m., 6-8 p.m., and 8-10 p.m. I did eight hours of teaching a day. Each class had between 40 and 80 students. I was teaching every day for three to four years. Mas Oyama told me that if I did not do the 100-man kumite, I could not go to America to teach. He said that the test would consist of two-minute rounds and no break between each person. There were 40 black belt students, so I fought about 120 times. I prepared by fighting the students in the classes that I taught. In each class, I would fight all the people who came to train. When I did the 100-man kumite, it was not a shock to me because I was totally prepared. However, it was not easy. I came to the U.S., and I had to receive a physical

examination for my green card. I had X-rays taken and discovered I had several broken ribs. It was a difficult test. I will never forget it.

Q: Can you give some insight on the 100-man kumite?
A: Well, it's the hardest thing I ever did in my life! You don't fight 100 men with your body; it's your spirit that keeps you going. After the 65th man, all of your physical resources are gone. You fight with your spirit. This is a big event for kyokushinkai practitioners. There are usually 50 opponents in a 100-man kumite,

"I'm sure that one day the leader of kyokushin will have blond hair and blue eyes!"

and you have to fight two minutes against each of them. In order to make it, you must fight smart. Of course, there are few tricks but they are more psychological than physical. For instance, I remember that I punched my first opponent in the face so hard that he collapsed in a pool of blood. This was not the right thing to do, but all the other fighters were shocked and intimidated by that. That gave me a psychological edge over them. On the other hand, I could say that opponents between numbers 60 and 70 are the hardest. After number 70, it's easy. You know and everybody else knows that you're going to make it. You feel confident. You get a smile in your face even if you can't feel your body anymore. Most of your opponents don't really want to fight you anymore, but I can tell you that there is always someone who wants to knock you down and see you fail.

Q: How did you prepare for the test?
A: I trained for a complete year in order to get ready. Three training sessions per day where I used to fight all the student at each class. Maybe 20 to 30 in the morning, 50 to 60 in the afternoon and 60 to 80 in the evening. I fought everybody no matter what, because the stamina that you need to go through the test is only gained from sparring, not from running or exercising. When I finished, my body was swollen and bruised. It took more than three months to totally recover from this. I couldn't walk, and I could only take liquids.

Karate Masters

"I fought everybody, no matter what, because the stamina that you need to go through the test is only gained from sparring, not from running or exercising. When I finished, my body was swollen and bruised. It took more than three months to totally recover from this. I couldn't walk, and I could only take liquids."

Q: What happened afterwards?
A: I received my 4th-degree black belt and came to United States. Kancho kept pushing me about coming, and I kept telling him that I didn't want to because I had a good job and a wife. Finally, I accepted for one year but mainly because he was saying to everybody that I was scared to go because the Americans were bigger than me. But like I said, it was after the 100-man kumite.

Q: How were your early days in the United States?
A: Well, I didn't know how to speak English ... just "good morning" and "thank you." I had to gain the respect from the students. Some of them were already black belts. I fought them, and they were shocked. After that, everything went OK. They liked me and respected me a lot, but I had to change my teaching methodology because I realized I was teaching too hard, the same way I was taught in Japan. Within three months, almost 95 percent of the students had quit. I realized how important it is to understand the culture of the people when you develop whatever activity you do. For instance,

in Japan we started to play baseball a fairly short time ago. Americans couldn't understand why we wanted to start baseball. But now we are doing pretty well. Why? Because in Japan we tried to understand the people who invented the sport. If you go to Japan, the referees yell in English, "Out!" "Strike!" or whatever. It's the same with the Oriental martial arts; you have to understand how the Orientals think and not just learn how to execute the physical techniques of punching and kicking. The physical is not enough. The cultures are very different so you have to train mentally, also. The right way to execute a punch or a kick includes the right way to use it and the right reason, as well. Attitude is paramount.

Q: Why didn't you go back to Japan?
A: Because I received a letter from Mas Oyama saying, "Don't come back. Stay in the United States and die in the United States." I said "Oh, boy!" I was worried, but everything went perfectly. I was treated nicely by a lot of people and later on I decided to open my own dojo in Connecticut, since I was teaching at Richard Bernard's school; he was the person who wrote Mas Oyama asking for a Japanese instructor.

"You have to understand how the Orientals think, and not just learn how to execute the physical techniques of punching and kicking. The physical is not enough. The cultures are very different so you have to train mentally, also. The right way to execute a punch or a kick includes the right way to use it and the right reason, as well. Attitude is paramount."

Q: What is your relationship with Tadashi Nakamura, leader of Seido Karate?
A: He's like a brother to me. We are very close. He is my junior and is about six years younger than I am. We have done many demonstrations together and have been close friends for many years. I think that if Tadashi Nakamura had stayed with kyokushinkai and Mas Oyama, he would have been the successor to Kancho Oyama. He left kyokushinkai, and I was sent to the U.S. to open a new kyokushinkai headquarters.

Karate Masters

"My reputation and name were becoming more popular in the organization. I was younger, my techniques were more advanced and this was creating problems for me."

Q: Was Mas Oyama as tough as everybody thinks?

A: Tougher. We had a lot of intense physical training for endurance and strength. Many times we would take a four- to five-hour drive and train in the mountains outside of Tokyo. Today, the level of training has greatly improved. This is because of videos, books, kickboxing, jiu-jitsu, et cetera. I think that the old karate spirit was much better than it is today. Many times, I was Mas Oyama's demonstration partner. Mas Oyama would always say, "Hit me harder!" He had great power in his body. I grew up free sparring with Mas Oyama. His style of fighting was pure power. Before the kyokushinkai organization, it was only the Oyama dojo. This was the beginning of his fighting style. All karate styles would train at his dojo. We allowed groin kicks, face contact, knee kicks, elbows, et cetera. Mas Oyama was preparing all of us for his full-contact tournaments. We did bare-knuckle, full-contact to the face. After fighting, we would soak our hands in cold water. Today, there are all types of protective equipment. I always think how lucky I was to train with him. Very few people have ever had such a great opportunity.

Q: When and why did you break away from Mas Oyama?

A: It was a long time ago. Many things were happening in the kyokushinkai organization. My reputation and name were becoming more popular in the organization. I was younger, and my techniques were more advanced; this was creating problems for me. Many countries were requesting that I conduct clinics for them. Mas Oyama was not happy about this. I did not want to leave, but I had no choice. I went to Mas Oyama, and we talked about this and decided that it was better if I would leave. I was with Mas Oyama for more than 30 years. It was a difficult decision. We remained friends, and he would send his top fighters to train with me. I was not against him; how could I be? We would sometimes talk on the telephone privately, but no one knew about our conversations.

Q: Did you have any personal contact with him?
A: We would only talk on the telephone. When he passed away, I attended his funeral.

Q: What is the difference between World Oyama Karate and Kyokushinkai Karate?
A: The Oyama karate organization is more creative. I created a lot more techniques. We do the basics and Oyama kata. Mas Oyama told me to eliminate the *heian* and goju-ryu kata. He said, "Create your own kata." After Mas Oyama died, the kyokushinkai did the same thing.

Q: Do you do *saifa, tensho, seipai* and *sanchin*?
A: No. The only naha-te kata is *seienchin*. I created a new series of kata, and we do *goju-shiho* and *kanku* kata.

Q: Do you place much emphasis on kata and bunkai?
A: Yes, we do a lot of kata and they have all the self-defense techniques, takedowns and choking techniques. I believe you just strike a balance. Also, you must train all the parts of your body and a variety of tactics and strategies. All the techniques used in kyokushin are very practical;

"I believe you just strike a balance. Also, you must train all the parts of your body and a variety of tactics and strategies."

there are few wasted movements. Mas Oyama studied different systems and incorporated what he considered to be effective. He was a very clever man. Kyokushinkai has no secrets; it's a very direct and open style. Kancho wanted things that way.

Q: Did you ever train with goju-ryu master Gogen Yamaguchi?
A: I trained with him for about six months, three days a week. At that time, an American by the name of Peter Urban was training with him and Mas Oyama.

Karate Masters

"The kyokushinkai dojo had many students from all styles, including shotokan, wado-ryu, goju-ryu and shito-ryu. I have studied with several senior students from goju-ryu. They came from all styles to practice full-contact fighting."

Q: Did you train with Peter Urban?
A: Many times when he was with Mas Oyama.

Q: How long did Peter Urban train with Mas Oyama?
A: I think about four or five years. Urban then became more involved with Gogen Yamaguchi's goju-ryu organization. Peter Urban would train one day in Mas Oyama's dojo and another day train with Gogen Yamaguchi. Later on, he went with Yamaguchi's organization and stayed in goju-ryu karate.

Q: Did Mas Oyama ever train with Gogen Yamaguchi?
A: Maybe they did in private. Gogen Yamaguchi would only come to Mas Oyama's dojo to give a lecture or demonstrate; sometimes his students would practice kumite.

Q: Did you ever train with any other goju-ryu karate masters?
A: The kyokushinkai dojo had many students from all styles, including shotokan, wado-ryu, goju-ryu and shito-ryu. I have studied with several senior students from goju-ryu. They came from all styles to practice full-contact fighting. When we formed kyokushinkai, Mas Oyama told me that we needed to have our own kata. We developed a list of kyokushinkai kata. When I left to form my own organization, I did the same thing. The goju-ryu students were from Gogen Yamaguchi's. Mas Oyama and Gogen Yamaguchi were good friends. They were advisors to each others dojo. When both organizations became bigger, they split them between each other.

Q: Kyokushinkai is perceived as dangerous because of the contact sparring. Is this a fair assessment?
A: It boils down to how the instructors teach. If you teach properly, with the correct basics, the students won't get hurt. Hard-style contact is not about beating people up; it's about perfecting basic techniques and learning control.

The contact in kyokushinkai is graduated: light, semi and heavy contact. You need to develop other qualities before sparring full-contact. That would be like driving a racing car without having the appropriate knowledge about how to operate the machine, the external conditions of the road and how to safely react under dangerous situations.

Q: How did you hear about Mas Oyama's passing?
A: I received a telephone call from one of my students in Japan. I made a decision to go to his funeral. I called my friend and former training partner, Tadashi Nakamura, and told him that we should forget about the past and go to the funeral. So we went to the funeral. All of the top kyokushinkai masters attended the services.

Q: What is your opinion of the current political situation of the Kyokushinkai Organization?
A: Mas Oyama was a very smart man. He chose the next generation Kancho before he died. The person was Tadashi Nakamura, before he left the Kyokushinkai organization. He then selected Shokei Matsui. Matsui is very young, he has a good heart, he is smart and Mas Oyama trusted Matsui. Matsui has done a good job as the Headmaster of the Kyokushinkai Organization. The organization has split into four groups. Matsui's organization is the biggest, and the most famous fighters have stayed in the Matsui group.

"It boils down to how the instructors teach. If you teach properly, with the correct basics, the students won't get hurt. Hard-style contact is not about beating people up; it's about perfecting basic techniques and learning control. The contact in kyokushinkai is graduated: light, semi and heavy contact."

Q: What is your relationship with Shokei Matsui?
A: We have a very good relationship. Matsui came to train with me before he fought in the world championships in 1987. I did not want to change his technique. I only wanted to concentrate on his stamina, endurance and mental training. I made him do repetitions to improve his techniques.

Karate Masters

"No one understood the point style and who or why a particular person was the winner. Mas Oyama started full-contact fighting. It was easy for someone to see who was the winner. The loser would be knocked down. The winner was the one standing at the end of the fight. The television and mass media began covering the tournament, and it became very popular."

Matsui won the world championship that year.

Q: Was Mas Oyama's wife active in the Kyokushinkai Organization when he was alive?
A: No. When I went to the funeral, she tried to grab me while I tried to stay in the background. I knew what she wanted, but I have been in America for too long and realized what she wanted to do. I have my own organization and want to continue promoting my own group.

Q: What was the key to Mas Oyama building such a large karate organization?
A: In Japan, people started to go to karate tournaments. They would see the point style and then Mas Oyama's full-contact style. No one understood the point style and who or why a particular person was the winner. Mas Oyama started full-contact fighting. It was easy for someone to see who was the winner. The loser would be knocked down. The winner was the one standing at the end of the fight. The television and mass media began covering the tournament, and it became very popular. There was a famous cartoonist who enjoyed the fights and became friends with Mas Oyama. Every week this man would create a cartoon story around Mas Oyama and kyokushinkai karate and this became huge and popular with the children in Japan. Every child wanted to train karate with the legendary Mas Oyama. The first world championship was held at the Budokan in Tokyo, Japan, and had 5,000 spectators. The next event had more than 10,000 spectators. People had never seen full-contact fighting. They really enjoyed this type of karate fighting. Mas Oyama received a lot of television coverage. The event became very big and was

great exposure for the martial arts. Then the Japan Karate Association, an organization that was very powerful in Japan at that time, tried to stop Mas Oyama from getting television coverage and from using the Budokan for this type of tournament. Mas Oyama was friends with a very powerful senator who helped him at that time. He also had friends in the Yakuza. Every championship was packed with a lot of action and filled to capacity. Mas Oyama authored more than 20 books and had many people finance his organization.

Q: What are your goals for the future?
A: Well, I like to teach everyone: men, women and children. Karate has to be for everybody. Training can't as tough as it used to be; people have to go back to work the next day, and children have to go to school. We can work hard but at the same time protect the students from possible injuries. Of course, we still have hard training for those who really want it. As far as my philosophy, Oyama karate is based on action; first we sweat, then we talk about it. I don't want anybody's intellectual grasp of karate theory to exceed his physical ability to execute the art because this will make the head bigger than the muscles. Sweat first, think later; you must be physical to reach your mind, then you try to reach your balance. Both mind and body must develop together, at the same rate. This is what we call in Japanese *shiki shin funi*, which means "the body and the mind are not different."

Q: Are you happy in America?
A: Yes, very happy. And no regrets at all. I think the United States has the potential to develop the best martial artists in the world. Most of the world's best instructors have come here. That's the reason I stayed here and why they call me "The American Oyama." I'm sure that one day the leader of kyukushin will have blond hair and blue eyes! O

Wally Slocki

A Straight Shooter

PRAGMATISM WAS THE ESSENTIAL CONCEPT IN KARATE-JITSU BEFORE IT GOT IMPREGNATED WITH SPIRITUALITY AND BECAME AN ART OF "DO." SENSEI SLOCKI EXEMPLIFIES THIS PRINCIPLE PERFECTLY. STRAIGHTFORWARD AND DECISIVE, THIS LEGENDARY KARATEKA FROM CANADA SET AN EXAMPLE AND OPENED THE DOOR FOR MANY NORTH AMERICAN PRACTITIONERS. HIS WORDS IN CONVERSATION ARE AS DIRECT AS HIS PUNCHES AND KICKS WERE IN FIGHTING. HE IS A MAN WHO LEARNED MOST OF HIS FIGHTING SKILLS BY EXPERIENCE. HE WAS RANKED THE NO. 1 FIGHTER FOR TWO YEARS IN FULL-CONTACT KARATE AND WAS THE FIRST CANADIAN TO REPRESENT KARATE ON TELEVISION. A MAN OF GREAT MANNERS, SENSEI SLOCKI INTRODUCED LEGAL AGREEMENTS FOR CLIENTS TRAINING IN THE MARTIAL ARTS IN 1967, AND AMONG MANY OTHER BUSINESSES, FOUNDED "STREETSMARTS," A TRADEMARK SELF-DEFENSE SYSTEM ACCEPTED BY THE TORONTO BOARD OF EDUCATION IN CANADA. A PIONEER BY NATURE, SENSEI SLOCKI WAS NOMINATED AS THE MAN OF THE DECADE BY INTERNATIONAL KARATE MAGAZINE AND RETIRED UNDEFEATED TO PURSUE OTHER ENDEAVORS. WHEN ASKED WHY HE DOESN'T APPEAR IN PUBLICATIONS THESE DAYS, HE SIMPLY ANSWERS, "I LOST MY EGO A LONG TIME AGO. I DON'T FEEL THE NEED TO BE IN MAGAZINES ANYMORE." HERE IS WALLY SLOCKI, A TRUE ONE-OF-A-KIND MAN.

Q: How long have you been practicing the martial arts?
A: I have been involved in the martial arts for more than 45 years; thirty-five of those have been dedicated to teaching, and I am still teaching. It has been a long time since I started, but I still enjoy the journey. My first love and my appreciation of the martial arts came from judo and jiu-jitsu, then from the Chinese, Japanese and Korean arts. I also learned a great deal from Western boxing, Greco-Roman wrestling, sambo and aikido. I went through many different styles, although my main art has always been Japanese karate. The study of other arts was for personal research and development.

I have been extremely lucky. Throughout the years, I have had the honor and the opportunity to learn and train with some of the world's best athletes. I acknowledge these great people with deep respect and due recognition. While some are still with us, many have unfortunately passed away. Frank Hatashita,

Karate Masters

"I am grateful to everyone I come in contact with in daily life. Each and every one of them has taught me important things that contribute to who I am. A teacher can be a situation — a certain moment in which you have the clarity to understand what is happening and gain knowledge from that to be use in your life."

Paul Chan, Matsumi Tsuroka, Mel Wise, Benny Allen, Teruyuki Okazaki, Richard Kim, Take Okiyama, Peter Urban, Aaron Banks, Robert Trias, Tony Facetti and Robert Daglish are among those who taught me the mechanics of body movement and important spiritual philosophies. I could go on and on, but the real teachers were my competitors, my real-world experiences, and the thousands of students who taught me what works mechanically and what doesn't.

I am grateful to everyone I come in contact with in daily life. Each and every one of them has taught me important things that contribute to who I am. Sometimes a teacher is not simply the person who taught you how to punch and kick or a new kata. A teacher can be a situation—a certain moment in which you have the clarity to understand what is happening and gain knowledge from that to be use in your life.

Q: What stands out from your early training days?
A: In the 1960s, I received a phone call from a jiu-jitsu teacher in Ottawa, Canada. He said his name was Georges Sylvain, and he asked me if I wanted to train with him. Georges was also a karate-ka and to get an invitation to train with someone who knew both disciplines sounded intriguing, so I accepted. Now you have to visualize Georges Sylvain; he's a former military police and an active police officer who is 6 feet 4 and 245 pounds. At the time, I was 5 feet 11 and 155. Georges seemed huge to me. As we were training, Georges asked me if I could help him with his flexibility and show him how I delivered and executed two techniques: a sidekick and a roundhouse kick. I gladly obliged, not realizing that this giant of a man—with a heart just as big—would win a grand championship tournament from me years later with these two techniques. But I don't regret that at all—on the contrary. That one phone call from him established a friendship that has

lasted for more than 30 years, and I am glad to be able to call Georges Sylvain a friend.

Overall, in the early years, Westerners welcomed traditional training with a positive attitude. It was something new and different. I believe that the people who were not afraid to work hard gained by training in the Japanese tradition. This is still true today. The traditional Japanese method is strict and hard, but if a student has the right mind and puts effort and time into his training, he will get good at it without a doubt. The Japanese approach is militaristic, but if you are capable of surviving it, the rewards are waiting for you.

Q: Who inspired you the most?
A: Mel Wise would have to be a key inspiration for me. He helped me to remain in the martial arts and to continue to train today. He was one of the best karate-ka I have met. What an honor it is to have him as a teacher. Mel would compete and win in kata whenever he entered a tournament. Knowing he had cancer, he always set goals and was an inspiration to others in the martial arts. I said goodbye to Mel six months before he passed away. Watching him win the grand kata championship in Florida will be with me always.

"Overall, in the early years, Westerners welcomed traditional training with a positive attitude. It was something new and different. I believe that the people who were not afraid to work hard gained by training in the Japanese tradition. This is still true today. The Japanese approach is militaristic, but if you are capable of surviving it, the rewards are waiting for you."

Q: Did the karate movements come easy to you?
A: Someone once said to me, "You were a natural and didn't have to work as hard as others." If he only knew the perspiration, the pain and the hours that I dedicated to my training each day —sometimes seven days a week at the beginning. Being gifted with talent for the sports doesn't mean anything. There are many people out there with great amounts of physical talent for sports, but they don't work as hard as other less-talented athletes. In the end, the guy with all that talent will end up doing something else and the one who worked hard because he wasn't as gifted is the one who will be successful. Talent without hard training means absolutely nothing.

Karate Masters

"Learning not only involves the mechanical aspects of punching and kicking. In order to learn right, you need a certain attitude toward what you are learning and the right state of mind. If you are not having fun, you are not going to last very long."

Q: How has your personal karate developed over the years?
A: It is very easy for me at this point not to waste time on things that I know are of no benefit to others or to myself. After so many years of training, I know what I need, what will be effective and why, so I don't spend time doing things that won't take me to my destination. When you are very young and you have the time, then you can play with things, but after a certain point in your life, you know what you want and how to get it so you just don't waste your time in useless things.

Q: What were the most important parts of your teaching?
A: Basic but very important things like hard work, discipline, diligence, focus, curiosity and having fun. Learning involves more than the mechanical aspects of punching and kicking. In order to learn right, you need a certain attitude toward what you are learning and the right state of mind. If you are not having fun, you are not going to last very long. It is very simple but very complicated at the same time. Your attitude will determine where you go in life. This not only applies to the martial arts but to life as well.

Q: With all the recent technical changes, do you think there are still pure karate styles?
A: The only time something is pure is when nothing is added or taken away. When *shotokan, shito-ryu* or other styles are taught to someone, and that person teaches it to another with their personal interpretation of a particular movement, then the style is no longer pure. So if that is true, then there are no "pure" styles anymore. Sensei Nakayama didn't teach the same thing Funakoshi Gichin was teaching. Egami wasn't teaching the same material Funakoshi taught. The same happened in shito-kai, goju-kai and wado-kai. Or, if you prefer, shito-ryu, goju-ryu and wado-ryu. All the top instructors add and eliminate certain things; they put their own flavor in their art; there-

fore, the final product is not the same as was taught to them. Maybe what they teach is 70 percent, 80 percent or even 90 percent, but it is not "pure" because modifications have been made.

I really don't understand this idea of practicing a pure system, because there is no such thing. The people who say this think that doing the same thing that Funakoshi, Ueshiba or Kano did is to practice a pure system. Let me tell you something. If you look at what Jigoro Kano, Gichin Funakoshi and Morihei Ueshiba did, they also modified what they were taught to suit their own preferences. Even they didn't have a "pure" system. They learned from different people—changed, altered, modified and created new material—anare d then gave their creation a name. It's that simple. In short, there is no "pure" system. That's a fantasy.

On the other hand, different styles are important because a person who is tall and thin with good flexibility may be better suited to one style, while a person who is short, bulky and perhaps not as flexible may be better suited for another. Training and learning different styles may be something that can benefit a person's growth as a martial artist because a style is the founder's point of view of how things are supposed to be. For instance, JKA shotokan karate is based on certain premises and its approach to kumite is completely different than in goju-kai. The former uses longer fighting distances while the later emphasizes close-range strategies and techniques. Both are reflections of what the founder and top instructors—in this case Nakayama and Yamaguchi—were trying to communicate in teachings. Neither is right or wrong; they are simply different.

"Different styles are important because a person who is tall and thin with good flexibility may be better suited to one style, while a person who is short, bulky and perhaps not as flexible may be better suited for another. Training and learning different styles may be something that can benefit a person's growth as a martial artist because a style is the founder's point of view of how things are supposed to be."

Q: What is your opinion of full-contact karate and events such as the UFC?
A: I see full-contact karate as a sport in which you have two people in superb physical and mental condition with the ability to entertain an audience. Full-

Karate Masters

"The West has caught up and surpassed Japanese karate with regard to physical aspects, but they still have a long way to go to equal the philosophy and history of Japanese karate. The meaning behind it, the attitude toward the art and the philosophical approach are still superior to the West."

contact karate, kickboxing and the Ultimate Fighting Championship have become entertainment, but you must have skill to keep your audience captive. All things evolve in life, and these sports are no exceptions. You may like them or not, but you can't deny that they have a place in today's martial arts and combat sports. You don't have to agree with them, but you can't deny them.

Q: Are there any fundamental differences between Eastern and Western karate-ka?
A: In my opinion, the Europeans have more hunger, a stronger work ethic, and are more eager to learn than the Japanese or North Americans. The West has caught up and surpassed Japanese karate with regard to physical aspects, but they still have a long way to go to equal the philosophy and history of Japanese karate. The meaning behind it, the attitude toward the art and the philosophical approach are still superior to the West. It has to do a lot with the different cultural backgrounds we have. In the West, in some ways, I don't think we'll never reach the level of the East. In other aspects, the East will never be as good as the West.

Q: Do you feel you still have further to go in your studies?
A: I am always mentally open to learn and to educate myself in all aspects of life. The martial arts are the same as life; you need to keep learning to improve the way you deal with things. Life is all about change. If you don't keep an open mind, then you are setting yourself up for failure.

Q: Do you think it helps to train with weapons?
A: Anything that a student can use, including a weapon, is good if it helps to increase strength, improve eye-hand coordination or help with balance. All of these factors are extremely important in empty-hand techniques. If weaponry training helps that, then it is a good thing to do.

Q: What is your opinion on *makiwara* training?
A: First, a person should find out what a makiwara is, how it is constructed, how to hit it, what to hit it with and why. That's a story in itself. Many people think makiwara training is simply to develop big calluses in the hands. That's wrong.

Q: Should an instructor's personal training be different from his teaching schedule?
A: Instructors have to focus on what students are doing and how they perform. It is difficult to train hard while you teach because you have to spend time correcting and taking care of the students in class. That's what they pay you for. Of course, there are some basic things you can do with the students when you demonstrate and explain techniques. You must to do the best you can because they all try to copy you. If you punch 20 times, you have to make sure these 20 punches are perfect because that image will be printed in your students' minds and they will try to duplicate you. Instead of wasting time training when you are supposed to teach, allocate personal time to train as hard as you teach.

"Instructors have to focus on what students are doing and how they perform. It is difficult to train hard while you teach because you have to spend time correcting and taking care of the students in class. That's why they pay you. Instead of wasting time training when you are supposed to teach, allocate personal time to train as hard as you teach."

Q: What is the most important element of teaching: self-defense, sport or tradition?
A: Let's get one thing straight. In my opinion, the art of karate is not the same as self-defense. Teach the art and the sport separately, the tradition separately and self-defense separately.

Q: What's the proper training ratio between kata and kumite?
A: In the art of karate-do, kata is kumite and kumite is kata. A serious practitioner should train both as equals because they complement each other. You need both halves in order to be able to see the whole picture and completely master the art.

Karate Masters

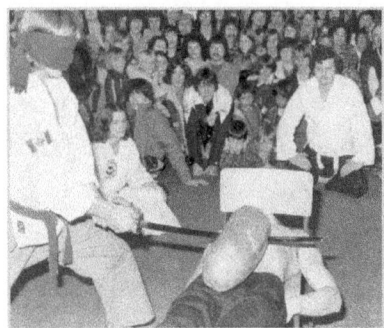

"There is a difference between kumite and trying to achieve good streetfighting skills. To me, karate as self-defense is a misnomer. Practice karate as an art and a sport, but don't take it to the streets. It won't work. Streetfighting is a whole different ball game. The sooner you accept this fact, the better."

Q: Do you think going to Japan to train is highly necessary?
A: Going to Japan to experience the culture is wonderful because you can get a lot of good insight. But from a simple technical point of view, I don't think it is necessary at all.

Q: What are the major changes in the art since you began training?
A: Changes in knowledge over the past 20 or 30 years have resulted in masters in Europe and North America making more money than ever before. Training costs more, you have more luxuries and the students are pampered. It is very different than the way things used to be. We gain some things, but we lose some things, too.

Q: With whom would you like to have trained with?
A: I would rather train with a person who is alive. The person I would like to train with in order to understand more about body control and mental preparation is Mikael Barishnikof. And he is still alive!

Q: What keeps you motivated after all these years?
A: As a person ages and grows, he sets different goals. Mine have always kept me motivated to improve and learn more.

Q: Do you think it is necessary to engage in freefighting to achieve good streetfighting skills?
A: There is a difference between kumite and trying to achieve good streetfighting skills. To me, karate as self-defense is a misnomer. Practice karate as an art and a sport, but don't take it to the streets. It won't work. Streetfighting is a whole different ball game. The sooner you accept this fact, the better.

Q: How important do you think *bunkai* is to understanding kata and karate?
A: Bunkai is a person's interpretation of what a movement means, and this interpretation differs from person to person. I believe that everyone should

break down a kata and see how many scenarios you can come up with. It's called "thinking for yourself." It is interesting to note that some people change and modify kata so they can find new applications to the movements. I don't think that is right. Another important point we should consider when looking into kata for answers to self-defense situations is the fact that kata were designed for self-defense and not for competition. The techniques the old master incorporated into the kata, and their technical solution to the problems, were based on the circumstances, environment and technologies of that particular time.

"Bunkai has its place in kata, and kata has its place in the art of karate-do. It is important to be knowledgeable about the bunkai of every kata, but we have to be careful. Why do you think modern anti-terrorist groups change their approach to an emergency situation and security systems are evolving all the time?"

Nowadays, attackers use other technologies for attacking people. They know much more about fighting than the muggers in ancient Okinawa and Japan. They have knives, and their knowledge of how to hurt you is 1,000 times more advanced than when Choki Motobu or Kanryo Higashionna devised the self-defense applications found in the traditional kata. This is a problem. Many people say that kata's bunkai is outdated, and to a certain extent it is true. Of course, all the kata movements have an application and a use in self-defense, but this doesn't mean that in a life-or-death situation these movements are what we should be doing. That could be fatal.

Bunkai has its place in kata, and kata has its place in the art of karate-do. It is important to be knowledgeable about the bunkai of every kata, but we have to be careful. Why do you think modern anti-terrorist groups change their approach to an emergency situation and security systems are evolving all the time? Because the terrorists are using new methods more advanced than those used 20 years ago. The same happens with kata, bunkai and the martial arts in general.

Q: What is the meaning of the practice of karate-do?
A: I believe that no one can explain the meaning of the practice of karate-do. What I can say is that I get great pleasure, enjoyment, and mental and physical benefits. It's a great tool to relieve stress and frustrations, to improve cardiovascular health and to get a complete body workout. It is

Karate Masters

"There are a lot of important values that are being overlooked by practitioners these days. If this is anybody's fault, it is the fault of the instructors. The instructor is responsible for how his students behave in the future, but it is also true that an instructor has much less control over his students than in the old days."

also a great social activity and a medium for self-expression. I am delighted to see someone I taught set goals and achieve them. Sometimes people ask spiritual question about karate, and I always answer with, "Go find a Buddhist monk and ask him." I don't get involved in discussing religion or politics. Karate, in my view, has always been an art and a sport. Looking at it as a religious thing is another story.

Q: Is there anything lacking in martial arts today?
A: Discipline, respect and etiquette. These are just a few observations. There are a lot of important values that are being overlooked by practitioners these days. If this is anybody's fault, it is the fault of the instructors. The instructor is responsible for how his students behave in the future, but it is also true that an instructor has much less control over his students than in the old days.

Q: What are the most important qualities of a successful karate-ka?
A: Honesty, loyalty, perseverance, humility, compassion and goal-setting. As a senior karate student, you should be an example of many different aspects. We all assume that practicing karate for many years, and being a senior in your dojo means that you have been successful in the art. It may be that way, but it also may not. On the physical side, a senior karate-ka should train hard to maintain the skills that they worked so long to achieve. If the body and mind are not worked, skills diminish quickly. Memory is all we have. Use this to train properly. My advice to a karate-ka is to have an open mind and ask questions of all styles and systems. They may have value to you ... maybe not immediately, but for sure in the future.

Q: Why do so many students fall away after two or three years of training?
A: Boredom, not setting goals and achieving them, and poor motivation. Teachers need to work on these important things with their students. A good

"I had the pleasure of associating with Bruce. He was a gifted individual, both in technique and expression. They say timing is everything, and he was in the right place at the right time. That is all there was to that."

student should display the same attributes of a senior practitioner, only at a lower level. The senior should lead by example.

Q: You were there when Bruce Lee was part of the American martial arts scene but not yet a movie star. What is your opinion of him?
A: I had the pleasure of associating with Bruce. He was a gifted individual, both in technique and expression. They say timing is everything, and he was in the right place at the right time. That is all there was to that.

Q: What are your thoughts on the future of karate-do?
A: All the information and so-called "secrets" of training have been passed down to people like myself and others. If these secrets go unlearned—such as the proper way to train the hand, the foot and the entire body as a lethal weapon—then the magic of karate will be lost forever. We need to try to preserve these important aspects so the art will live forever. These principles go beyond the mere pure physical techniques. If you lose these principles, you will lose the essence of karate. O

Alex Sternberg

A Focused Determination

ALEX STERNBERG, WHO BEGAN TRAINING IN THE MARTIAL ARTS IN 1962, STARTED WITH JUDO. AFTER TRYING IN A KOREAN STYLE, HE THEN CHANGED TO THE JAPANESE STYLE OF SHOTOKAN IN 1966 UNDER GEORGE COFIELD'S GUIDANCE. SINCE THEN, HE HAS TRAINED UNDER THE TOP SHOTOKAN MASTERS IN THE WORLD AND HOLDS AN IMPRESSIVE TOURNAMENT RECORD. HOWEVER, STERNBERG CONSIDERS HIS MAJOR ACHIEVEMENTS IN THE MARTIAL ARTS TO BE "PROMOTING KARATE TO THOSE WHO NEED IT." HE BEGAN TEACHING IN 1966 AND OPENED HIS OWN DOJO IN 1967. SELECTED AS A MEMBER OF THE U.S. DELEGATION TO THE WORLD CHAMPIONSHIPS SINCE 1977, SENSEI STERNBERG HAS ALSO PUBLISHED BOOKS AND CONTRIBUTED ARTICLES AND COLUMNS TO INTERNATIONAL MAGAZINES AROUND THE WORLD. A CHIEF REFEREE AT MANY U.S. AND INTERNATIONAL CHAMPIONSHIPS, ALEX STERNBERG CURRENTLY TEACHES THE ART OF KARATE-DO IN NEW YORK. WITH A DETERMINATION TO UPHOLD THE TRUE SPIRIT OF KARATE, SENSEI STERNBERG HAS BEEN ONE OF THE ANCHORS OF THE MODERN SHOTOKAN MOVEMENT AND AN EXAMPLE OF THE TRUE MEANING OF BUDO.

Q: When did you start the martial arts?
A: I started in 1962 with judo. I did this for one year, then switched to mook-doo-kwan tang soo do under Richard Chun, a local instructor. His dojo had some notable people training, such as Gregory Hines, the actor and dancer—who also switched to George Cofield later on—and *Black Belt* Hall of Fame fighter Joe Hayes. I trained with Mr. Chun for more than three years until I reached red belt, and then I switched to shotokan karate with George Cofield, who was under JKA master Okazaki (ISKF) at the time. I began to train with Mr.Cofield around 1965 or so.

In addition to those two styles, for the last 10 years I have also practiced *Hayashi shito-ryu*. I personally trained with Mr. Hayashi and other members of his inner group. Hayashi Sensei was a true *kata* encyclopedia. His historical and technical knowledge was second to none—a true master of his own right. But this training was mainly so I could become familiar with the kata from other styles, per WKF kata requirements. My main style is still JKA shotokan, but I appreciate the overall understanding that learning kata from another

Karate Masters

"I learned karate from people who were forced to use their techniques daily for survival due to the neighborhood they lived in. There was very little theory and a lot of physical and hard training."

style brings to a karate practitioner. It opens a lot of possibilities and helps you to look at your own style in a different way.

Q: What was your training under Sensei Cofield like?
A: When I began to train in karate, I was a student in a rabbinical academy, studying religion. It was a great culture shock to say the least. But when I reached George Cofield, I was one of two or three white kids in an all black and Hispanic dojo located in one of Brooklyn's worst slums. I learned karate from people who were forced to use their techniques daily for survival due to the neighborhood they lived in. Sensei Cofield's brand of shotokan was extremely practical-minded. There was very little theory and a lot of physical and hard training. Whatever he taught us had to work or it was useless. I remember that during the very beginning of my training in Sensei Cofield's dojo I got kicked through a wall with a mirror on it and made a quick trip to the hospital.

We had people from the streets coming in almost daily to test our skill. We fought real fights very often, sending many to the hospital. Those were the 1960s; many didn't believe that karate worked, and they had to be convinced. We were able to convince many. Sensei Cofield broke away from the JKA at that time. He was out to prove that one could train as hard as the Japanese without being Japanese. We trained three hours every single day. The training was extremely demanding and tough, and it was unusual for us to walk out of the dojo without bleeding. There were no major injuries, but the way we were taught was to be able to use the art in a real fight. It was not a game, and not a sport.

Q: How were the post-WWII years when karate was introduced to the U.S.? Were the teachers mainly Japanese?
A: Not "mainly," but all of them! Nobody knew karate but them, so they were the teachers. Karate was distinguished at that time by its hardness, toughness and the idea of practical application. Every single technique we learned was meant to work in a real encounter. No sport, no games. The people practicing at that time were not interested in competition or finesse; they were interested in pure fighting. Most of the students were men between 20 and 30 years old, and there were no women or kids in the classes. It was a tough game. There were very few Americans teaching and those who did were direct students of a Japanese teacher. There were not too many *dojo* and not much advertising or publicity. We used to train long hours, and the teachers wouldn't charge those who had no money. The teacher's attitude was, "You have to do the technique the way I'm telling you. This is the way I want you to do it. If I tell you to punch a brick wall, you do it. No matter how hard the training is, you have to do it. And if you drop, then you have no courage, discipline or perseverance." They were right to some extent, but that is definitely not the right way to teach today. People won't accept this attitude anymore. The

"Karate was distinguished at that time by its hardness, toughness and the idea of practical application. Every single technique we learned was meant to work in a real encounter. No sport, no games."

Karate Masters

"If you punched someone and knocked him down, you were awarded the point because you had a strong technique. The judges were not going to disqualify you because of lack of control. You showed a superior technique. You showed superiority over your opponent."

instructors didn't really care about how the art was being perceived by the masses or the media then. They taught the way they knew and that was it.

Q: How were the competitions?
A: Really tough. The whole idea of karate was as a self-preservation art ... not as a sport. The points were only awarded when the technique actually hit the opponent. The fighters were fighting and not playing a game. It was, by and large, much more bloody than any competition today. As a matter of fact, in today's tournaments, it is very rare to see blood; and when it happens, it is just by accident.

Q: There were no rules controlling excessive contact?
A: There were rules, but the emphasis of them was on real application—so the judges looked for a "strong technique" and not necessarily for the safety of the fighters. If you punched someone and knocked him down, you were awarded the point because you had a strong technique. The judges were not going to disqualify you because of lack of control. You showed superior technique. You showed superiority over your opponent. Therefore, you were the winner. That simple. The criteria was totally different from the one used by today's judges. They wanted to see who was the stronger fighter, not simply who could score a point.

On the other hand, you as a competitor never wanted to show any sign of weakness. If you were punched in the mouth and started bleeding, you tried to prevent the referee from disqualifying your opponent because you didn't want to win by disqualification. It was not honorable. And at that time, honor was important. Today, you see competitors that make it to the semifinals of a world championship because three or four of their opponents were disqualified along the way. That's not honorable, and honor is part of karate, part of *budo*. If you get hit, deal with it; don't lay on the floor with your hands in your face to see if the referee disqualifies your opponent so you can pass to the next round. But I also understand that at that time competition was no more than a civilized version of streetfighting. In fact, some people though the best idea was to not have rules at all!

Q: How do you rate yesterday's champions compared to today's?
A: Well, today instructors are educated people with a lot of experience and knowledge about different physical aspects of training and the human body, but things are different these days. Champions today are the legacy product of that particular era, but they are also a more refined product, bringing together the extremes of both decades. Maybe the top fighters of the 1960s were tougher than the top champions of today, but I believe

"I believe today's fighters would probably defeat the best that the 1960s could offer. The present champions have much more skill, they understand more about training, muscle control, psychology, and tactics and strategies, and their physical techniques are on a higher level than they were 20 or 30 years ago."

today's fighters would probably defeat the best that the 1960s could offer. The present champions have much more skill, they understand more about training, muscle control, psychology, and tactics and strategies, and their physical techniques are on a higher level than they were 20 or 30 years ago. Today, most of competitors are great fighters, great athletes and great technicians.

Karate Masters

"Lewis was a very unique individual. He earned his black belt in under a year's time and he was smart enough to exploit his extraordinary physique by always wearing a gi that was about three sizes too small. As a result, it didn't quite fit around his torso and his huge chest muscles were always very prominent."

Q: Who were the fighters you were impressed with at that time?

A: Chuck Norris and Joe Lewis. Norris was an exemplary champion in that he was both a tough fighter and a true gentleman. He was looked up to by the public and his fellow competitors for sportsmanship and skill. To me, and to many other teenagers just coming into our own in the mid-1960s, Norris was an inspiration. As a fighter, he was very clean, and he never took advantage of an opponent other than what sportsmanship allowed. When he lost a match, he never complained about the referees, got mad or created a difficult situation. His answer was to go back into training, come back and totally vindicate himself by beating all his opponents. His philosophy was that if he lost, the fault was his. Period. He never complained or bad-mouthed anybody to their face, behind their back or any other way. His style was a combination of Korean and Japanese methods. He adapted techniques from different styles to develop an effective and practical fighting system. As a result, you couldn't really pinpoint Norris as being exclusively a Japanese or Korean stylist. He definitely was one of a kind, both as a *karate-ka* and a human being.

Q: What about Joe Lewis?

A: Joe was Norris' nemesis. They brought out the best in each other during their matches. Lewis occasionally beat Norris, but it was Norris who came out on top at the end of their careers with a decisive edge in the number of matches won. Lewis was a very unique individual. He earned his black belt in less than a year's time, and he was smart enough to exploit his extraordinary physique by always wearing a gi that was about three sizes too small. As a result, it didn't quite fit around his torso, and his huge chest muscles were always very prominent. The sleeves on his jacket would just barely come down to his elbows so that his massive forearms would be constantly exposed, along with his outsized knuckles and fists.

This really made a mental impact on his opponents. By the time you were in front of him, you knew that you didn't want to get hit by this guy. In the ring, he was all action, although with a very different personality than Norris. At a tournament, he would remove himself from everyone, sit by himself in a corner and remain there to concentrate on his strategy for the evening ahead. Both men, in different ways, were pioneers that subsequent *karate-ka* emulated. In this respect, they both drew a great many students to the martial arts.

Q: Are there are any fundamental differences in mental or physical capabilities of Japanese karate-ka in comparison to their European or American counterparts?
A: The fundamental difference between the Japanese and the Europeans is social, historical and cultural. Look at the tea ceremony in Japan: it takes about 20-30 minutes to gracefully prepare the bowls and the tea, boil the water, mix the ingredients and then gracefully serve the tea. Now look at the Western way: boil water, throw in a tea bag, put it down and there you have it ... five minutes at the top. The Japanese are very rigid socially and their karate reflects this attitude. The techniques they use must be just so. The toes on your foot must be exactly 17 degrees to the right or the left, the posture must be just so and so on. In Western boxing, in comparison, you hit the opponent with power and knock him down. If you decisively beat him, then it is good. How you stand is your choice, provided you deliver power. You don't have to fit in a rigid mold created by "early masters." The bottom line is most important. You know how every Japanese fighter will fight; he will charge forward. This is very different from every other culture. There is strength in flexibility, but there may also be strength in one dimension. Whatever works is good. All things work at the right time with the right opponent. The skill is to know when the right time has arrived ... and the right opponent.

"As an instructor, you must set up a training schedule or you stop training. Teaching is not training. Your personal development makes you into a better teacher. If you stop developing, you will stop teaching new, fresh concepts."

Physically, the Japanese can be just as good as the Westerners at the right weight and height, but look at the results from international competitions; they speak for themselves. Japanese karate is well entrenched in the Western world, taught by many excellent Western masters who fully understand not only the concept of combat but who also understand the Japanese learning process and the Japanese cultural issues. Some of them are far superior to any Japanese sensei; some are not.

Q: Do you teach karate with a sport approach or as traditional budo?
A: Karate is a sport *or* a martial art; it is what you make of it. Think of target shooting as opposed to sniping in warfare—same skill, different application.

Karate Masters

"There are many components in finding a good teaching program and everything depends, in the very end, on what you are trying to accomplish with that particular group of students. Karate is not an art for privileged people; it is an art for everybody."

When I started teaching many years ago, I experimented with different teaching methods and programs. The success of any particular program depended on whether my students were able to master a set number of specific techniques within a certain time limit. If I saw that the majority of students couldn't master them, I changed the format and order for the next class.

This trial-and-error method produced students far superior to those who graduated from my school 12 or 15 years ago. There are many components in finding a good teaching program and everything depends, in the very end, on what you are trying to accomplish with that particular group of students. Karate is not an art for privileged people; it is an art for everybody. So everybody needs to have the same opportunities to achieve excellence in its practice. Therefore, karate is *budo* that can be practiced as a sport at a younger age.

Q: Do you feel that you still have further to go in your studies?
A: Most definitely! I must learn what my body is capable of at the age of 50 and beyond. I am well trained—as well as anyone else. Some are younger are sharper, but I was sharp too 10 or 20 years ago. We study until we die, and we keep developing new insights. Hopefully, the younger *karate-ka* are listening. As an instructor, you must set up a training schedule or you stop training. Teaching is *not* training. Your personal development makes you into a better teacher. If you stop developing, you will stop teaching new, fresh concepts. Your body tell you what you feel in your training, and you pass that onto your students. So if you are stale, they will be also.

Q: Do you like traditional training methods such as the *makiwara* and the *kobudo* arts?
A: I think they are positive if you know how to use and approach them. Weapon training can give an added dimension to one's understanding of empty-hand concepts, as well as improve your perception regarding timing

and distance. It is true that some of the methodology in the use of the weapons may be obsolete, but the idea is to learn what was communicated from the old masters through kata and analyze the meaning and principles behind the weapon and its use. Only then can you apply it in a natural way to our modern environment.

"The fundamental difference between the Japanese and the Europeans is social, historical and cultural. The Japanese are very rigid socially, and their karate reflects this attitude. The techniques they use must be just so."

I see people thinking kobudo is outdated, such as karate's kata. The problem is not with the art, though, but with the observer's understanding. Although many people would disagree, I believe makiwara training is indispensable to developing power, but it must be approached carefully with an understanding that we don't want to deform or disfigure our hands or damage them and then develop arthritis, which is often a by-product of such training. Makiwara not only teaches the right kime but also the right distancing and the right impact feeling. It's hard to explain, but those who normally train with the makiwara will understand my words. Many of the traditional methods were developed by the ancestors to enhance the karate technique, not to simply look good. The old training methods were created to improve karate technique and to make the human body a more efficient weapon ... not to win a beauty contest.

Q: What is the most important element of karate: self defense, sport or tradition?
A: All three ... with the emphasis decided by the student. The sensei can encourage, but who are we to dictate? Students come to our *dojo* for differ-

Karate Masters

"Kata is a composition of basic movements. The purpose of kata is to teach the body to move in a variety of ways, using different type of techniques. Once you understand that, you'll see that kumite is just having the ability to move your body freely like in kata—but this time against an opponent."

ent reasons. Let them chose what appeals to them from our teaching. After all, there is nothing the instructor can do but share the art in the right way and let the student decide what he wants to do with it.

Q: What is the proper ratio for kihon, kata and kumite?
A: One third each, and you must cycle every month. Practice kihon for the correct basics, kata for balance, coordination, and spirit, and kumite for an understanding of the application. There must be harmony between all three. If you look deeply into the essence of each part you'll find out that they are all the same. Kata is a composition of basic movements. The purpose of kata is to teach the body to move in a variety of ways, using different type of techniques. Once you understand that, you'll see that kumite is just having the ability to move your body freely like in kata—but this time against an opponent. There is an interrelation between all these three elements. It's important to always understand what you are doing when you practice, how this gives more meaning to your skill and how this will help to make you into a more effective fighter.

Some people think you have to go to Japan to become a good karate-ka; but that's not totally true. It may be helpful, but mainly because you will have no other distraction and you will train only. But you can do the same in Europe by training with a good team for a few weeks or months. The right training is the right training, no matter where you are.

Q: What are the major changes in karate since you began training?
A: The development of the sport concept. When I trained at the beginning, karate was a martial art. Period. We had some tournaments but no equipment—no gloves, no mouthpieces, no groin cups, no headgear, no boots and plenty of contact. Also, the amount of young children practicing karate today is different from those days. Also, students are free to ask questions and those inquiries are welcomed by the instructors.

Q: What is your opinion about practicing several martial arts and mixing styles?
A: I think it's OK to practice different arts, but you really need to define what a master is in relation to learning any art. Most people who teach

many different styles are actually not masters of *any* art, though they may make a lot of money at it, and they are certainly not masters of several arts. Most serious people, when they see a business card with a listing of many arts the person has supposedly mastered, dismiss that person as a braggart. Even those who train in 20 different arts are not really respected by those who taught them in the first place. It's like the idea of having seven Ph.D. degrees; it's ridiculous. If I need surgery, I want a doctor who is an expert in his field, not someone who has been jumping from one field to another.

Q: What is the philosophical basis for your karate training?
A: The technique must work and you must be able to make it work for yourself. We need to define why we train. Is it for conditioning or is it for fighting? *Tae-bo* is not a martial art the way most people practice it, but if you apply the moves with more power and follow-through, you have a martial art. Conversely, if you take a martial art and speed up the moves and work mainly for conditioning, you have tae-bo. We need to define our concepts. I personally derive great satisfaction from training and teaching karate and most importantly from learning new concepts. I wish I had the opportunity to train under Funakoshi Gichin and Masatoshi Nakayama. I truly believe they have been the two major turning points in the evolution of karate from the old times in Okinawa to our modern days.

"The technique must work, and you must be able to make it work for yourself. I personally derive great satisfaction from training and teaching karate, and most importantly from learning new concepts. I wish I had the opportunity to train under Funakoshi Gichin and Matayoshi Nakayama."

Q: Do you have any memorable karate experience that inspired your training?
A: In 1973, I was at the Top 10 Nationals, having been selected as one of the nation's top competitors that year, and I saw Master Hohan Soken perform a demonstration. He was 93 years old, yet he still moved gracefully. His movements were precise, with a perfect flow and rhythm, and you could see the very essence of true karate in his actions. It was an unforgettable experience. I hope when I am at that age I can still move at least 10 percent as well as Honan Soken did that day!

Karate Masters

"I practice and study karate and am inspired to live a good life by the teachings of my religion. Everyone should find inspiration where he best can. The practice of karate-do is the continual attempt at self-perfection, pushing the physical limits as far back as possible at every age."

Q: How much spiritual understanding does a karate-ka need?

A: Spiritual understanding comes from spiritual training. Mine comes from a lifelong commitment to orthodox Judaism and the study of the scriptures contained in the Torah and the Talmud. For some, it's a commitment to Christianity or other organized religions; and for others, it comes from studying the philosophical writings of Musashi Miyamoto, Lao Tse or others. Karate training can only bring one to the doorstep of self-inspection. "Seek perfection of character," Funakoshi wrote. Where did he get his philosophical inspiration? I practice and study karate and am inspired to live a good life by the teachings of my religion. Everyone should find inspiration where they best can. The practice of *karate-do* is the continual attempt at self-perfection, pushing the physical limits as far back as possible at every age. It is using karate practice for meditation as "Moving Zen," as it was once described by Mr. Nicol of England and deriving personal satisfaction from the practice of it. The practice of karate is filled with excitement as you get older. You practice because you want to, due to the feeling of satisfaction you derive. As I practice, I feel like I do when I slip into my favorite shirt: I am comfortable with the familiarity. Karate practice is similar for me. It is what I do. I practice karate. I am an artist just the same as one who plays a musical instrument. I make a certain melody appear; I create a certain mood. And when I get together with my fellow musicians, other martial artists, we all want to check out each other's melody. I want to "jam." When I train with other sensei, I get inspired and the workout gives me a feeling of fulfillment.

Q: How much training should a senior karate-ka do to improve?

A: As much time and energy as he is capable of devoting to it. Our lives often get in the way. Our careers, families and responsibilities come first. Our karate practice is more personal toward our development, and we must have a balance. Our body changes, sometimes due to injuries incurred during our younger training days. Therefore, the way we do our personal training has to adapt to these special circumstances. It would be stupid to do the same kind of training when you are 50 years old that you did when you were 25. We have to be smart enough to adapt the art to ourselves. That's *budo*; that's why karate-do is a way of life.

Q: What qualities does a good karate-ka need to display?
A: The successful karate-ka is on the road to self-fulfillment. As I said before, we are artists, our canvas is our mind and body. As we practice, we mold our mind and body so it begins to emerge as a figure. The longer we practice and the more correctly we practice, the more the figure is defined. The image becomes sharper and sharper until we achieve our masterpiece. The successful karate-ka is on the road to achieving his masterpiece, but it is a long road; we can improve as long as we are on the road.

Some people may think that we lack something in our modern-day training, but I think there is nothing lacking. Today we have millions practicing compared to a few thousand back in the old days; today we have tens of thousands of dojo compared to a handful then. We now have all sorts of dojo specializing in every aspect of the martial arts. Students must find what interests them and match the dojo to that.

"Our karate practice is more personal toward our development, and we must have a balance. Our body changes, sometimes due to injuries incurred during our younger training days. Therefore, the way we do our personal training has to adapt to these special circumstances. It would be stupid to do the same kind of training when you are 50 years old that you did when you were 25."

Q: Do you recommend supplementary training?
A: First define what skills you want to improve and then select another activity that enhances those skills. For instance, lateral shifting is also done in basketball and tennis and football. So if you practice on the school football, tennis or basketball team while you practice karate, that can be a good combination. The same goes for gymnastics to enhance balance and upper body strength. Of course, strength training is ideal for improvements in muscle strength.

Karate Masters

"The student should be patient and trust the instructor with his training and progress. When you feel the need to tell the instructor what he should do with you, its time to find a new instructor. Just make sure you know what you are talking about."

Although weight training is perceived as a negative activity for young children, many parents, and even some coaches, have some old fashioned misconception about it "stunting growth." This is, of course, not true and has been disproved in scientific testing and research. Yet some old ideas take time to disappear. The student should be patient and trust the instructor with his training and progress. When you feel the need to tell the instructor what he should do with you, its time to find a new instructor. Just make sure you know what you are talking about. Many students leave karate because they lose interest, because it is "no longer fun." In a recent study of 10,000 high school athletes, it was determined that the No. 1 reason to be on a team and to be involved in sports was to have fun and get enjoyment. When it is not fun, these kids quit. We need to motivate our students and keep them interested, as well as teach them the value of discipline, but it's not so easy.

Q: You do not thrive on publicity like some martial artists. Why?
A: Magazine exposure doesn't enhance my knowledge, nor does it bring more students to my dojo. It is a pure ego trip. Now, I would love to be on the cover of all the magazines, but it is not important enough for me to spend time and energy to pursue it. What I am interested in is participating in forums in which we explore different aspects of karate development, where I can share experiences with others eager to learn. Years ago, I did receive lots of publicity and had my share. Now it is someone else's turn. My interest these days is in gaining knowledge and helping to bring the art of karate to a higher level.

Q: You had some serious injuries. Did you ever fear you'd have to stop training?
A: Yes, when I recently received a knee injury, I was afraid that I might not be able to perform the techniques as I did years ago. I also considered stopping when I once sent someone to the hospital in a match with a serious injury. I see those situations as growing experiences, but only now, looking back after everything has passed. It's very difficult to develop the ability to look at things from a certain perspective in order to turn a problem into a growing experience.

Q: You have been a dedicated competitor in both kumite and kata. What advice would you give to a new competitor?
A: Well, let's start with *kumite* first. Sparring is the goal towards which you have been working ever since you began training in karate, and sport competition is the closest you'll ever get to actual street fighting—the noise, the pressure, the intensity, et cetera. The only difference between the two situations lies in your intent; you are not trying to maim or kill your opponent in the ring; instead, you are effectively trying to use karate techniques to score points and hone your fighting skills.

"Years ago I did receive lots of publicity and had my share. Now it is someone else's turn. My interest these days is in gaining knowledge and helping to bring the art of karate to a higher level."

I would recommend using a variety of techniques derived from the bread-and-butter basics. I emphasize this because it is your ability to consistently use the basics with imagination and skill that will enable you to win with a greater degree of regularity and with a minimum number of injuries. Sport karate is not a series of spectacular techniques for a very simple reason; they leave you in incredibly vulnerable position. I remember when I was young and tried to impress my opponent with a flashy spinning back-kick. Well, my opponent punched me in the back of my head as I spun around to deliver the kick. Complex, high-risk techniques are not necessary in sport karate. The idea is to show how precise and effectively you can hit, not how many fancy techniques you can throw at your opponent.

Karate Masters

"Performing kata in a competition is something that you have to train for in a very specific way. Longer and harder training sessions with more criticism from your instructor is the beginning. As in the rest of your karate training, you must put in the hours and the effort to succeed."

It's also important that you know the rules of the tournament. Because we are dealing with a sport situation, it is wise to use the rules to your advantage, but be fair to the art of karate as well.

Q: How important are the psychological aspects?
A: Extremely important. There are a lot of psych games that top competitors play outside the ring to defeat their opponents before they even step onto the mat. Everything you do in competition is important, not merely the moment when you finally step into the ring. Just remember that there are always psych games going on—even if they are not so obvious—so make sure that you don't become a victim of one. Look to and learn from the other fighters with more experience. Practice some things you feel might suit you and try them out in competition. The more you practice them, the more accomplished you will become. You will soon reach the point in which no one will notice the fact that you are playing mind games on them. In combat, never show any signal of pain or anger. Never. This can be used by the opponent to put more pressure on you. Don't ever let your emotions show in the ring, whether you are in pain because you made a mistake and got tagged, or are ecstatic about executing a superb technique. Never give yourself away.

Q: From a pure tactical point of view, what advice would you give?
A: Tactics and strategy are very complex aspects to try to explain in few words. There are many variables that determine what you should do, but I can give you some pointers, though. Before you step into the fighting area, make sure you are loose—not just physically—but mentally as well. The tighter you are, the more upset you are likely to get and the less you are going to see—both what your opponent is doing and what you are doing. Consequently, you are going to get hit. Look at your opponent at all time. The more you look at your opponent, the more you are going to learn about him and the less you are going to be surprised. You are going to learn the techniques he likes to use and how he reacts under pressure. Of course, there are many tactical considerations based on your opponents' stances, footwork and *kamae*; we could go on and on.

Q: You were one of the most efficient karate-ka at using sweeping techniques in competition. Is that still a good technique?
A: Sweeping is a great technique, but it can be very dangerous if you don't know when and how execute it properly. I have seen a lot of people injure themselves trying to sweep their opponent's leg. There are many factors to take into consideration before trying to sweep someone: the stance, the rhythm of his movements and footwork, weight distribution, center of gravity, the tempo and cadence of actions, et cetera. To make a sweeping technique work, you have to know how to read your opponent and be able to time the move perfectly. Just don't forget to stick to the basics. Basic karate may not be very flashy, but it works … if you use it. So keep it simple and direct.

Q: Can you talk about the kata aspect of competition?
A: Unlike the kata that you do in the dojo to meet your instructor's rank requirements, performing kata in a competition is something that you have to train for in a very specific way. Longer and harder training sessions with more criticism from your instructor is the beginning. As in the rest of your karate training, you must put in the hours and the effort to succeed. There are six essential areas that you must master before you can enter in a tournament. One is the floor where you are going to perform the form. The different surfaces create difficulties if you are not used to them. Make sure you train on the type of floor you are going to compete on, or you'll be surprised how easily you can lose your balance. The second is not to get mixed up about your direction. Try to perform your kata facing different directions. Don't rely on one single direction. The place where you will perform your kata won't be your dojo, so it is very likely that when you make a move-

Karate Masters

"Think of yourself as a performer at all times because that's exactly what you are. Don't get nervous and rush through the kata; perform it. Let the kata bring out your personality. Believe in the form. You can't convince anyone that your performance is good unless you are convinced of it!"

ment and change directions you'll be disoriented. The third aspect is the pacing of the form. Make sure you know and understand the rhythm of the different sequences and the overall pace of the kata; otherwise, even if your technique is good, your kata won't be acceptable to the judges. Fourth is the bunkai. A deep understanding of the kata's bunkai will help you to bridge the gap between theory and practice. By practicing bunkai, the coordination you develop in doing the moves is going to take on a much greater significance. Beccause kata is now removed from the realm of the abstract, your movements are going to have more speed, power and meaning. The fifth is proper decorum. Your performance begins the moment your name has been called. Show the right attitude. Be confident but not cocky. The judges, who are human beings, are going to be affected by the way you behave. The sixth and final aspect is being thoroughly acquainted with the rules.

Think of yourself as a performer at all times because that's exactly what you are. Don't get nervous and rush through the kata; perform it. Let the kata bring out your personality. Believe in the form. You can't convince anyone that your performance is good unless you are convinced of it!

Q: Do you consider yourself a traditional teacher?

A: Well, yes. I think I am a traditional teacher for two reasons: I teach all the traditional values intrinsic to the art of budo, and I have not changed either the kata or the approach of Funakoshi Sensei to karate training. On the other hand, you can describe me as a modernist because I use all the modern approaches to physical and mental training. I haven't closed my eyes to the more current training sciences and research that allows the modern athletes to be better than the "old-timers."

Q: What are your thoughts on the future of karate-do?

A: We need to organize one group that will contain every organization representing karate. Each practitioner should demand this from their sensei and their organizations. We practice and teach that karate gives confidence, yet I see countless sensei scared to tell the truth to their leaders. They are afraid they will lose whatever meager positions they have been given, and allow themselves to be humiliated and their students shortchanged as a result. The different sensei ought to start practicing what they teach their students about courage. We need unity in karate, not hundreds of groups. We need more education and research in karate. We need everyone with experience to be included, not excluded, from the family of karate. Only if we do this will we grow as one. I would love to see all the masters under one big organization but I know it is an impossible dream—too many politics and personal interests will prevent that from ever happening. I just plan to keep training, teaching and working for the art of karate. Meanwhile, I'll keep dreaming—just in case. O

"We need everyone with experience to be included, not excluded, from the family of karate. Only if we do this will we grow as one. I just plan to keep training, teaching and working for the art of karate. Meanwhile, I'll keep dreaming—just in case."

Masahiko Tanaka

The Legend

THIS MAN TOOK THE WORLD OF KARATE WITH HIS DYNAMIC AND POWERFUL TECHNIQUES. EXTRAORDINARILY FAST AND AGILE, TANAKA SENSEI IS ONE OF THE MOST IMPRESSIVE AND DEMANDING INSTRUCTORS UNDER WHICH ANY KARATE PRACTITIONER CAN TRAIN. FORMED AT THE FAMOUS HORNET'S NEST AT THE KENSHUSEI IN THE JKA HEADQUARTERS, MASAHIKO TANAKA BECAME A LEGEND TO ALL HIS CONTEMPORARIES WITH HIS UNIQUE AND CHARISMATIC PERSONALITY, PERFECTLY CONTROLLED POWER AND FLUID FLEXIBILITY OF MOVEMENT. WHEN ENTERED IN COMPETITION, HE WON EVERY POSSIBLE TITLE. WHEN COACHING THE JAPAN NATIONAL TEAM, HE DID THE SAME. HIS ACT AND WORDS ARE A TRUE INSPIRATION, AND HE IS A LIVING EXAMPLE OF KARATE PHILOSOPHY. "THERE ARE TWO ASPECTS TO KARATE TRAINING," HE SAYS. "THE TECHNIQUE OF THE BODY AND THE WAY OF THE MIND. THE MENTAL TRAINING CENTERS ON THE DEVELOPMENT OF ZANCHIN AND THE ABILITY TO CONCENTRATE FULLY ON THE OPPONENT, WHICH [BOTH COMBINE TO] POINT YOUR CONSCIOUSNESS TOWARDS THE HARA." WORDS OF WISDOM FROM ONE OF THE BEST KARATE MASTERS IN THE WORLD.

Q: Sensei, tell us about your youth.
A: I have always been a loner. My family was constantly moving, and I didn't have any opportunity to make friends and stay with them for a long period of time. I would pack my knapsack and go hiking into the mountains alone. I believe this influenced me greatly. I chose rugby at my school because it seemed like it was the toughest activity, and I wanted to prove that I was a man. This experience was all happiness for me. If I wasn't bleeding or scraped, I would feel unhappy with myself, but I did well. In fact, I can say that all my karate power comes from those sprints during my rugby years because everything was ankles, knees and hips. Rugby helped to mold my legs in those early years.

Q: What university did you attend?
A: I went to Nihon University. I studied economics in the footsteps of my father who died when I was 19. That was a very important turning point in my life because everything changed [at that point]. I decided to switch

Karate Masters

"I did have a favorite strategy when facing foreign opponents. Despite their size and strength, most of them had a weakness in their initial speed and in between their waza. I would wait for such an opening to occur so I could score."

courses. Not only did I begin to study veterinary medicine, but I also studied to become an expert in forestry. I dreamt about having a farm in South America.

Q: How did you got involved in karate?
A: A friend of mine at the university took me to a karate dojo. Yaguchi Sensei was the teacher there. I joined, but I never told my mother that I did. I didn't want her to worry about me learning how to fight! Later on, someone saw me fight and invited me to participate in the Kanto Area Championship. My team took first place.

Q: When you graduated, why didn't you pursue your dream of going to South America?
A: Well, karate was really important to me already. It was my life. I was a *sandan* at the time, and I really wanted to take the courses for *kenshusei* [student instructor] at the JKA Headquarters. They refused my request because there weren't enough funds to support a student instructor at the time. However, if I could support myself, they said that I would be allowed to enter the course. Of course, I started to look for any kind of job that would allow me to pay my bills, and it didn't matter to me what kind of work it was. I was everything from a river man to a real estate agent. For a year I transported logs along canals. When doing this, you have to actually ride the logs, so I thought of it as a training for my legs. Gradually, as my balance improved, I fell into the water less and less.

Q: Did the JKA send you abroad?
A: Yes, I was sent to Denmark in 1975 for approximately a year, but I kept training so I could compete in the World Karate Championships that were held that year in Los Angeles, California. I used some of the Danish karate-ka to prepare myself for that tournament, and I found out later on that they weren't enjoying the training with me at all. It turns out that they thought I was very hard with them and with myself, but that was the only way I knew how to get better ... training as hard as I can.

Tanaka

"Karate is an art, and art is—more than anything—an expression. When you see a kata performed well, you realize that immediately. As artists, we all strive for perfection."

Q: What happened in the championship?
A: I won the world title. In the final, I had to face Oishi Takeshi Sensei, and he was one of the best in the world. His nickname was "Mr. Lightning" because he was so fast, and he was the kumite champion the previous four years. To be honest, the rest of the fighters were also very strong and dangerous. There were never any easy competitors … unless someone made an error. One fighter was always very hard to beat, at least for me. His name was Norihiko Iida. In fact, I lost seven times to him in competition matches. Only once, the eighth time, could I beat him.

Q: When you weren't fighting Japanese opponents, what kind of approach did you use?
A: I did have a favorite strategy when facing foreign opponents. Despite their size and strength, most of them had a weakness in their initial speed and in between their waza. I would wait for such an opening to occur so I could score. I was very successful at it.

Karate Masters

"Karate is a martial art and a way of life, not only a physical activity that has a sportive side to it. Master Funakoshi said karate should be used as a tool to develop and perfect one's character ... both physically and mentally."

Q: You came out of competition retirement in 1986 and entered the 29th JKA Championship. Why?
A: It was a good challenge for me. I was 45 years old, and I knew I presented a challenge to all the young fighters. It was a tough challenge for me, too! I was defeated in the quarterfinals. I was a little disappointed, but I wanted to prove myself that I could contest the young champions in competition ... not just in the dojo. I did this for my own satisfaction. I love to fight and that urge was with me for some time. Now that I have it out of my system, I don't get upset about the outcome of a fight. The ultimate aim of karate lies not in victory or defeat.

Q: What does karate represent to you?
A: Karate is an art, and art is—more than anything—an expression. When you see a kata performed well, you realize that immediately. As artists, we all strive for perfection. In our case, we should strive for perfection in technique, even though we will never achieve it. A lot of high-ranking instruc-

tors have expressed their concerns about how many karate dojo around the world have become competition minded. Yes, it is true that I have competed many times, but competition was always down on the list of my priorities when it came to the true values of karate.

Karate is a martial art and a way of life, not only a physical activity that has a sportive side to it. Master Funakoshi said karate should be used as a tool to develop and perfect one's character ... both physically and mentally. When we talk about karate as a way of life, we open the possibility of many interpretations. It is interesting that, regardless of how people understand it, there are some fundamental truths to it that don't change. Through many years of intense training under our teachers, we learn the basics of both the technical and spiritual side of the art. We follow our sensei, and by watching and listening to him, we reach a high level of skill and understanding. So, in some sort of way, we are following the way of life that has been handed down through the years. Now it is up to us to find our own way or put it together in a personal format that applies to our life. The quest is now to make it our own. It is important to respect and give credit to the teachers, because without them, our spiritual growth probably would never come about. And without their guidance in training, we wouldn't be who we are today.

"In the JKA, we worked hard to develop a form of karate that uses the human body in the best possible way when it comes to utilizing all muscles and joints in the body to generate power. It is a very simple concept, but it is a difficult task to achieve."

Q: Sensei, why is it so important to keep our heels flat on the ground when we do techniques like gyaku-tsuki but not when we spar?
A: This is very simple question to answer. In the JKA, we worked hard to develop a form of karate that uses the human body in the best possible way when it comes to utilizing all muscles and joints in the body to generate power. It is a very simple concept, but it is a difficult task to achieve. Keeping the heel down when performing kihon teaches the body to use all the power from the ground and get the right feeling of the movement. We strive to keep it down while doing kata, kihon, makiwara, et cetera because it is the best way to develop the feeling for body power. Once you have the

Karate Masters

"JKA Shotokan is more a method or approach to karate than a separate style. Unfortunately, many people don't understand this."

correct technique and feeling for how the body must move and absorb the impact, you can do it any way you want. By lifting the heel up when punching in combat, you get an extra few inches that can be useful in a free fight. You can also put more body torque in the action, if necessary. This is something often seen in competition, due to obvious reasons. You can't teach this to a beginner because he doesn't have the right body feel for the technique. In the past, old masters never did any kind of competition, and that is why we always see pictures of them with the back heel flat.

Q: So you generate more power with the heel down than with the heel up?
A: No. You can generate the same amount of power in both cases. But this only works when you have the right body feel, a sense of the technique and all the lines of power in your body are in perfect coordination. For instance, when punching, always keep your shoulder and chest relaxed. You should only tense these muscles at the moment of impact. The kime should be over in a split second and not stay tense after the technique has been thrown. All these elements are important to understand. Things like kime, zanchin and hara don't come without hard training and dedication. The secret is the body. There are no other secrets in karate.

Q: How would you describe "JKA Shotokan"?
A: Very simple. It's a straight down-the-line karate that places emphasis on good form, speed and kime. Is not that what any karate should be? JKA Shotokan is more a method or approach to karate than a separate style. Unfortunately, many people don't understand this.

Q: Shotokan is a very straight-line method of karate, isn't it?
A: What is the shortest distance between two points? The straight line is always the simplest path to reach your target, but I guess I understand what you are implying in your question. When you are young, the strong, straight-line approach to combat is more suitable because of the physical

characteristics of the individual. Unconsciously, young people rely more on strength, so running over the opponent when you have a powerful technique seems to be the best way. It is when your body and interpretation of the art changes—and this usually happens when you get older—that you realize other venues of dealing with a powerful attack. At a senior level, to be linear is not enough. In the fundamentals of JKA karate, we work on making the technique better. This includes punches and kicks. Every single punch and every single block and kick must be fast, powerful and precise, and they should have kime and power. These are the tools the artist must use. Considering this, it is not difficult to incorporate softer approaches to use the "tools" because the elements are already there. You may add a circular motion to the way your body moves, but when you punch, block or kick ... you do it with power and determination.

"Fighting has always been and always will be an important part of karate because that is where the true spirit of budo is absorbed."

Q: Do you see karate as a fighting art for self-defense?
A: I believe it is fair to say that not all karate-ka have confidence in their ability to fight in a real self-defense situation, but those using the "do" aspect of the art in their lives should, at least, have a total different and level-headed approach to these kinds of encounters. Foresee where the problem may arise and avoid it before it happens. Karate is not just a sport or a physical activity; it is a martial art and a way of life. A way of life is always part of us in every minute of our existence.

Q: Sensei, these days we can see many different karate organizations around the world. What is your opinion of this?
A: It is all politics and personal interest. Period. Many people want to make money with karate, even if they are not fully qualified to do it. Associations and federations are the same. For me it is more rewarding to study the art, follow your teacher and try to be the best human being you can. This is traditional budo, and this is what I believe. If karate training teaches us anything, it teaches us that the truth is always harder to take and less attractive than we would like.

Karate Masters

"The traditional training method of doing a high number of repetitions for kihon techniques is boring for the new generations. They don't want to repeat the same punch or kick 1,000 times. You can't treat the new students the way we were taught in the past."

Q: Why do some practitioners modify and create different methods of training?
A: Young practitioners try to develop new methods of doing things without first mastering the old. Their foundation is not good and not strong enough to build other new things on top. I think that true traditional karate will [eventually] be lost if there aren't any instructors or students who adhere to the traditional methods and values of karate and budo. Unfortunately, students want to learn everything fast; therefore, instructors have to teach more than the student can chew, because otherwise he will leave the school and then the instructor will have financial problems. The traditional training method of doing a high number of repetitions for kihon techniques is boring for the new generations. They don't want to repeat the same punch or kick 1,000 times. You can't treat the new students the way we were taught in the past. Yes, it is true that there are more scientific approaches to training, but what happens to the spirit of karate? Punching 1,000 times trains the spirit—not only technique. I know it is boring, but the spirit needs this kind of training. If you don't like training like this, you'll be missing an important part of who you are because you'll never understand the other side of yourself. Karate must be followed the way it is, and you cannot try to change it. When you get into your car to go to work, you follow the street, right? You don't create new streets or simply go ahead because you don't like curves! You follow the streets. That's the way karate is and the way it should be practiced.

Q: Do you recommend special training sessions like *gasshuku* and *kangeiko*?
A: I do. Your techniques get better and your spirit gets stronger. The JKA instructor's course is a constant special training program. You need to push your body to the limit and then use the spirit to reach further. If you don't put yourself at your very limit, how do you know how far can you go? How do you know how strong you are and how far your spirit will take you?

"Karate was created and developed as a self-defense method. Funakoshi Sensei saw the flaws in trying to keep a warrior mentality in times of peace and developed a new approach to the art."

Q: Sensei, one of your special techniques is the use of the lead leg to score on your opponent's attack. How did you develop this?
A: This is not my *tokui-waza*, but I did use it in competition very much. It is basically an interception movement, and it is performed with the lead leg. Most of the time people use a roundhouse kick in this capacity, and it is called *saya-mae- mawashi-geri*. The idea is to stop the opponent in his tracks. It is a very tricky movement because you have to coordinate the timing of the opponent's entry with your own action. You don't retreat with your back foot. You bring your lead leg toward you and snap the kick. To generate power, you need a strong ankle on your supporting leg and the ability to snap your hip out so you can put all of your power behind the kick. Don't forget. Your opponent is charging you, and he is bringing force and momentum behind him.

Q: Are modern practitioners focusing too much on the martial aspect of karate and forgetting the element of art?
A: It is possible that this is happening. Karate was created and developed as a self-defense method. Funakoshi Sensei saw the flaws in trying to keep a warrior mentality in times of peace and developed a new approach to the art. Fighting has always been and always will be an important part of karate

Karate Masters

"You must learn not only how to make karate natural to you but also how to strengthen your body without stressing it more than necessary. Wrong technique brings a lot of injuries."

because that is where the true spirit of budo is absorbed. Therefore, karate-do is an art because it allows us to reach higher levels of existence as human beings. It is also an art because the students need to learn the principles, work hard and develop their own way of expressing karate through their bodies. Art is not something that you develop by simply copying others. I can copy a Picasso's painting, but it doesn't make me an artist. To be an artist, and every karate-ka should be one, we need to learn how to express—in our own words—what we have learnt from our teacher. If the art is to survive, this is the only way.

Q: Injuries are part of the game if a practitioner trains hard. What are your thoughts on that?
A: Well, injuries are a risk for anyone doing any kind of physical activity. Karate, because it involves fighting between two or more individuals, can be dangerous because of a lack of control or technical ability [someone may have]. What is interesting to me is that most of the injuries that longtime practitioners suffer result from the wrong technique—not from fighting! If you don't understand how to use and relax your body properly, you may experience problems in your joints and lower back when you get older. You must learn not only how to make karate natural to you but also how to strengthen your body without stressing it more than necessary. Wrong technique brings a lot of injuries.

Q: Does modern society influence the way new generation of practitioners look at the art?
A: Definitely. In modern society, things are obtained instantly. Everything is about now. Fast food, fast cars, e-mail, et cetera. This is good because it allows us to do things in less time and with less effort, but karate-do has nothing to do with this. In fact, for a complete understanding of what karate implies as an art of budo, we need to look in the opposite direction. Funakoshi Sensei clearly explained that the goal of karate is perfection of character. Therefore, we have to look at it as a lifetime training and philoso-

phy that involves the body, the mind and also the spirit. In life, the goals that are worth keeping are the ones that take time and effort to achieve. Those things are not achieved quickly and require sincere dedication and good character.

Q: What final advice would you like to give to the practitioners?
A: They should all think about this. If you are training in karate as a simple physical activity, you will derive less benefit as you get older. And there is a very simple test that you can do to determine this. If you are getting less [benefit], then you are not following the right way of karate. This is not the way of the art. Karate training is a mirror of life, and the way you live your life must go hand in hand with the way your train. Your mind must grow as your muscles when you are young and strong. Don't neglect one side of your training because you are too busy trying to improve the other. No matter who you are, what your skill level is or how much you progress, you'll realize, generally after 40, that regardless of how many times you train and repeat the movements, the techniques won't improve. They will get slower as you grow older, and they will get weaker. Are you ready to put all the time, effort, sweat and blood during your young years only to find out that everything you have worked for is gradually becoming less effective? Well, remember that balance is the key. And by balancing both side of the coin [physical and spiritual], you'll find the answer. O

"Karate training is a mirror of life, and the way you live your life must go hand in hand with the way your train. Your mind must grow as your muscles when you are young and strong. Don't neglect one side of your training because you are too busy trying to improve the other."

Keiji Tomiyama

The Challenges of Budo

HE IS ONE OF THE ICONS OF TANI-HA SHITO-RYU KARATE. A DIRECT STUDENT OF FOUNDER CHOJIRO TANI, TOMIYAMA WAS CHOSEN BY TANI SENSEI TO SPREAD THE ART IN EUROPE ACCORDING TO THE ETHICAL AND MORAL PRINCIPLES OF THE OLD JAPANESE TRADITIONS. ONCE KNOWN ONLY FOR HIS FEROCIOUS FIGHTING SKILLS, SENSEI TOMIYAMA HAS MATURED NOT ONLY AS A KARATE-KA, BUT ALSO AS AN INDIVIDUAL. WITH THIS MATURITY HAS COME A PHILOSOPHY THAT PUTS A PROPER PERSPECTIVE ON WHEN TO FIGHT AND WHEN NOT TO FIGHT. HOWEVER, HE STILL BELIEVES THAT THERE ARE TIMES WHEN A MAN MUST NOT RETREAT. "TO FIGHT WITH ANOTHER IS WRONG," SAYS TOMIYAMA, "BUT TO LOSE A FIGHT WITH ANOTHER OVER PRINCIPLES YOU DEEM HONOURABLE IS WORSE. TO FIGHT WELL IS AS PROPER AS BEING ABLE TO STUDY CORRECTLY OR WALK PROPERLY. BY LEARNING TO FIGHT, YOU ARE ACTUALLY EDUCATING YOURSELF TO AVOID BATTLE." DESCRIBED AS A TEACHER WHO GIVES AS MUCH AS HE DEMANDS, TOMIYAMA CONTINUES HIS DEDICATED TASK OF SPREADING THE MESSAGE OF HIS TEACHER. HIS SCHOOLS AROUND THE WORLD CONTINUE TO FLOURISH BECAUSE THEY HAVE BEEN ESTABLISHED ON A NUCLEUS OF LOYAL INSTRUCTORS AND STUDENTS WHO LIVE BY THE SAME BUDO PRINCIPLES THAT FOSTERED THE SPIRITS OF THE ANCIENT WARRIORS OF JAPAN.

Q: How long have you been practicing the martial arts?
A: I started karate at the age of 17, so I have been practicing for 35 years. However, I did a little *kendo* at the age of 13 and *judo* at 16, as they were compulsory at school. I hold a 7th dan in *shito-ryu* and a 6th dan in *goju-ryu,* but I do not actively teach goju-ryu as everything I have learned because it is included in my shito-ryu teaching. Shito-ryu is a broad style which includes both *shuri-te* and *naha-te.* Moreover, my teachers learned their goju-ryu from master Kenwa Mabuni, the founder of shito-ryu, who also taught goju-ryu just to my teachers. I still practice with my teachers in goju-ryu every time I go back to Japan. Also, I have been practicing *shinto muso-ryu jodo* for the last 10 years or so.

Karate Masters

"At the university club, we trained for three hours every day; there was one hour of fitness training, one hour of basics and kata and one hour of kumite. Sit-ups were an important part of fitness training, and we did a minimum of 500 every day. We jokingly called ourselves members of the Doshisha University Sit-Up Club. When you do so many sit-ups, inevitably the skin around your backside forms a callus."

Q: Who were your first teachers?
A: I started with my cousin who was studying shito-ryu, but my serious training started when I entered Doshisha University in Kyoto and joined its karate club at the age of 18. The teacher there was Sensei Fukuda. Master Chojiro Tani, one of the senior students of Kenwa Mabuni and the founder of *tani-ha shito ryu*, was the technical director and came to the dojo and taught regularly.

Q: What do you remember most of your early days in karate?
A: I was boxing in high school. At the same time my cousin, who is two years older, was studying karate. So one day we decided to fight to see whom was better. I was beaten conclusively. He just kept kicking me, and I had no answer for that. At that point, I gave up boxing and started learning karate!

At the university club, we trained for three hours every day; there was one hour of fitness training, one hour of basics and kata, and one hour of kumite. Sit-ups were a important part of fitness training, and we did a minimum of 500 every day. We jokingly called ourselves members of the Doshisha University Sit-Up Club. When you do so many sit-ups, inevitably the skin around your backside forms a callus. At public baths, which were quite common in those days, we could recognize members of the karate club by just looking at their backsides! At training camps, where we practiced three times a day for one week, we used to do 1,000 sit-ups in the morning, another 1,000 in the afternoon and another 1,000 in the evening. Our record was 2,500 sit-ups at one time. We also had training camps at Sensei Tani's dojo in Kobe.

Smoking was the norm in those days and almost every adult male smoked. It was a sign of adulthood and almost every male student started smoking upon entering the university. Sensei Tani, myself and everybody else in the dojo were smokers. There was a big ashtray, maybe two feet in diameter, at the end of the dojo and, at the break in the middle of training, everybody, including Sensei Tani, sat around the ashtray and smoked while discussing techniques. On finishing a cigarette, we resumed training. Both Sensei Tani and I stopped smoking quite soon after those university years, and the dojo became a non-smoking zone several years later.

Q: How has your personal karate has changed over the years?
A: I was fairly successful in competition, winning second place in the All-Kansai Individual Championships, so I was one of the top university fighters. Master Tani tried to modernize karate and developed a unique theory consisting of many new ideas such as "double-hip twist," "zero-tension-zero," "kick shock," "recoil," "changing weight," "dropping body" and more.

"I was fairly successful in competition, winning second place in the All-Kansai Individual Championships, so I was one of the top university fighters. Master Tani tried to modernize karate and developed a unique theory consisting of many new ideas."

Following his instruction, I developed very good speed which helped me to be successful in competition. When I came to Europe by Master Tani's request in 1972, after graduating from the University, I realized that European people were thicker and heavier than the Japanese. So I tried to develop more power. Luckily, Sensei Yasuhio Suzuki, chief instructor for Europe, had very powerful techniques, and he taught me how to use body weight more effectively.

When I visited Japan in 1980, I met Master Yamashita and Master Uehara of goju-ryu at the university dojo. To enable you to understand the situation more clearly, I will briefly tell you the history of the Doshisha University Karate Club. In the 1930s, some students from Doshisha University and Ritsumeikan University, both situated in Kyoto, got together and sought instruction from

"I was also very lucky to be able to train with Master Fujimoto, the most senior instructor on the goju side of the tradition, who had refused to teach previously. I absorbed a lot during this period. I also managed to train with Master Tani quite regularly, learning many more shito-ryu kata."

Master Chojun Miyagi, founder of goju-ryu. These two universities are the birthplace of goju-ryu in mainland Japan. The famous master Gogen "The Cat" Yamaguchi and most of the other senior instructors of Japanese goju-kai are graduates of the Ritsumeikan University Karate Club. On the other hand, Doshisha University Karate Club sought instruction from Master Kenwa Mabuni, who had settled in nearby Osaka, following the advice of Master Miyagi who could not stay in mainland Japan all the time.

To show respect to his fellow master, Kenwa Mabuni only taught naha-te at Doshisha University, thus the club remained a goju-ryu school. Master Tani, a graduate of Doshisha University, eventually became a shito-ryu stylist and, with permission from Master Mabuni, started tani-ha shito ryu. So the university club was basically goju-ryu, but I followed Master Tani and became a shito-ryu stylist. Both masters showed and explained some goju kata as taught by Kenwa Mabuni, and I was quite impressed by the theories and wisdom contained in these forms. Master Tani must have also learned these, but his instruction was more geared towards his modern theories so their explanation was quite eye-opening to me.

In 1982, my father fell ill, and I had to go back to Japan to look after him and his business. I stayed there for three years and, during these three years, trained with both masters every week. I was also very lucky to be able to train with Master Fujimoto, the most senior instructor on the goju side of the tradition, who had refused to teach previously. I absorbed a lot during this period. I also managed to train with Master Tani quite regularly, learning many more shito-ryu kata.

Upon returning to Europe, I had to train and think hard to combine Master Tani's modern theory with goju's traditional wisdom. The answer came to me fairly quickly because it had already started to form within my body during my three years in Japan. The key lay in Master Tani's teaching. When he had taught his theory, he had always said that once mastered, these movements would become smaller and smaller and eventually invisible. Once these invisible, or internal, movements were mastered, there was no conflict between his modern teachings and the traditional teachings. In 1990, I wrote my book "Fundamentals of Karate-do," explaining these traditional teachings in a more modern approach.

"When I went to Europe for the first time, I was in Paris, and I could not speak a single word of French. I was also young and inexperienced. So I just kept training normally and everybody had to follow and copy me. I remember the language barrier, but I do not remember any differences in training between the Westerners and the Japanese."

For the last 10 years or so, I have started realizing that one has to reach a high spiritual level in order to reach a high technical level. So that is what I am trying to achieve at the moment. Although I have almost all of the information material needed, I have to further refine my techniques and reach a higher level. The border between spiritual and physical states gets blurred at the higher levels. So I still have a long way to go.

Q: How did Westerners respond to traditional Japanese training?
A: Very well, actually. When I went to Europe for the first time, I was in Paris and could not speak a single word of French. I was also young and inexperienced. So I just kept training normally and everybody had to follow and copy me. I remember the language barrier, but I do not remember any differences in training between the Westerners and the Japanese. It is rather impossible to categorize Western karate and Japanese karate. There are many kinds of karate and karate-ka in the West as well as in Japan. Some Western people are far more advanced than some Japanese. What I can say is that there are a small number of old generation karate-ka in Japan who reached quite a high level, just because they practiced for a longer period and were closer to the source.

Karate Masters

"It is very difficult to define what pure shito-ryu, goju-ryu or even shotokan is. I believe in my version of shito-ryu, but another shito-ryu instructor will probably disagree with me. Also, my goju-ryu is quite different from other goju branches."

Q: How has your teaching philosophy evolved?
A: Until 1982 I was teaching what I had learned from Master Tani and Sensei Suzuki. I was just a messenger. However, when I came back from Japan around 1985, I started to teach my own ideas, which does not necessarily mean my creations but rather my understanding of what karate should be. I had to explain and convince my old students of the validity of the teaching, as my approach was different from my pre-1982 period. The majority understood or trusted me, but some failed to understand and left, which did not bother me too much as I was convinced that my new approach was far superior to the old one. In 1990, I decided to spread the word outside Western Europe and started to travel the world. Within a few years, I had established branches in Eastern Europe, Southern Africa, the Middle East and the Indian sub-continent.

Q: With all these changes, do you think there is still pure shito-ryu and goju-ryu?
A: It is very difficult to define what pure shito-ryu, goju-ryu or even shotokan is. The first established shotokan club was the Keio University Karate Club. Their techniques are different from the JKA, for example, but nobody can question their pedigree. I believe in my version of shito-ryu, but another shito-ryu instructor will probably disagree with me. Also, my goju-ryu is quite different from other goju branches. Having said that, there are distinctive differences between the shotokan group and the shito group, and between the shito and goju groups. When you see people from reputable shotokan organizations, although there are some differences, you can recognize them as shotokan people from their movements. The same can be said for shito, goju, wado, uechi, shorin, et cetera. On the other hand, I admit that there are some people whose style we cannot recognize by just observing their movements. Generally speaking, the technical standard of these unrecognizable people is poorer.

Tomiyama

"I do think that different schools are important because one cannot just learn one style of karate. There is no such thing as a standard karate. Different styles exist because of different historical ideas and principles. There are many paths to climb a mountain."

I do think that different schools are important because one cannot just learn one style of karate. There is no such thing as a standard karate. Different styles exist because of different historical ideas and principles. At the higher levels, all styles become quite close and similar. It is like climbing a mountain. There are many paths to climb a mountain. Although all paths lead to the same summit, one has to choose a path to climb. On the other hand, there are people who are only interested in competition fighting. They train only how to move around and how to score points. For them, different styles are not important.

Q: What is your opinion of full-contact karate and kickboxing?
A: People who are engaged in full-contact karate and kickboxing are very committed and very strong. I respect them very much. Although these activities are combat sports, they are not budo. So they lack the philosophical aspects that balance their existence as human beings.

Karate Masters

"Karate is a whole package—physical, technical, spiritual and cultural. Therefore, etiquette and discipline are quite important. Karate has been in the West for quite a long time now, so it is quite diversified."

Q: What are the main characteristics of your shito-ryu method compared to other branches?
A: Master Kenwa Mabuni taught shurite first in order to acquire basic fighting skills. Then, he taught naha-te to develop power. So all other shito-ryu groups are shuri-te based and put naha-te on top of the shuri-te base. On the other hand, Master Tani and myself learned naha-te or goju first, then shurite was added on top of the naha-te base. This is the main difference. As I explained earlier, I now practice the invisible version of Master Tani's theory and, as a consequence, our movements may be slightly smaller and more subtle than other shito-ryu groups. Moreover, as our techniques do not require great muscular strength or big dynamic movement to produce power, it is well suited to older practitioners who have started to reach limitations in their external power.

Q: Do you feel there are any differences between Western karate-ka as compared to Japanese karate-ka?
A: None whatsoever. Japanese people used to be smaller than Westerners, but the younger generation Japanese are now quite tall due to the change in lifestyle and nutrition. Also, Japan is no longer a poor country with strong social discipline whose people readily accept harsh discipline.

Q: How do you see Japanese karate in the West compared to the rest of the world?
A: For me, karate is a whole package—physical, technical, spiritual and cultural. Therefore, etiquette and discipline are quite important. There are many Japanese instructors resident in the West who teach this wholesome karate. Many Western instructors who learned from them also teach this kind of

karate. But there are many instructors who did not learn properly or did not like this kind of approach. They usually teach karate as just a physical and technical exercise. On the other hand, there are some people who have gone in the opposite direction and teach mystified karate which, in my opinion, can be harmful to one's mental health. Karate has been in the West for quite a long time now, so it is quite diversified.

Q: Do you think it helps to train with weapons?
A: It generally does, although it is not essential to train in weapons to progress in karate. One has to have good stances and postures as well as the correct distribution of strength in order to handle weapons properly. So training with weapons will help to develop the aspects which are equally essential for karate. On the other hand, people who are already quite good in karate can learn weapons fairly quickly, as they already possess these qualities.

"The quality of your karate is determined by the quality of your basics, so you have to practice basics regularly and try to improve them whatever level you are at. This does not mean you can neglect kata and kumite practice. You should practice kata and kumite to improve your karate, but do not neglect the basics. Tradition is the most important element."

Q: What's your opinion about *makiwara* training?
A: Makiwara training is good for developing focus and power and strengthening the body, but it should be done correctly. Moreover, a makiwara board should be flexible.

Q: Do you think an instructor's personal training should be different than what he teaches to his students?
A: Definitely. When you teach people, what they need for their development should be your main concern. This can be quite different from your own needs. These are two completely different things which need to be approached separately and individually.

Karate Masters

"I have great respect for many of the Japanese instructors teaching outside of Japan. They are much better than the average instructor in Japan, and moreover, can speak the local language."

Q: What's the proper training ratio between kata and kumite?
A: In general, I would say 50-50.

Q: What determines a karate-ka's level?
A: The quality of your karate is determined by the quality of your basics, so you have to practice basics regularly and try to improve them whatever level you are at. This does not mean you can neglect kata and kumite practice. You should practice kata and kumite to improve your karate, but do not neglect the basics. Tradition is the most important element. Tradition includes self-defense techniques, self-development exercises and personal ethics.

Q: Is going to Japan to train necessary?
A: Not really. It depends who you are learning from in your country and who you are going to learn from in Japan. Of course, it is nice to visit Japan and see the culture, but whether it is highly necessary or not depends on each person's circumstance. I have great respect for many of the Japanese instructors teaching outside of Japan. They are much better than the average instructor in Japan, and moreover, can speak the local language.

Q: What are the major changes in the art since you began training?
A: During the last three or four decades, karate has spread around the world and become one of the major combat sports. So this worldwide development of karate as a sport can be seen as the major change, although traditional karate is still mostly unchanged.

Q: With whom would you like to have trained with that you have not?
A: I consider myself extremely lucky to have met and trained with so many legendary teachers. I do not feel a need to have trained with any other teachers, although I try to learn something new from everyone I meet. As a shito-ryu stylist, you might expect me to say Master Kenwa Mabuni, but

because all of my teachers are direct students of Master Mabuni and I learned a lot about him, I do not feel a need. Perhaps the only person I would like to have trained with is Master Choki Motobu.

Q: What would you say to someone who is interested in learning karate-do?
A: Well, I would say, "Karate is good for you, so start straight away." Some people are very natural when it comes to any kind of physical activity, but It was never this way with me. Even if you are gifted, I always believed the factors to determine the quality of your karate were the quality of instruction you received and the amount of work you put in. At the University Club, we did several hundred repetitions in each technique with senior grades constantly correcting junior grades. If we did not correct ourselves following their instruction, senior grades did not hesitate to slap our face or kick our stomach. So, to avoid getting hurt, we learned fairly quickly.

"There are styles which are compatible and others which are not. I do not think practicing two incompatible styles is beneficial. For example, I myself train in shito-ryu, goju-ryu and uechi-ryu. I have no problem with this because the underlying principles of these styles do not conflict."

Q: What keeps you motivated after all these years?
A: My teachers have constantly given me inspiration and motivation. I have formed ideas about what karate should be, and I try to implement it in myself. It is the main motivation for my own development. On the other hand, I would like to help others to develop themselves. That is why I keep traveling and teaching.

Q: What is your opinion about mixing karate styles?
A: There are styles which are compatible and others which are not. I do not think practicing two incompatible styles is beneficial. For example, I myself train in shito-ryu, goju-ryu and uechi-ryu. Moreover, some *ryuei-ryu* kata were included in the shito-ryu list in recent years. I have no problem with this because the underlying principles of these styles do not conflict. On the other hand, I think I would have a problem with mixing shotokan and shorin-ryu. Some branches of goju-ryu are also too different from mine, and thus incompatible. As I explained earlier, shito-ryu is a very broad style,

Karate Masters

"One has to empty one's mind to be able to understand the opponent's intention and get rid of ego to harmonize with the opponent in order to control him. In other words, the principles are 'understanding' and 'harmony.' It is easy to say but not that easy to achieve."

and I teach all these styles or kata under one roof of shito-ryu. To avoid confusion or conflict, I teach all of these with the same principles.

Q: How important do you think *bunkai* is in the understanding of kata?
A: Originally, to learn karate meant to learn kata and their bunkai. It still applies to traditional karate. Although practicing a kata and improving its techniques is most important, the performance becomes incomplete and hollow without understanding and practicing its bunkai, and that is exactly what is happening in competition kata. To combat this, the World Karate Federation has put kata bunkai in the finals of the team kata event. So we shall see what happens.

Q: What is the philosophical basis for your karate training?
A: In common with most Japanese martial artists, I have learned, and am still learning, the budo philosophy of the samurai, which is based on Zen Buddhism, Confucianism and Shintoism. But I believe the majority of its virtues are universal and can also be found in other religions and philosophies of the world. Although they also apply to life in general, I believe the most important virtues specifically to martial artists are *mushin* or "no mind" and *muga* or "no ego." One has to empty one's mind to be able to understand the opponent's intention and get rid of ego to harmonize with the opponent in order to control him. In other words, the principles are "understanding" and "harmony." It is easy to say but not that easy to achieve.

Tomiyama

Q: Do you have a memorable experience that inspired your training?

A: Yes, when I saw Master Fujimoto for the second time. When I saw him for the first time, I was still a white belt and could not understand what he was doing. But when I saw him for the second time, many years later, I was actively seeking knowledge, and I can still remember the shivering which went through my spine with excitement and elation. I get a similar inspiration every time I train with him.

"One has to incorporate daily life with karate practice—how to walk, how to breathe, how to speak, et cetera. Karate is not only a way of simply punching and kicking; it is a way of life and as such affects all the facets of your existence. At least this is the way it should be."

Q: What does the practice of karate-do mean to you?

A: Another grand question! In short, it is the continuous betterment or improvement of one's technique, understanding and personality. But the baseline is to enjoy the training and to achieve your goal—whatever it may be. It can be to get fit, to pass the next grading, to master a technique, to learn a new kata, et cetera. Once your current goal is achieved, set a new goal and keep enjoying the training. Hopefully, this contributes to improving the quality of your life, for which the social side is also quite important.

Q: How can a practitioner can increase his understanding of the spiritual side of karate?

A: Primarily by reading relevant materials containing correct information, and meditating and practicing kata with the right attitude and state of mind. One has to try to achieve the state of mind I explained earlier—*mushin* and *muga*. But if you behave aggressively with a big ego in daily life, the higher levels of spiritual development are impossible to achieve.

Karate Masters

"Although it is very good to strengthen the whole body, I have seen too many people who started to use brutal force rather than technique as they grew stronger due to weight training. This is detrimental to karate practice."

Q: How much training should a senior karate-ka be doing to improve?
A: Everything, every single day, has to be impregnated with the spirit of karate-do. One has to incorporate daily life with karate practice—how to walk, how to breathe, how to speak, et cetera. Karate is not only a way of simply punching and kicking; it is a way of life and as such affects all the facets of your existence. At least this is the way it should be.

Q: Is there anything lacking in the way the martial arts are taught today?
A: I am still learning, you know. Well, again it depends on the instructor. As I said earlier, maybe etiquette and discipline are missing in some dojo. But the world and its people are changing constantly, and there are varied cultures and customs in the world, so certain changes are inevitable.

Q: What are the most important qualities of a successful karate-ka?
A: Perseverance and modesty. Open-mindedness to absorb the teaching and friendliness to get on well with fellow students also helps. Enthusiasm is also important, but many over-enthusiastic students burn out quickly and leave. Steady students who keep coming regularly and persevere are the winners.

Q: Do you recommend supplementary training?
A: Stretching and running are very good and very important for the overall physical condition of the karate-ka, but one has to be careful about weight training. Although it is very good to strengthen the whole body, I have seen too many people who started to use brutal force rather than technique as they grew stronger, due to weight training. This is detrimental to karate practice. It is very important to remember that it is "supplementary" training and that you should put the primary emphasis on karate training—not on the other aspects.

Q: Why do many students fall away after two or three years of training?
A: There are so many things to do these days and many people tend to do a little of everything rather than stick to one thing and reach a high level. Also, there are some barriers to break through in order to progress in karate. The first barrier is to become a brown belt and the next is to become black belt. Two to three years is the time when students face these barriers. Probably these barriers are too much for some students. There are also people who successfully overcome the barriers but have no energy left to carry on. The next barrier is between 3rd and 4th dan. People can progress up to 3rd dan with plenty of spirit and enthusiasm, but refinement is needed to pass to 4th dan and many people find this quite difficult. Those who made the 4th dan grade generally continue to train for the rest of their life and keep progressing.

Q: There is very little written about you in magazines. Do you avoid publicity?
A: My two main teachers, Master Tani and Master Fujimoto, did not like publicity, so perhaps that influenced me. Master Tani could have gotten an important position within the Japan Karate Federation, but he declined it. Master Fujimoto was positively against publicity and believed that those who wanted to learn from him had to seek him out. Although I would like people to know what I am doing to a certain extent, as I might be able to help some of them, self-glorification is against my beliefs.

Q: Have been times when you felt fear in your training?
A: At the university club, our seniors did not use control at all during free sparring. Talking to them after graduation, I found out that they had sincerely believed that it had been beneficial to us. Many of us got broken noses and teeth because of the free-sparring sessions everyday. We all felt some kind of fear as the free sparring session approached. Having once started fighting, you are too busy dealing with the job at hand and have no time to feel fear.

Q: What is the key to gaining a deep understanding of karate principles?
A: Time is an important element in one's progression. If you do not understand something straight away, you have to keep practicing it. Then one day, if you remain diligent, you will suddenly understand like a ripe fruit dropping off a branch. If you do not keep practicing, you will never understand. It is important to give yourself time, be patient and just keep practicing. O

Dominique Valera

Long Live The King!

Born in Lyons in 1947, Dominique Valera is the king of European karate. He is a legend who has dominated the world karate scene for many years. When he was performing or fighting, everyone in the competition would stop and watch. His speed and sense of timing were nearly perfect, and he became the first Caucasian to earn respect from the Japanese champions. The son of Spanish immigrants, Valera channeled his innate aggression into judo, which he began at age 7 and attained black belt rank at 13. "The attitude I have now," says Valera, "is definitely a reflection of everything I had to go through during my youth."

In 1961, he began training karate mainly from books, and as soon as an instructor was available, he went to learn. In his hunger for knowledge, he studied all the karate methods he could put his hands on. Styles were not a limitation for him, but just a vehicle to learn more about his loved art. He decided go to Japan, where he visited legendary masters such as Matayoshi Nakayama, Gogen Yamaguchi, Mas Oyama and Choju Tani.

After years of dedication to traditional karate, Valera was part of an incident that would change his training and teaching direction forever. In the 1973 World Karate Championships in Long Beach, California, Valera was disqualified after landing a heavy punch. Incensed by their subjectivity, he proceeded to throw kicks and punches at the officials. After that, Valera decided that he had had enough of point karate and would move into a more realistic arena. True to himself, he went to the United States to train in full-contact karate under Bill "Superfoot" Wallace. After grueling training sessions, Valera went back to France and showed the Europeans what full-contact was. He won the European title and earned two shots at the world title, although greats Jeff Smith in 1978 and Dan Macaruso in 1980 prevented him from winning.

He is an icon—the man that every karate-ka in Europe imitated and looked upon as the perfect karate combatant. He became the leader of a generation that many describe as the best group of fighters that European karate has ever seen.

Karate Masters

"The teachers were very few and everything was very limiting. The spirit was very different than today. It was more of a martial art and less of a sport. The training sessions were tough and 'martial' compared to what we have in today's karate. To be honest, I never really bothered with the spiritual and mythical aspects."

Q: You began your training in judo. Why did you change to karate?
A: I didn't like the idea of being that close to my opponent. I didn't enjoy fighting at close range. I prefer to have greater distance between my opponent and myself.

Q: What do you remember about your beginnings in the art?
A: The teachers were very few and everything was very limiting. The spirit was very different than today. It was more of a martial art and less of a sport. The training sessions were tough and "martial" compared to what we have in today's karate.

Q: How did you get involved in karate?
A: I started my karate training with Francoise Sanchez and Jean Perrin in Lyon, France. I remember that my first class was on January 5, 1960. A little after that, in 1964, I began to train under Henry Pleé and Yoshinao Nanbu. Sensei Nanbu didn't speak a single word of French, and it was very difficult for him to communicate. We simply tried to copy whatever he did. At that time Jacques Delcourt, who became the president of WUKO years later, was a brown belt.

Q: What attracted you to karate?
A: The competitive aspect is what I really enjoyed the most. To be honest, I never really bothered with the spiritual and mythical aspects. For me karate was competition. It was a good and efficient way to compare myself with other competitors and find out what my level was. On top of that, it gave me the opportunity to travel around the world. In fact, my trip to Japan in 1966 is one of the greatest moments of my life. My friends and I bought a car to drive to Japan. My friends were Patrick Baroux, his brother, Jean Pierre Fisher, Jean Pierre Lavorato and Alain Setrouk, who unfortunately died later. Both Nanbu and Setrouk decided they wanted to take a plane,

but the rest of us were very stubborn and we went by car! We never planned an arrival time. No rush; we simply enjoyed the trip. It was great and is one my favorite memories.

Q: Was driving to Japan difficult?
A: Of course! That trip was a real adventure! We jumped into the car and began driving toward Russia. We had almost arrived at the Russian border when one of the wheels broke. We changed the wheel and 50 miles later the car caught on fire! We had to accept the fact we couldn't keep using the car. So we left the car there and jumped on a airplane. But since we were looking for adventure, we decided not to go straight to Japan. After a short flight, we took a train and then spent two more days on a boat until we reached the Japanese coast. The whole trip took five months!

"We went to Gogen Yamaguchi's dojo to train, but he didn't accept us. We politely told him that it would be an honor for us to train in his dojo, but he refused to allow us participate. Before we left his school, he mentioned that he had 8mm films that we could buy from him in American dollars. So much for the gods."

Q: Did you enjoy meeting the legendary Japanese masters?
A: During our training days in France, Japanese karate-ka were almost considered gods. Once we arrived, we went to Gogen Yamaguchi's dojo to train, but he didn't accept us. We politely told him that it would be an honor for us to train in his dojo, but he refused to allow us participate. Before we left his school, he mentioned that he had 8mm films that we could buy from him in American dollars. So much for the gods.

Q: Where did you go afterwards?
A: We went to Mas Oyama's school to train. He was a little strange but was a very kind man and we felt very well-received. The teacher who spent more time with us and really made us feel at home was Yoshinao Nanbu's instructor, Sensei Tani. He spent time with us and truly accommodated us.

Karate Masters

"I initially had that illusion of perfection. I really wanted to be impressed, but the truth is that I wasn't impressed at all. Don't get me wrong. I liked it, but I wasn't impressed with the teachers. It was no different than what we were already doing back home."

Meeting him was a pleasant experience, and it was very different from the other Japanese teachers we met.

Q: Weren't you impressed with what you saw there?
A: I initially had that illusion of perfection. I really wanted to be impressed, but the truth is that I wasn't impressed at all. Don't get me wrong, I liked it but I wasn't impressed with the teachers. It was no different than what we were already doing back home. Maybe the spirit and the whole Japanese cultural thing was fun, but technically I wasn't impressed.

Q: Don't tell me the teachers weren't good, because that's hard to believe.
A: No. I'm not saying the teachers weren't good from a technical point of view; some of them were. But they couldn't transmit their knowledge. In the end, it was irrelevant how good they were. On the other hand, I didn't see them do anything impressive either. I don't care how good you are, if you can't transmit your knowledge to me, I simply don't care. The wearer of a black belt must be capable of transmitting the art. It is paramount that he knows how to communicate his knowledge and techniques to his students.

Q: What do you remember about the first karate world championships held in Tokyo?
A: That championship was a joke. There were 50 referees and 42 were Japanese. Japan had three teams and the rest of the countries were only allowed one national team. Why? Personally I got third position, which was the bronze medal. During my fight against Wada, who later on became the world champion, he didn't move. He didn't do anything at all. No pressure, no intention, nothing at all. When the match finished, the referees asked for *hantei* and guess what? They decided the Wada was the winner! What a joke. You cannot tolerate something like that in a world championship. It was embarrassing.

Q: Did the things change during the next world championships in Paris?
A: A little, but not much, to be totally honest. Of course, it wasn't an ambush because we were in France and not Japan. Even today, the sport of karate has problems with the referees in *kata* and *kumite*. Karate won't be an Olympic sport until the art is unified. The problem is that in karate we have many different styles and this creates a split and division among practitioners.

When you practice basketball, you practice basketball; when you practice tennis, you practice tennis; but when you say that you practice karate, everybody asks, "What style?" And if you don't practice the same style, then the answer is, "Oh! It's not the same." This attitude creates segregation among the people. Then when you are a black belt, these differences are bigger than when you were a beginner. The styles tend to separate practitioners instead of unify them.

"Karate won't be an Olympic sport until the art is unified. The problem is that in karate we have many different styles and this creates a split and division among practitioners. What really surprises me is that after all these years we still have the same problems. Nobody has realized what the problems are and prevented them."

Taekwondo people do taekwondo and judo people do judo, but karate people do shotokan, shito-ryu, kyokushin-kai, et cetera—and herein lies the problem. Without unification, we'll never reach the Olympics. Even today, the big karate organizations are still trying to unify criteria about kata and kumite. What really surprises me is that after all these years we still have the same problems. Nobody has realized what the problems are and prevented them.

Q: Weren't you one of the first who tried to make people understand that the Japanese don't necessarily have to be better than the Westerners in karate?
A: Yes, definitely. Let me tell you a very interesting story. I started to travel to Spain to teach, thanks to the former president of the Spanish National Karate Federation, Mr. Celestino Fernandez, and Prince Adam Czartoryski

Karate Masters

"Just because you are Japanese you are not going to be better than a European or an American. Fortunately, everybody understand this now. But 30 years ago, it was a different story. Now Americans think as Americans and Europeans think as Europeans—not as Japanese."

de Borbón, who happens to be the cousin of the King of Spain, his Royal Highness D. Juan Carlos de Borbón, a legitimate black belt in karate. I emphasize "legitimate" because he truly trained hard to reach that rank; it is not an honorary title. At that moment, the Spanish karate section was under the Spanish National Judo Federation. Due to my popularity in Europe, the Spanish representatives invited me to teach classes at the National Council for Karate Trainers. This was a course that black belts had to go through in order to get their official teaching license from the Spanish government. This way the quality of the instruction for the students was assured, not only in technical aspects of karate, but also in physical education and overall fitness curriculum.

Anyway, after one of the classes on theory, I decided to spar with a few of the instructors. I began with some of the top Spanish practitioners, and the Japanese started to laugh as I dominated my opponents. Then I decided that it was the turn of the Japanese, and I began to play with them. I did the same sweeps and other techniques that I did with the Spanish fighters. The rest of the teachers at the class thought I was crazy. They asked, "How can he be doing these things to the Japanese?" The answer was that I did it because I could.

Then I addressed the whole group and said: "As you can see, you are all equal here. Now let's start to work." President Celestino Fernandez told me that he was thinking, "What is this crazy French guy doing?" But deep down he told me that he was extremely happy. Karate is for everybody. Just because you are Japanese you are not going to be better than a European or an American. Fortunately, everybody understands this now. But 30 years ago it was a different story. Now Americans think as Americans and Europeans think as Europeans—not as Japanese.

Valera

Q: Speaking of D. Juan Carlos de Borbón, the King of Spain, did you ever train him?

A: Yes, I did. He mainly trained under Yashunari Ishimi, a 8th dan shito-ryu teacher from Madrid, but I taught him some extra classes. He had very good reach with his hands and although he needed a little bit of extra flexibility in the legs, he knew how to use them skillfully at *chudan* level. He is a great human being. When you talk to him, he doesn't act like a King; instead, he acts like a normal person. He makes you feel very good. He is famous in Spain for being very accessible to the people.

Q: Were you intimidated the first several times you met him?

A: Worse than intimidated. One time I didn't believe him! I was going to fight for the European title in Madrid against Angelo Jaquod. I was at my hotel resting when the phone rang. I picked it up and a voice said: "Dominique, it's me. Juan Carlos, the King of Spain." I thought that someone was playing a practical joke on me so I answered, "Sure you are. And I am Brigitte Bardot." He started laughing and continued: "No, it's true. Do you remember this and that?" And I said, "God! I'm sorry your Highness, I was sleeping." I was really embarrassed, and he kept laughing at the Brigitte Bardot thing. He wished me luck and said that he was going to be there that night. And he was. He arrived with all his security, watched the fight and came down to personally give me the trophy as European Champion. It was really great.

"I was going to fight for the European title in Madrid against Angelo Jaquod. I was at my hotel resting when the phone rang. I picked it up and a voice said: 'Dominique, it's me. Juan Carlos, the King of Spain.' I thought that someone was playing a practical joke on me so I answered, 'Sure you are. And I am Brigitte Bardot.'"

Q: You fought against Yoshinao Nanbu in the 1966 French Cup. What is your opinion of him?

A: Truthfully, I have the greatest respect for him. He came to Europe and instead of hiding behind the Japanese aura of mastery, he stepped onto the mat and competed in national tournaments. He was the first Japanese who

Karate Masters

"I'd rather hit a face than a wooden post. I see the use in practicing with a punching bag, but not with punching the makiwara. It is one of the stupidest things ever invented in karate. It ruins your hand and reverberates in your body, which is very bad for your internal organs."

really impressed me with his training. The first. Period. No other Japanese has impressed me the way he did. He was a true fighter and put himself to the test without hiding. My respect goes out to him to this very day.

Q: Who was your toughest opponent?
A: Gilbert Gruss, hands down. We faced each other in 10 finals of the French Championships. He is not only a great karate-ka but a great man, too.

Q: How has karate evolved technically in the last 20 years?
A: To begin with, let me tell you that karate is karate and will always be karate. A *gyaku-tsuki* hasn't changed because it can't change; it is the way the individual uses the technique that may change. You can use it offensively, as a counterattack, with a long step and slide on the spot or moving backward. You can always find some subtle details that affect the way you deliver the physical movement, but in the end, a good and solid *mae-geri* is a good and solid *mae-geri*, regardless if it was delivered in 1973 or in 2005.

Q: Did you ever use the makiwara?
A: Why? I don't see any point in using it. I'd rather hit a face than a wooden post. I see the use in practicing with a punching bag but not with punching the makiwara. It is one of the stupidest things ever invented in karate. It ruins your hand and reverberates in your body, which is very bad for your internal organs. I'm sorry if I hurt some people's feelings, but that's what I think.

Q: Do you practice kata?
A: They say kata is fighting against an imaginary opponent. Well, when I want to fight, I fight against a live opponent. That's why I don't believe in kata. It has its place in traditional karate, and I practiced them like everybody else, but I don't believe they teach you how to fight. Not at all. They have a reason to exist as a vehicle to re-transmit techniques from the ancestors. I like to watch them for their beauty, but as a training aid they are very, very outdated and outmoded. I have always preferred an opponent in front

of me. That to me is real training ... matching skills and minds.

Q: You are known for your specialty—foot-sweeps. What made you start using them?
A: I got the idea from ice-skating. I saw the way the skaters turn around, and I thought about using the movement against kicks. I devised certain ways of using a similar body movement, and every time someone threw a roundhouse kick to my face, he ended up on the floor. I have always enjoyed fighting from a separated distance; I don't like to be too close. Because of this, I began to use foot sweeps to unbalance my opponent and cut the reaction time when I was entering to punch. I felt more comfortable with leg techniques because they allow me to keep a greater distance. I'm physical, big and strong, so I kept the distance and used my kicks and foot-sweeps to get in and end that fight with a punch and a takedown. I was never bothered by the physical contact.

"I have always favored the idea of having a certain amount of contact. In fact, when top-level karate competitors punch to the chest in a European or world championship, they actually hit hard; it is not a joke; there is body contact. You should see the chest after receiving a punch; it is red."

Q: You never agreed with the idea of simply touching an opponent to get a point. Why?
A: If you going to score a point, then score a point. I have always favored the idea of having a certain amount of contact. In fact, when top-level karate competitors punch to the chest in a European or world championship, they actually hit hard; it is not a joke. There is body contact. You should see the chest after receiving a punch—it is red. I remember many people saying, "Oh, they simply touch." Then they enter a competition themselves and are not able to breathe after receiving a good reverse punch at *chudan* level. That is what karate is all about. If you score, then make contact. If you don't make contact, then it can't be counted as a point.

Unfortunately, that's what happens with punches at the face. The judges should do something about this because it is very confusing and it's getting worse. They can't give a point if the opponent doesn't touch you. In order to score, you should hit, and, of course, it is going to be contact. That is karate. It is not fencing. I don't mean you have to knock you opponent down, but

Karate Masters

"Competition is a challenge, and that's why it is interesting. It is a test of your own capabilities against a live opponent. You put yourself on the line. I always liked to win, but what I really enjoyed was the experience. That's what every competitor should focus on ... gaining experience from the competition—a constructive experience that helps you for the rest of your career."

there has to be a certain amount of contact. On the other side, I never liked that a guy could beat me in competition simply by touching my gi or grazing my hair. That is what happened at the 1975 World Championship in Long Beach, California, and that was one of the reasons why I left traditional karate competition.

Q: What happened?
A: It's been a long time ago and people still ask about that. There was a problem, and I hit a couple of officials. People talk more about that incident than about the fact that I was world champion. It's a pity. I think is better to talk about positive things; it is more interesting for young people.

Q: Why do you think competition is so good?
A: Competition is a challenge, and that's why it is interesting. It is a test of your own capabilities against a live opponent. You put yourself on the line. I always liked to win but what it really enjoyed was the experience. That's what every competitor should focus on ... gaining experience from the competition—a constructive experience that helps you for the rest of your career. In my competitive days, I always liked to work on spectacular and difficult technique instead of using the old boring *gyaku-tsuki* and *mae-geri* that everyone is fed up with seeing.

Q: Did you ever spar with any legendary American karate fighters?
A: Yes, I did. I had just arrived in the United States and went to a school to train. A translator there said that I was the current European champion. Then a man who was training there said, "Sure you are, buddy. We'll see about that!" He came up to me had and we sparred. He was very good and tried to knock me down, but I had a lot of mobility for a fighter of my weight. Anyway, after two or three attempts, I swept the guy, and he ended up on the

floor in front of everybody. He was shocked and said, "Man, nobody but nobody ever put my butt on the floor. I know you're coming from France, but what is that you just did?" I answered, "It's a special technique." And then I showed it to him. He was the great Thomas LaPuppet from the New York Fire Department. What a gentleman, what a great fighter and what an amazing human being. He passed away, and I truly treasure the time we spent together.

"My good friend Bill Wallace invited me to train with him, and I had the hardest time of my life. He did all his training and stretching routines on me and took me to a different level. The time I spent with Wallace was like spending four or five years training under other guys. I was a fast learner because I had natural physical ability, and I guess he enjoyed that part, too."

Q: How did you get involved in full-contact karate in the mid-1970s?
A: I wanted to put myself to the test—start from zero in another combative aspect of the martial arts. In full-contact I was nothing, and I ended up at the top. My good friend Bill Wallace invited me to train with him, and I had the hardest time of my life. He did all his training and stretching routines on me and took me to a different level. He showed me boxing hands and a different way of applying my kicks. The months I spent training with him were brutal. He had a very specific way of training and was very demanding. The time I spent with Wallace was like spending four or five years training under other guys. I was a fast learner because I had natural physical ability, and I guess he enjoyed that part, too.

Q: Did you have to unlearn a lot of things?
A: No. What it is really different is your mental approach to what you are doing. Now you are hitting for real, and you don't control your punches and kicks. You throw more combinations, but at the same time, you need to be able to take some punishment, too. You have to be ready to get hit and to hit your opponent. In traditional karate, because of the rules, you don't think you are going to get hit. Then bang! There you go! The opponent just hit your face, and you are bleeding. In full-contact, you know what you are getting into from the very first moment you step into the ring. I was hit many times

Karate Masters

"Karate is a journey; you have to keep looking and searching for things. Just make sure that whatever you are looking for makes you feel good inside. Because karate is, after all, simply the ability to uniquely express your inner thoughts with your exterior body."

because in karate you are taught to keep you head up; in boxing, you tuck your chin into your chest so you don't get knocked out. Your shoulders must be up for protection and the guard is totally different.

Q: What happened in your attempts to become world champion?
A: Against Jeff Smith in 1978, a few hours before the fight, some rules were changed. I was using a lot of sweeping techniques and out of the blue, one hour before the fight started, the judges decided sweeps were not allowed. I reacted to an attack unconsciously and I did one. I got a warning from the referee, and I realized that I had to knock Smith down to win that fight. I couldn't do it, but I smashed a roundhouse kick to the face that send his mouth protector to the seats fifth row.

My next title fight against Dan Macaruso was a nightmare! I had scheduled to fight against a heavyweight so I beefed up four pounds. All of a sudden that guy pulled out due to an injury. The organizers called and said that I could fight Dan Macaruso, but that I had to lose more than 25 pounds! They said that if I couldn't lose the weight that it was my problem, and they were going to look for another fighter. I bit the bullet and accepted. For the next five weeks I trained like crazy, not technically, but simply to lose weight. I was weak—really, really weak. I went to the weigh-in room, and the doctor asked me, "Are you OK? You look weak and pale." I was dead. To top it off, my specialty, the sweeps were not allowed, and they authorized the use of the spinning backfist, which was Macaruso's strong technique.

After the second round, I couldn't move my legs, let alone kick. It was very hard to give, up but I couldn't continue. They put me on an oxygen mask, but they did it too late, so some brain cells died, and I lost part of my normal motor skills. I had to regain muscle function through a lot of rehabilitation training. For almost three months, I couldn't walk or talk properly. And I had to do all this in front of my daughter. Like I said, a nightmare.

Q: What style are you practicing today?
A: When I have a gi on, I do traditional karate. But when I put the gloves on I hit, and I hit hard. Would you like to see? All kidding aside, the key is not what you are wearing. The competitive life of an athlete, either in traditional karate or in full-contact, is very short. It is a simple passage of time. Karate is much more than simply a tournament or a kickboxing bout.

Traditional karate should be designated as the first stage of full-contact. Karate can be practiced by amateurs, but full-contact or kickboxing requires a lot of training, not simply three hours per week. These more combative approaches are limited by the age of the practitioner. Karate can be practiced all your life but not kickboxing. Due to the rules in traditional karate competition, you are often not certain why you lost. In full-contact, however, the consequences of defeat hit you immediately and directly. Sparring is something that instructors should know how to introduce to their students. It has to be progressive and not be taught using the old swim or sink approach. Once you get hit a couple of times and don't get damaged, your confidence increases and you relax. That's when you get a lot out of your training. I love to spar hard. You liberate your body if you train hard!

Q: Where are you going in karate?
A: If I knew, I'd be there by now. Karate is a journey; you have to keep looking and searching for things. Just make sure that whatever you are looking for makes you feel good inside. Karate is, after all, simply the ability to uniquely express your inner thoughts with your exterior body. O

"Traditional karate should be designated as the first stage of full-contact. Karate can be practiced by amateurs, but full-contact or kickboxing requires a lot of training, not simply three hours per week. These more combative approaches are limited by the age of the practitioner. Karate can be practiced all your life but not kickboxing."

Tamas Weber

Budo on the Battlefield

A DECORATED VETERAN OF THE FRENCH FOREIGN LEGION, TAMAS WEBER HAS USED KARATE-DO TO PREVAIL IN LIFE-OR-DEATH COMBAT SITUATIONS AND ALSO TO DEAL WITH EVERYDAY LIFE. FEW PEOPLE IN THE HISTORY OF KARATE ARE MORE RESPECTED THAN TAMAS WEBER. POSSESSING A COMPLETE KNOWLEDGE OF KARATE LORE AND EXPERIENCE, SHIHAN WEBER HAS PUT HIS LIFE ON THE LINE ON MANY OCCASIONS, IN MANY WARS, WHILE SERVING WITH THE FRENCH FOREIGN LEGION. HIS BATTLEFIELD EXPERIENCE IS PUNCTUATED BY THE MANY BULLET SCARS ON HIS BODY. IT IS IN HARD MEN LIKE HIM THAT THE TRUE CONCEPT OF LIFE AND DEATH IN THE MARTIAL ARTS TAKES FORM. HIS KARATE-DO TRAINING HAS BEEN HEAVILY INFLUENCED BY HIS APPROACH TO THE BATTLEFIELD; AND ALTHOUGH HE APPRECIATES THE SPORTIVE ASPECTS OF THE MARTIAL ARTS, KARATE FOR HIM IS SIMPLY *BUDO*. AS A MASTER OF THE ART, THE EXTERIOR STRENGTH AND INTERNAL POWER HE DISPLAYS ARE UNDENIABLY APPARENT. HOWEVER, HIS WARRIOR SKILLS ARE COMPLEMENTED BY HIS DEEP LOVE OF FAMILY AND A GENUINE CONCERN FOR THE STUDENTS UNDER HIS TUTELAGE. AS ONE OF THE HIGHEST RANKING MASTERS IN THE WESTERN WORLD, TAMAS WEBER IS RESPONSIBLE FOR COACHING MANY OF THE OUTSTANDING CHAMPIONS OF EUROPE. CURRENTLY LIVING IN SWEDEN, BUT POSSESSING SPIRITUAL QUALITIES THAT CROSS ALL SOCIAL AND POLITICAL BOUNDARIES, TAMAS WEBER IS A TRUE ICON OF WHAT REAL *BUDO* SHOULD BE.

Q: How long have you been practicing karate-do?
A: I started my training in the martial arts in November of 1951, more than a half-century ago. My first teacher was Masafumi Kawata, who was *nidan* at that time; the highest rank in those days was *godan*. Straightaway, I had a good feeling for the art, but it was never easy for me. After some time of hard and dedicated training, my personal understanding and knowledge of the art increased very much. The *kata, bunkai* and *kumite* aspects became part of a complete new dimension, compared to my previous understanding. I improved my technical skills and developed more speed and power, and a mature way to move. This was much better for focusing power and controlling distance. Today, my karate is like a tidal wave— with high-explosive power mixed harmoniously with the calm of the ocean. I strive to

Karate Masters

"I don't think that a pure style has ever existed in real terms during the history of karate. Like painting or writing, nothing can be described as a "pure" art; everything is a combination of several influences."

develop deeper and more focused types of movements based on internal strength and not muscle power.

Q: Was your early karate training difficult?

A: I remember when we were training *ippon-kumite* (free sparring) very late at night; we would nearly fall asleep. To wake up, we kept a bucket of cold water in the middle of the small dojo. Every 15 minutes or so we each dipped our head inside the bucket to avoid falling asleep. Despite dripping water all over the floor, we kept on training. Often the dojo was in half darkness. The purpose was to give us an instinct and feel against unknown attackers. We were totally devoted to the art; the attitude and approach to training was very different than what you see today.

Q: With all the technical changes during the last 30 years, do you think there are still pure styles of karate?

A: I don't think that a pure style has ever existed in real terms during the history of karate. Like painting or writing, nothing can be described as a "pure" art; everything is a combination of several influences. You often have a strong and charismatic personality who serves as a basic initiator and reference of a particular style, but if you compare the previous forms performed by the old masters, you will find a huge difference between their way of interpreting the techniques and the way the modern karate is perform today. For instance, there are now very deep stances and unnecessary movements with no meaning at all; these movements have been added simply to make a more visually attractive performance. In the old times, the main purpose of the art was self-defense, and it was based on each individual's capability to adapt karate to his body structure, understanding and knowledge. Karate was a highly efficient fighting tool that used the entire body as a weapon. Because of its killing efficiency and the great danger of misuse, it became necessary to restrict abuse. For this reason, a set of strict rules of honor, respect and humility were established. Karate today has lost part of is fighting fluidity; the stances are more like movie choreography ... very deep and stiff with a limited correlation to practical fighting.

I sincerely think that natural development and adaptation is the natural essence of all life on earth; why should karate be any different? Every sensei has his own interpretation. This interpretation is transmitted to the students who, hopefully, will soon take their teacher's approach and raise the art to a higher level. It is a fact that the execution of techniques and movements have special flavors peculiar to each style. However, it is not the physical difference of technique that makes the distinction in style; instead, it is the mind of the student. The thinking and strategy dictate the technique to be used, which in turn requires a special way to initiate the application of power suited to the tactics. It is this means of applying strategy in combat that creates different styles.

"Karate today has lost part of is fighting fluidity; the stances are more like movie choreography— very deep and stiff with a limited correlation to practical fighting. I sincerely think that natural development and adaptation is the natural essence of all life on earth; why should karate be any different?"

Q: What is your opinion of full-contact karate, kickboxing and no-holds-barred?

A: Basically, kickboxing and full-contact karate are very demanding sports. You need a high level of physical conditioning, but they are still sports with rules, gloves, referees, and judges. In the true art of combat, there is only one rule—to defeat your adversary as fast and efficiently as possible. The NHB events are very hard, violent and physically demanding. For the audience, it is like the Coliseum was for Rome. There was a reason why the Romans had the gladiators fighting and there is a reason why these kind of events fit into our society today. The smell of blood makes the audience feel the savagery of combat without actually bleeding or suffering pain from

Karate Masters

"Kata *has nothing to do with the acrobatic performances that we see today. Changing the technique to make it more appealing to the judges and increasing the breathing volume to pretend to have more* kime *is a joke to the real art of karate-do."*

wounds themselves. They use these events to release the aggression they have inside and can express their violent feelings about their home and working lives. Like the gladiator, the purposes of the fighters in this brutal game is to survive the match and make money. I wonder if all this is really worthwhile, though. Are we getting something of real spiritual value out of it or just watching Roman gladiators without the lions?

Q: Do you think Western karate has caught up with Japanese karate?
A: In the sportive aspect, definitively yes. The European teams are much better in kumite than their Japanese counterparts. However, as far as understanding the principles and essence behind the art, probably not, besides a few rare and exceptionally knowledgeable and experienced Westerners. Unfortunately, when a Westerner wins a world championship, he immediately thinks he is better than the Japanese in the art of karate-do—not in the sport but in the art. This is not the case. Many Western kumite champions don't really know how to execute a perfect zenkutsu-dachi, for example. In the kata aspect, just because a Westerner wins a world title it doesn't mean he is better than a Japanese or Okinawan performing kata. Kata has nothing to do with the acrobatic performances that we see today. Changing the technique to make it more appealing to the judges and increasing the breathing volume to pretend to have more kime is a joke to the real art of karate-do. In the martial arts, you can learn a simple movement quickly, but knowing the correct usage of the body in relation to the movement takes a few years.

Q: So you don't think of karate as simply a sport?
A: Karate is not, and will never be, simply a sport. If we allow that to happen, then we'll be responsible for a major crime. Of course, the scale and range of techniques will always include the techniques needed to score in tournament *kata* or *kumite*. But karate is a martial art and a martial art

includes many lethal techniques such as the finger-jabs to the eyes and attacks to the throat that are very valuable self-defense weapons. This makes it too dangerous to become only a sport. The bottom line is that karate-do is a violent art. Because of the times of peace we are living in, however, a part of that art can be used as an enjoyable sport activity. The important point here, though, is not to lose the direction and real meaning of the training.

"Karate is not, and will never be, simply a sport. If we allow that to happen, then we'll be responsible for a major crime. The important point here, though, is not to lose the direction and real meaning of the training."

Q: What connection do you see between the art of karate-do, budo in general and the life-and-death battlefield environment?
A: Like on the battlefield, a warrior should be well-prepared for the coming battle by good training basics. When the first explosions detonate and the first bullets whistle in the air, there is a short moment of surprise and stress before you can assess the situation, control your fear and go to immediate action. This control is only possible because of your military and technical skill, your inner strength and the confidence in your own knowledge. Reflexive action is based on systematized training learned through a wide range of drills and exercises. The martial artist, before a fight begins, should feel like a warrior in the battlefield and have a short moment of stress mixed with fear. Then when you control your fear and stress, you turn it into a source of a positive energy and use it as a power source to neutralize and destroy the challenger or the target. All of your internal power and all of your physical energy should be released in an attack or counterattack. This ability to move efficiently and quickly, and adapt to a combat situation, will depend very much from your preparation, basic training, knowledge and self-confidence in your capabilities. This is what is incorrectly called "reflexes."

There is no difference, in principle, between the martial artist and the soldier on the battlefield. The only difference is the goal for the actions and

"There is no difference, in principle, between the martial artist and the soldier on the battlefield. The only difference is the goal for the actions and the tools used in combat. The warrior, like the soldier or the true martial artist, feels the same stress and fear before he starts the battle."

the tools used in combat. The warrior, like the soldier or the true martial artist, feels the same stress and fear before he starts the battle. But when the combat action begins, the technical skill, the readiness to go to action, the first move and the readiness for an ultimate sacrifice of life is the difference between victory and defeat.

Q: Did your experiences as a soldier help you to understand the concept of "one killing blow" in karate?
A: I sincerely think that the "one killing blow" concept is one of the myths of the martial arts. On the battlefield, nobody know exactly how an enemy was killed. In an assault, everybody fires in all directions and hundreds of bullets have to be fired for one kill. Why does the martial artist or karate-ka think they can kill with one blow when bodyguards and police officers always fire two bullets to the chest? Of course, it might happen that one blow can kill—but it is not guaranteed—and what will happen if it doesn't? You will get killed in return. *Makiwara* training and a fast and strong technique do not guarantee that you will efficiently deliver a lethal blow to your target. The way you train is the way you fight; and if the way you train is traditional, chances are the way you fight will be effective.

Q: Do you think that dealing with a life-and-death situation changes the whole concept of karate as a sport?
A: Yes. The basic concept of karate is to use all the mental and the physical abilities of the human body as a tool for self-defense. To achieve that goal, an arsenal of techniques was created and combined and the human body was transformed and reshaped by an intensive and systematical training method into a lethal weapon. The purpose was to severely defeat any challenger with a graded response from a harmless disarm up to a lethal blow.

Karate was too dangerous to be taught to everyone because it could easily be misused. This is why it was necessary to frame the training with a code of values, honor, humility and respect. This code is similarly to the military and *bushido* code. Karate was a way of life—a life of training and devoted commitment with great respect for the sensei.

The purpose of sport, in contrast, is to score. To score, you need a very limited arsenal of non-lethal techniques authorized by the rules. You can only score if the judge agrees to give you the points; the criteria is often very subjective

"The basic concept of karate is to use all the mental and the physical abilities of the human body as a tool for self-defense. Karate is a way of life ... a life of training and devoted commitment with great respect for the sensei."

and is a game involving you, your opponent, the judge and the referees. Today you are on top, and tomorrow you are history. You will never know if your techniques will work for real; it is not a way of life ... just a game for children. The rules change not to make the fighter more efficient in combat, but rather to make the competitions more attractive to the spectators.

The whole picture of karate has evolved in two totally different directions. One direction is a sport, and the other is trying to keep the old concept of martial art. These two different and distant concepts can't be evaluated with the same criteria. Sport misuses the karate traditions when the competitors insist that they are practicing a martial art. The titles and the medals should be enough. Why should sport fighters keep a ranking system related to more formal achievement, technical skill and combat fighting experiences? For me, personally, after my experiences on the battlefield, it is very difficult to take the powerless scoring techniques seriously. I feel that I am not a part of that game. I like a more realistic and useful approach to combat, but I am a dinosaur.

Karate Masters

"After my experiences on the battlefield, it is very difficult to take the powerless scoring techniques seriously. I feel that I am not a part of that game. I like a more realistic and useful approach to combat, but I am a dinosaur."

Q: You are one of the highest-ranking karate practitioners in the Western world; do you feel that you still have more to learn?

A: Rank has nothing to do with the idea of learning. The higher your rank, the more time you have to dedicate to the art to reach higher levels of understanding. I think that in any subject you should analyze the past to avoid the previous mistakes. Stagnation does not develop human skill in any field or science. There is no limitation in the understanding or technical development you can achieve in karate. The teacher should always try to improve his skill level by gaining new experiences, more knowledge and a deeper understanding of what he is doing. When you just transmit your knowledge to the students, you may be losing part of your sharpness and the necessary physical condition you need to master the art. Therefore, it's paramount that the instructor dedicate a certain amount of time to his personal training and not mistake his teaching time as his training time.

A good karate-do instructor teaches the students the way to teach themselves how to take all the elements of the art and weave them into their own experience and self-realization. The teacher, of course, cannot kick or punch for the student; he can only show, tell and do everything necessary to make the student aware of what punching and kicking is. We live in a world in which everything seems to be done for us, but the art of karate-do is not that way. It doesn't follow those rules. In fact, it's just the opposite. It's extremely important that the instructor has a firm grasp of all the fundamental elements of his style. His understanding should be deep enough to interrelate all the philosophical and technical principles of the art and show the student how to incorporate those into his training and life. This will take him to a higher level as a teacher himself. A good instructor is not greedy, and his goal should be to make his students better than himself. That's the real challenge. He should love the success of his students, not be threatened by it.

I have always devoted time for my personal development and my private training. I like to push beyond my physical limitations and go further in my research of the relationship between muscle power, technical skill and devastating concentration. In a way, it is a great fight between the inner part of myself and the natural aging process. It's a challenge between my body and my spirit. Time will tell who is the winner!

"I have always devoted time for my personal development and my private training. I like to push beyond my physical limitations and go further in my research of the relationship between muscle power, technical skill and devastating concentration."

Q: What are the major changes in the art since you began training?

A: The art didn't change as much as the people did. The mentality is different these days when compared to what we used to have 20, 30 or 40 years ago. Before, the world of karate was very mysterious. It was a strange form of superpower that provided skill to face any challenge and confront anyone earth. The people who were attracted to the training were stronger physically and mentally. Everyone was ready to undergo many years of hard practice and have a great respect for the sensei. Today, the practitioners are only interested in the physical appearances, superficial knowledge, and a fast black belt guaranteed and signed by a famous teacher who is only known in his small city. More often than not, that "master" promoted himself to higher degree. The rank and not the knowledge become a major tool for the economical competition between the different dojo.

Karate Masters

"Today, the practitioners are only interested in the physical appearances, superficial knowledge, and a fast black belt guaranteed and signed by a famous teacher who is only known in his small city. The rank and not the knowledge become a major tool for the economical competition between the different dojo."

Q: With whom would you like to have trained?
A: I regret the fact that I never trained under the supervision of Motobu Choki. I grieve the fact that Fujiwara disappeared in the early 1970s. I truly believe that a lot of knowledge has been lost, not in a technical sense, but in a more philosophical one. Losing these old masters is not about losing an unknown *kata* or secret application, but about losing the right training spirit, the correct attitude and the proper state of mind to train karate-do.

Q: Do you think it is necessary to engage in freefighting to achieve good self-defense skills?
A: Free sparring in the dojo gives you the opportunity to improve, in a practical way, your technical knowledge. Of course, you have to really understand what you are doing. You can't lie to yourself. All psychological conditions are not the same in sparring as in a real situation, in which panic and stress are at a very different level. But it is true that freefighting is the closest to a real fighting situation you can come to in the dojo. Just like hard military exercises are not like real war, but they are useful because they bring a certain kind of experience, feeling, and a knowledge that prepares you mentally and physically to adapt yourself to a real war situation. The truth is that you never know how you are going to react until that moment arrives. In karate-do, *kumite* is very important for the development of efficient, economic footwork, precise alignment, and fast, fluid action. It also trains the acceleration of body parts to deliver maximum power and gives you a highly refined sense of timing and rhythm for the development of proficient combat skills that might be used in a self-defense situation.

Q: What is your opinion on mixing karate styles?

A: Every style and every instructor has a unique character, profile, personality and way to teach. To be a sensei means having the ability to transfer your knowledge to students in an appropriate way. The emphasis of every particular style is mostly due to a charismatic leader and his capability to emerge among the others and pave the way for his approach and concept. So it was the case for Funakoshi Gichin, Mabuni Kenwa and others. All of them—with their own way of understanding—have contributed to a common karate history that brought benefits to the entire karate community. No style stands alone today like in 1922. What we know about the history of each style is a series of tales with few eyewitnesses and foggy memories. What is the truth? Every student starts his own history with his first sensei. For him, the style of his teacher is of no meaning at all. What is more important is the student's physical compatibility with the characteristics of the chosen method. For the practitioners, the style is an abstract reference with very little value beside the fact that you will feel safe when you belong to a group that uses a reference code and a emblem or symbol to tell you apart from others. This belonging is something usual for all of mankind, and its role in the martial arts world is simply a reflection of our society.

"The emphasis of every particular style is mostly due to a charismatic leader and his capability to emerge among the others and pave the way for his approach and concept. No style stands alone today like in 1922."

Q: What is your philosophical basis?

A: My philosophical basis is very simple, and I understand it may not fit into everyone's mind. Through the hardship of training, through the continuous challenge against your personal physical and psychological limits, through pain and discipline, every individual develops self-control and an internal harmony that leads to a higher quality of life. The discipline in the dojo, and the way you learn to respect the rules and your partner or opponent, will be reflected in the way you handle your private life outside of the dojo. It will give mankind a noble attitude in society. I believe that karate gives everyone a code of honor that can and should be used in his approach to life.

Q: Did you have a memorable experience that inspired your training?
A: One of the karate experiences I remember most is when I came back from the war. All my friends in Paris were talking about a new master who had just arrived. They described him as fast, strong, impregnable and very impressive. I was waiting to see some Japanese giant—a kind of superman from the *rising sun* empire. When I came to the dojo, I didn't find that at all. I only saw a very short man with a massive body structure that made him look shorter than he actually was. I was totally disoriented because of my preconceptions about things. That man was recognized today as one of the greatest karate masters in the world, and he is a true icon of what tradition, science and evolution means within the art of the "empty hand." His name was Taiji Kase. Enough said.

Q: What is the meaning of karate-do for you?
A: The meaning of karate-do and budo is a way of practice with no real end or beginning; it is a perpetual stream of conceptions and principles. Everyone should try to read and educate himself about the art of *budo*. Historical facts, geographical influences, style particularities, different philosophies and correct attitudes are all very important things to learn if one wants a complete education in karate as a way of life.

Q: What are the most important qualities of a good karate-ka?
A: I think that the most important aspects for a karate-ka is humility, respect and devotion to the art. The strength should be inside yourself and not a attribute you display in front of others to show off. You only reveal your strength when needed. Endless training is good, but rational training is much better and will help to reach higher goals in the art and in the sport, as well. Karate is a lifetime commitment. It is not something to be done for a few years and then quit, like they do in the universities in Japan or in the Western world after getting the rank of black belt. I understand that there is an enormous gap between that philosophy of *budo* and our modern way of life, but everything should be enjoyable and not evaluated in terms of money. Unfortunately, karate is a very demanding activity that requires a lot of involvement and dedication if you really want to reach the higher levels

of the art ... and it returns no money at all. Very soon, training becomes one of the last priorities and people leave. The fear factor is important in training, and the student should be able to deal with it in a positive manner. Feel it but control it in such a way that you'll be able to do great things.

Q: What is the future of karate-do?
A: The future is very a big uncertainty, but I firmly believe that true karate will survive our generation; the question is for how long? It's sad, but in many ways I represent an old guard of instructors who accept the new direction the art is taking as a sport, but yet are struggling to keep the old traditions and principles of *budo* on the battlefield alive. Karate-do is something that we own ourselves. It doesn't belong to any association or federation. It's ours. It becomes part of our own texture, learned in the bones, a kind of fixture of heart and body in cooperation with the mind. Karate is a vehicle which, used in the proper way, will set us free as individuals because we do it ourselves and for ourselves ... allowing us to know ourselves and understand other people as well. We must continue on as students and teachers because, in the end, the candle is not there to illuminate itself. O

"The discipline in the dojo, and the way you learn to respect the rules and your partner or opponent, will be reflected in the way you handle your private life outside the dojo. It will give mankind a noble attitude in society."

Goshi Yamaguchi
Protecting the Legacy

DESPITE HIS MANY INTERESTS AND GOALS, GOSHI'S FIRST LOVE IS KARATE. HE CONSIDERS IT AN ART AND ATTRIBUTES ALL HIS SUCCESS IN LIFE TO WHAT HE CALLS THE GREAT "EXPERIENCE OF KARATE PRACTICE." UNLIKE SOME INSTRUCTORS WHO PROFESS TO BE EXPERTS, YAMAGUCHI SENSEI MINIMIZES THE SENSATIONAL AND MELODRAMATIC ASPECTS OF KARATE. "KARATE IS A SKILL THAT REQUIRES TIME AND THOUGHT," HE SAYS. "ONE WHO INTENDS TO USE IT AGGRESSIVELY IS ONLY DISILLUSIONING HIMSELF. HUMILITY AND SELF-RESTRAINT ARE VERY IMPORTANT IN TRUE KARATE-DO." WHEN IN ACTION, HIS MOVEMENTS ARE RELAXED, YET ONE CAN SENSE THE UNBELIEVABLE SPEED AND FORCE AT THE TERMINATION OF EACH TECHNIQUE. THE APPARENT DESTRUCTIVE POWER OF EACH ACTION IS OVERSHADOW BY THE BEAUTY OF THE CONTINUOUS FLOWING MOVEMENT THAT IS TYPICAL OF THE GOJU-KAI SCHOOL. THIS CALMLY FORCEFUL KARATE SENSEI RECOGNIZES THE DIFFICULTY OF DESCRIBING THE ART IN A CLEAR-CUT FORMAT FOR EVERYBODY TO UNDERSTAND. "IT IS EXTREMELY HARD TO TELL PEOPLE WHAT KARATE IS BECAUSE IT IS SOMETHING THAT MUST BE EXPERIENCED TO BE UNDERSTOOD—NOT JUST DISCUSSED. WHAT YOU LEARN IN THE ART OF KARATE CAN ALWAYS BE USED IN YOUR DAILY LIFE."

Q: Shihan, how old were you when you started karate training, and what are some of your memories of that time?
A: I started karate at eight years old. At that time, we had no class for the children, so we trained with the adults, and the classes started late at night. What I remember most is that I could not eat supper if I didn't take class. So, every night I had to train or my parents wouldn't give me food! When I was in high school, I thought about how to commit to the art and study karate better. It was very stressful growing up as the son of one of the most famous Japanese karate-ka, Grandmaster Gogen Yamaguchi, because everybody said, "You are the son of Gogen Yamaguchi." So, I couldn't choose my own life. At that time, I was under a lot of self-imposed pressure all the time. I'd think things like, "I have to do my training; I have to be strong." Actually, this was very good for me, because my brother kept reminding me or menacing me about what things would be like when I was grown up.

Karate Masters

"What I remember most is that I could not eat supper if I didn't take class. So, every night I had to train or my parents wouldn't give me food! It was very stressful growing up as the son of one of the most famous Japanese karate-ka, Grandmaster Gogen Yamaguchi, because everybody said, 'You are the son of Gogen Yamaguchi.' So, I couldn't choose my own life."

Q: As the son of Gogen Yamaguchi, was the training tougher for you?
A: Yes, of course. When I was a child, I couldn't say "daddy" all the time. I had to say "sensei" or "*hanshi.*" It was always something like that. It was not like father and son; it was always teacher and student. It was difficult.

Q: Have you ever studied any other martial art?
A: Yes, I have. I did Chinese kung-fu. When I was a child, my brother also taught me judo, and I did kendo, too.

Q: In regards to karate, are you going to bring up your son like your father brought up you?
A: No, it will be quite different. That type of relationship is very difficult, so I have changed it. When I grew up, however, it was OK because I had older brothers, and everyone had it the same way.

Q: How about outside the dojo. What was life like with your father and mother?
A: My mother loved me and always took care of me. I believe my father loved me very much, but he didn't show it. So, I have no memories about playing with my father. I always had to say, "Good morning, teacher." When we walked together, I had to step back from him. That is what it was like. It was not like daddy and children.

Q: Your father went to Manchuria (a mountainous region of northeastern China) during World War II. What do you know about his experience and why he went there?
A: At that time, I was not born, so I know what my father told me. One of the reasons he went there was to see General Ishihara, a very famous general and shogun. He wanted my father go with him to Manshu (Manchuria). His group was a special organization—not the military—and it was throughout the Manchuria country. He had a very special position. You could say that it was underground, and he got news or intelligence in this manner. Of course, he taught karate, so he had good connections for Manchurian

Chinese kung-fu and different martial artists he had taken to Japan. Everyone was able to communicate with each other, so they used to demonstrate the respective arts. As a result, on two occasions, the general took members from China to Japan.

Q: When you started your karate training, who was your first instructor?
A: My brother taught me very well at the outset. When I started in class, of course, my father taught, but my brother had already taught me well.

Q: Was your father a Shinto priest, and what did that mean?
A: Yes, he was. A high position, too. He liked to meditate, and he did this every morning. He also liked to pray, because Shinto is, as most Japanese people know it, like a culture. He also liked to use Shinto ideas in his karate.

"I believe my father loved me very much, but he didn't show it. So, I have no memories about playing with my father. I always had to say, 'Good morning, teacher.'"

Q: How did his Shinto spirituality and practice influence you and the goju-kai today?
A: A lot, of course, but these are different ideas. He liked to use Shinto in all aspects of his training, but he didn't say that everybody must do that, because this [Shinto] is a religion. He believed everyone had a right to his own religion, so he never told anyone he had to do it. Some people liked to follow him. I studied with him, but the influence of Shinto is not the same as training in goju-kai. Shinto reflected his personal ideas.

Q: How and when was he introduced to yoga?
A: He knew a very famous yogi, but I don't remember the name. I do know that he was from India. In Japan, there was a big organization that studied yoga, and my father had good connections through that group. So, he studied with the instructor from India and one from Japan for a long time.

Q: Did the yoga influence goju-kai? If so, where were the influences?
A: Yes, of course, he liked to put it all together. The yoga and the Shinto, too. This was his idea. We believe yoga is good for your breathing, and this

Karate Masters

"We believe yoga is good for your breathing, and this comes in handy when you are working on your breathing. In the goju classes, my father taught the students how to do breathe properly ... as they would learn in yoga. If there's good breathing in yoga, there's good breathing in karate."

comes in handy when you are working on your breathing. In the goju classes, my father taught the students how to do breathe properly ... as they would learn in yoga. If there's good breathing in yoga, there's good breathing in karate.

Q: Is that where *ibuki* breathing comes from?
A: No, goju breathing comes originally from Okinawa and there might be some Chinese influence, too. My father called it ibuki because the Okinawans and yoga heavily influenced him. We didn't say ibuki.

Q: How would you describe the state of goju-kai around the world?
A: Let me start by saying that I'm the president of the *All-Japan Karate-do Goju-kai* and of the *International Karate-do Goju-kai*. We have blocks in Oceania, Europe, South America, Africa and North America. Goju-kai also has many members. Outside of Japan, the Australian block has the oldest history.

Q: In the martial arts, we see many styles split and instructors break away from their masters. Why does this happen?
A: Some people say that this natural, and it follows from the concept of *shu-ha-rei*. "Shu" means that you study well continuously and "ha" means ideas. Finally, "rei" means to leave. As you know, we have many different styles of martial arts. Some martial arts start within one group. Then people have different ideas so they make many groups. This is the truth. If you teach well and maintain a good responsibility over your school, you can keep it attractive for all the members, even for some who are considering starting different groups. My father had many students and some formed new groups, some of which are now gone. But my father agreed that they could start or go their own way. Mas Oyama Sensei, of kyuokushin, is an example of one who broke away. He was a member of goju-kai a long time ago. He and my father discussed many things and expressed many ideas. Of course, Oyama Sensei studied goju-ryu extensively, but one of his ideas was to start his own group, which my father approved. As a result, he started kyokushin. Even now there is still a very good friendship between the groups.

Q: What is the most important job of an instructor?
A: Well, of course, he has to teach well technically, but he also has to teach about life, such as how people can do well for their country and how they can contribute or work toward world peace. Every instructor must develop his own, good personal style.

Q: Some instructors who break away to create their own style don't have a complete understanding of "do" or neglect it in their teaching. To a student who isn't being fed the philosophy of the martial arts, what would be your advice?
A: If an instructor focuses only on the technical and doesn't think about this side [philosophy] anymore, a student might have to think about moving to another instructor. In karate, however, you can learn many things from technical training. Not only can you learn technique, because karate is self-defense, you can also mature, grow up and learn to become your own person without copying someone else. In goju-kai, many instructors stress technical training, but there aren't enough who focus on proper spirit for self-development. If there were, there would be more harmony in the teaching. Somebody mean by how good the teacher, the suggestions from the teacher.

"My father had many students and some formed new groups, some of which are now gone. But my father agreed that they could start or go their own way. Mas Oyama Sensei, of kyuokushin, is an example of one who broke away. He was a member of goju-kai a long time ago."

Q: What does karate-do mean to you?
A: Karate-do, in my personal view and in my own way, means you should study the art from a more technical perspective. If you do this, it enables you to find out who is stronger. Whether I am stronger than you is irrelevant. What is important is whether I am stronger. This happens all the time. Sometimes I may want to escape, and I may want to look after just myself, but that is not correct. If I do karate, I have to be big, all the time. So karate is good for friendship and personality. It's also good for communication between countries and groups … in a sports way. So I believe karate-do is good for training and for self-defense.

Karate Masters

"In karate, however, you can learn many things from technical training. Not only can you learn technique, because karate is self-defense, you can also mature, grow up and learn to become your own person without copying someone else."

Q: Is the emphasis of your teaching on sport karate or the traditional art?

A: We don't need to separate sport and the traditional element. Many young people like to have a chance to participate in sport karate competition, and it is very good for them. In the process, they make friends and grow up. But people cannot neglect the mental aspect of training. It's just as important as the technical aspect. It's important to note that being a champion does not mean that the individual is the best [all-around] competitor. Of course, in sport, the champion is on top of the mountain. When you talk about traditional karate, however, the objective [top of the mountain] is not that at all. This confuses people. Karate-do is more than just how well you can do for yourself personally. It is also how well you interact with the public.

Q: Do you ever see karate becoming an Olympic sport?

A: The idea is good, but if it becomes an Olympic sport, I'm concerned that something [traditional ideals] will be lost. Ideally, we'd find a way to get it into the Olympics and maintain the ideals. The instructors and organizers have to look at both ways. In Olympic competition, people think of one thing and one thing only, and that is how they can get a medal. Of course, the Olympic games are very good for contributing to world peace, but we need much more respect for the other things. The art is much more than training, competing, winning a medal and setting a record. Some practitioners who win medals are very good, but if they only think only about competition, they are not thinking about their attitude and manners.

Q: Do you encourage your students to compete?

A: Of course, because I was an international referee. I also think it would be good for the art to become an Olympic sport. When I teach, I teach both the way of sport and the traditional martial art.

Q: Did you compete in your younger days?
A: Yes I did. When I was young, I participated in kata and kumite. I wanted to try more, but my father said, "One day you have to change. If you participate in tournaments, it's likely that you are always thinking about how you lost or how you can win." So my father told me to stop competing. My last tournament was a goju-kai tournament.

Q: Was your father in favor of sport karate?
A: I don't think so. He didn't like it because when he started training for kumite or real sparring, my brother started *jiyu-kumite*. At that time, my father didn't think about competition like we are doing now. I think he would have accepted the idea of training in traditional karate first and then competition later. If you do competition karate, you are not using real karate. In competition, you are only seeing who is faster and who scores the point.

"Karate-do, in my personal view and in my own way, means you should study the art from a more technical perspective. If you do this, it enables you to find out who is stronger."

Q: Have events like K-1, Pride and the UFC affected the martial arts?
A: Any martial art sport must have rules. In K-1, people fight to see who is the strongest. I don't mean to say that this is bad. In fact, it is OK for some different groups. But goju-kai is nothing like these events. We must throw controlled punches. Of course, in training, we study how to throw a hard punch with the intent of killing. But of course, we do not actually do that. Now there is peace in the world, and I don't believe we need to show how strong we can kick and punch in the ring. We won't stop anyone else from doing that, but that is a different philosophy than what we have.

Q: For the last decade, there has been a growing trend among students to cross-train in different arts. How do you feel about this?
A: This is a good thing. Of course, some people say you should stick with only one art … whether that is karate or some other martial art. But my father told me that it is not good to concentrate on just one art. In the budo, a long time ago, every samurai could study many different ways. My father felt the same way.

Karate Masters

"I also think it would be good for the art to become an Olympic sport. When I teach, I teach both the way of sport and the traditional martial art."

Q: In terms of self-defense, does goju-kai have any particular strengths or weaknesses?
A: Although goju is very dangerous, my brother taught me the art is not for fighting in the street. Nevertheless, we have some other techniques ... not just punching and kicking. I think goju has many techniques that make it good for self-defense. As you advance in your studies, you learn the more advanced bunkai from the kata.

Q: How have the martial arts and karate training changed?
A: Some have maintained the traditional way, but karate came from China and then it went to Okinawa, where it was changed. Then it went to Japan, where it became modern. Now we can learn many different martial arts. As the training used to be, we do not only follow the traditional way. So goju has the old way in it, but then tournaments came along. Because tournaments have high kicks, we now have to teach high kicks for competition training. Without the competition influence, goju does not have high kicks ... only low kicks. So I think we've changed most for the sports angle.

Q: Do you feel kata is still necessary in training?
A: Kata is of the utmost importance. When people study freely—everything, including kata—gets changed. Kata is like the culture for this school. Goju has goju ideas, and these are in the kata. That is why we must study one standard. Afterwards, we can do more development. If there were no kata, there would be no standards. We would have fighting in the street. Practitioners must train in kata every day. Sparring is about somebody having strong muscles; a strong body can be good, but kata is different. You need to train [to improve]. Kata is about the battle within yourself. This is why everybody can start karate and study little by little. Sometimes people think, "I'm a good fighter." Well, that's not enough. In kata, nobody attacks. It's just about your-

self. When I show myself, this is fighting myself. When a beginner's kata is not so good, it's like his opponent is not so strong. When they advance to green or brown belt, of course, they are much better than before. Now they have to show that their kata is much better than before.

Q: Has bunkai, the practical application of kata, always been a part of the goju system?
A: Okinawa has always had bunkai ideas, but at that time there were only some kata techniques. In goju-kai, we used to do all the movements in the application. Of course, this is not the only way; some people have different ideas. Now in goju-kai we decided to standardize it in a format. Of course, when grading for instructors, we ask, "Show your application for some kata."

"Kata is of the utmost importance. When people study freely—everything, including kata—gets changed. Kata is like the culture for this school. Goju has goju ideas, and these are in the kata. That is why we must study one standard."

Q: Like a "textbook" of the system, are all the techniques of goju contained within the kata?
A: Yes, and some goju instructors came up with this idea. They studied many things and put them in the kata. So kata, as you said, is like a technical training textbook.

Q: What are your plans for the future of goju-kai?
A: It's not only important to make many branches and grow, but it's important that Gogen Yamaguchi was the founder of these. Of course, I hope in the future there are many members and many branches, and I hope people will study the ideas from Gogen Yamaguchi and myself. We have the WKF, which is like a sports organization that members from all the various countries can enter. Thus, they can grow up all together. But goju-kai is like a private organization, so everyone has a different reason for putting on tournaments and winning is not always the main thing. It's not so important if you take a medal, but it's how we keep going.

Q: What is the biggest problem currently facing the martial arts?
A: People think that the martial arts are only for fighting or self-defense. If you only study how to fight and become strong, this is not the true way. The most

Karate Masters

"I do believe that goju-kai is developing, growing up. In many ways, it's like kobudo, which is something that cannot change. The philosophy must be the same, but there could be some minor adjustments in some areas."

important things, in the study of any martial art, are how to personally develop and keep your life good. When something happens, some people use punches, a sword or something else. The next thing you know they are in jail. Karate is about how you can have a good life, but I'm not talking about money. I mean how you can be at peace with yourself. When my father was alive, he told me, "You must die when you die." He first mentioned this to me when I was a small child, but I didn't understand. When I graduated from a university, I asked him what he meant. He explained by telling me that some Russian soldiers took him while he was in Manchuria and said, "We will kill you, because you are good at the martial arts. You are dangerous." My father was extremely nervous. He could not move because they said they would kill him. But then he changed his outlook; he said, "If I must die, I must die. OK, it's no problem." So he stood up and followed them. Soon, they stopped somewhere to kill him. He said, "If I believe I'll die, I cannot get life again, so it doesn't matter." If you study the martial arts, you must understand how to die. Everybody must die, right? But nobody thinks about it. Nobody knows when he will die. My father said in the martial arts that bushido is thinking about this.

Q: Many instructors have no idea about the code of bushido in the martial arts. How important is it to you?
A: In bushido, it's not how much you think about yourself. That's the most important point. At the same time, there is a king or a lord in bushido, and everybody must follow somebody. Thus, the rule in bushido is that members devote their lives to the leader. When the leader in the group is killed, the members have to do something. They cannot say that it is not their problem. In

bushido, you don't think about yourself. You think about your boss and your country. That is the main idea. My father said that I must go higher than him. He said, "I'm getting old. You're young. When you study in the future, you'll have more than me, because I have taught you. It's not enough for you to study from me. You must study on your own. Then you will grow further than me." This is one idea he expressed to me. He also said that I trained on my own, so we could both grow together. Many people think, "I study from some teacher, so now I am better than my teacher. [Now it's time that] I study with some other teachers." I am not saying that this is wrong, but it's only looking one way.

Q: Loyalty is lacking in many dojo nowadays. Hence, there are many breakaways. What's your opinion on this?
A: In Japan, bushido must be a way of a loyalty. The Japanese have the concept of *giri*, which is an obligation to loyalty. Thus, for yourself, if you believe there's someone better—with more knowledge, stronger or whatever—this is better for your humility. Many people who break away from their teachers believe they are best ... even better than the teacher. They've lost the plot because suddenly they believe they are the best. Of course, they don't have any loyalty.

Q: When grandmasters die, organizations often break. When your father died, however, goju-kai was reasonably intact. There were not too many problems. Why?
A: After my father died, many students asked me the same question. I told them, "You already respect my father very much. Now my position has changed. I will be the president. My brother's position will also change. You can choose. If you would like to go, you can." Everybody wanted to stay with me, so I'm very happy. They had good memories of my father. [Despite his death], they could study happily to keep a harmonious life. I was not going to pull at people. Because they support me, goju-kai is still strong, I believe.

Q: How do you think goju-kai will be practiced in 50 years?
A: It probably won't be the same, but the main ideas won't change. Things will stay like they were under Gogen Yamaguchi. There might be some new training methods, and instructors will have to teach separately for sport and the traditional way. I do believe that goju-kai is developing, growing up. In many ways, it's like kobudo, which is something that cannot change. It will always be the same. The philosophy must be the same, but there could be some minor adjustments in some areas. O

Kiyoshi Yamazaki

The Perfect Balance

BORN IN CHIBA PREFECTURE ON AUGUST 16, 1940, KIYOSHI YAMAZAKI EMIGRATED TO THE UNITED STATES IN 1968 AND HAS BEEN A RESIDENT AND INSTRUCTOR IN ANAHEIM, CALIFORNIA, SINCE. ALONG THE WAY DURING THOSE YEARS, HE RECEIVED A CERTIFICATE OF EXCELLENCE FROM THE ALL-JAPAN KARATE-DO FEDERATION (FAJKO) AND COMPETED IN THE ALL-JAPAN KARATE CHAMPIONSHIPS, WHERE HE WAS A KATA AND KUMITE FINALIST. YAMAZAKI SENSEI HAS A REPUTATION FOR OUTSTANDING TECHNIQUE AND A DEEP KNOWLEDGE OF THE JAPANESE TRADITIONS. HIS SKILL AND PROFICIENCY HAS LED TO MANY JOBS IN THE FILM INDUSTRY AS BOTH AN ACTOR AND TECHNICAL ADVISER. SOME OF HIS CURRENT POSITIONS INVOLVE BEING THE JAPAN KARATE-DO RYOBU-KAI OVERSEAS CHIEF INSTRUCTOR, USA NATIONAL KARATE-DO FEDERATION TECHNICAL CHAIRMAN, PAN AMERICAN KARATE-DO UNION TECHNICAL CHAIRMAN AND MEMBER OF WORLD KARATE-DO FEDERATION TECHNICAL COMMITTEE. AS A PROMINENT TEACHER, YAMAZAKI SENSEI DISPLAYS THE QUALITIES THAT ARE EXPECTED OF A TRUE MASTER. EMBRACING THE FUTURE, HE FEELS THAT A GREAT RESPONSIBILITY LIES ON HIS SHOULDERS. BUT WITH DEDICATED PASSION AND AN AMICABLE ATTITUDE, KIYOSHI YAMAZAKI KNOWS THAT A PERFECT BALANCE CAN BE ACHIEVED—A BALANCE IN WHICH THE ART OF KARATE-DO BECOMES AN INTERNATIONAL SPORT AND AT THE SAME TIME, MAINTAINS THE TRUE SPIRIT AND LEGACY OF BUDO.

Q: How long have you been practicing the martial arts?
A: I have been practicing karate for more than 40 years. My father was a kendo instructor. He was very traditional and very strict. My brother and I began our training under him at an early age. We would arise in the morning and, whether it was summer or winter, we were outside to practice our basic technique. Cut, cut, cut. Practice, practice, practice. After morning practice, we would go to school. During our lunch break, we would return home for more practice. After school ended, we would practice once more under my father's supervision. He was very strict. If you made the slightest mistake, BAM!—he would strike you with the shinai. He struck very firmly; there was no question of discipline. Sometimes I wondered if I really had a father. He would strike us so often, I would wonder, "Is this man really my

Karate Masters

"This integration of Funakoshi's, Motobu's and Mabuni's teachings provide the ryobu-kai practitioner with a very flexible and adaptable method. Jiu-jutsu and aikido allow a great deal of flexibility and effective techniques in close-range self-defense situations."

father?" And needless to say, I was not too eager to return home and commence the afternoon practice session.

Q: In how many styles of martial arts have you trained?
A: My first teacher was Master Yasuhiro Konishi, and I have trained in two different styles of karate: *shotokai* and *shindo jinen-ryu*. *Ryobu-kai* was founded by Master Konishi. He was a practitioner of *Takeuchi-ryu jujutsu,* and he was also a student of Morihei Ueshiba. Master Konishi's background then was in jujutsu and aikido. Master Konishi studied under Gichin Funakoshi, so ryobu-kai is influenced by *shotokan.* But Choki Motobu, a relevant Okinawan teacher and fighter, and Kenwa Mabuni—who was one of the main instructors in Japan and recognized as an encyclopedia of *kata* because of his combination of *naha-te, tomari-te,* and *shuri-te* methods in the creation of *shito-ryu*—were Master Konishi instructors. Ryobu-kai combines Master Konishi's experiences as a practitioner of aikido and jujutsu, but the karate-do aspect is a highly evolved form of three major Okinawa styles. The approach of these three karate masters — Funakoshi, Mabuni and Motobu—gave Konishi Sensei a very peculiar approach and allowed him to develop a very efficient style that he named ryobu-kai.

This integration of Funakoshi's, Motobu's and Mabuni's teachings provide the ryobu-kai practitioner with a very flexible and adaptable method. *Jiu-jutsu* and *aikido* allow a great deal of flexibility and effective techniques in close-range self-defense situations. Konishi's goal was to create a well-balanced system without losing the friendship he had with all karate-do masters. Once Yasuhiro Konishi passed away, his son, Takehiro Konishi, took over as the leader of the style. In iaido, I studied the *omori-ryu* and *kashima shinto-ryu* methods.

Q: How did you get involved in *kobudo* training?

A: My instructor was a very good friend of Master Nakazato Shugoro of *Kobayashi shorin-ryu.* Nakazato Sensei was also a master in iaido and kobudo. In order to broaden my training, he arranged for me to study kobudo under Nakazato Sensei in Okinawa. We practiced several times a day and into the evening. A great deal of our practice was conducted outdoors, on all types of terrain. It was a great addition to understanding karate technique. Also, thanks to my instructor being a friend of Nakazato Sensei, he gave me special instruction in kobudo;he taught me a favorite sai kata of his. But the actual training was very hard, intense training, good for technique and spirit. We would practice well into the night—and often kata special training was conducted at night to give the feel of using karate in the dark—and in

"A great deal of our practice was conducted out of doors, on all types of terrain. It was a great addition to understanding karate technique. We would practice well into the night—and often kata special training was conducted at night to give the feel of using karate in the dark—and in different spaces."

different spaces. I was very fortunate indeed to study under him. My kobudo training, of course, was focused on the bo, tonfa, sai, nunchaku and kama.

At the time of my training in Okinawa, I met Tadashi Yamashita, one of Nakazato Sensei's best students. We trained together there and became great friends. Then, of course, I returned to my studies in Japan. I did not see Yamashita Sensei again for nearly 20 years. Then, one day at a tournament in Southern California, I turned around and saw him—what a surprise. It was one of the most ironic moments of my life.

Q: Would you tell us some interesting stories of your early days in karate training?

A: While a student at the University of Tokyo, I studied shotokan, but I should say I studied with the *shoto-kai* group. There is a difference between the shotokan practiced in the Japan Karate Association and the shotokan of

Karate Masters

"Only when you give up the idea of rank will you realize that the study of karate is the study of your true self. In every moment of your life—not just the art of karate-do or the art you are involved in—you must be ready to act."

the shoto-kai. Shoto-kai is a branch of shotokan that traces its lineage directly to Shigeru Egami, one of the top Gichin Funakoshi students and a legend in karate history. Training in shoto-kai was very different. We never heard of tournaments; it was unthinkable. We practiced karate conditioning and kata training, but sparring was something very different than what we understand today. We did not practice *jyu-kumite*. Our sparring was limited to one-step sparring or *ippon-kumite*. At the highest level, there was free one-step sparring ... free in the choice of technique. And, of course, when we sparred, we sparred very hard to attain kime and proper *ma-ai* (distance). The training was geared to developing explosive power—power delivered with one blow. This also helped us develop a sense of feeling our opponent's opening, the right moment to attack decisively. When I first began to train, it was a totally different kind of training than you see today. It was traditional Japanese ... very strict and you never questioned your instructor. This philosophy made things difficult, and I flunked my shodan test three times. I never knew why and did not dare ask Konishi Sensei why. More than 30 years later, he finally told me why I did not pass; he said I was overconfident! Back in those days, you didn't know you would test until a day or two before. You didn't know what you would be tested on either. You didn't have three or four months to prepare your kata and sharpen your timing in kumite. The idea was that a real martial artist should be prepared at all times. Only when you give up the idea of rank will you realize that the study of karate is the study of your true self. In every moment of your life—not just the art of karate-do or the art you are involved in—you must be ready to act.

Q: How did Westerners respond to traditional Japanese training?
A: When I came to the United States in 1969, Westerners thought that karate was only about breaking boards and concrete blocks. I did do that to get people interested in what I was doing because at that time that was all people were interested in. Once they saw me do those things, I was able to

slowly teach them real karate-do. The first question I was always asked back then was, "Can you break boards? How many?" I would respond to them by saying that usually wood and concrete don't attack people; therefore, that issue was irrelevant. People may attack you, and that is why you need to learn real karate-do ... not just a simple trick of breaking boards to impress people. Fortunately, today most people understand karate either as sport or as budo, so there's no need to break boards and do crazy things to get attention.

It must be kept in mind that Japan has a cultural tradition and educational background solidly etched in the martial arts. Training attitudes, therefore, are very different. Young people are not surprised to have their mistakes corrected by being struck by a shinai. Of course, this tradition is not the same as the cultural background and educational approach in America. There must be adaptations to make. This is a very interesting point. In Japan, one does not question the purpose of a certain technique or move from a kata. Westerners are eager to study the martial arts but in their own way. They also have a different attention span and attitude to training, and they are very interested in "how to" and applications, which I think is simply a reflection on the Western culture.

"Fortunately, today most people understand karate either as sport or as budo, so there's no need to break boards and do crazy things to get attention. Training attitudes are, therefore, very different."

For instance, iaido is a good example of this. It is well understood in Japan that the art is a form of meditation. It is not a teaching of fighting technique with a sword; it is a form of moving meditation. But my students in America want to know what this movement is and what the kata means. To keep their interest in training, it is necessary to elaborate on the application. For example, there is what is known as tate or *tate-do* in Japan. This dates from the development of *kabuki* theatre, which contains many dramatic stories and incidents which call for swordplay. The movements are dramatic but are extrapolated from traditional fencing movements. That is what I do to keep my students' interest; I elaborate on tate-do and show them the application that can be drawn from an iaido kata. But this is an intermediate stage, something done after the student begins. The student begins to train

Karate Masters

"Today, I focus on improving my spirit. When you reach a certain age, it is the spirit that keeps you going. Your body is left behind and your mind truly knows the limitations of your body. It is then that your spirit really pushes you forward."

very enthusiastically, but then there comes a point in which he questions what he is doing. Tate helps to provide an answer. Then it becomes very important to move beyond that stage.

There is a great difference between choreography and the moving spirit of iaido. It becomes necessary to insure that form is correct and that a deeper, truer understanding of the art is reached. One may adapt training to the student; for example, it was common during my day to restrict kobudo training to advanced levels. This is not practical in the Western world. I think kobudo is an important part of training because it helps coordination and balance. The more you train, the better your spirit and confidence becomes, which helps your overall control. You introduce weapons gradually to the student to keep his interest, to lead him further into the true budo. But then you become strict. You should adjust the pace to the student's capability and his background, and then introduce the art.

Q: How has your personal karate has changed over the years?
A: In the beginning, I had to train very hard. Because I started very young, it is difficult to say whether I was natural at the art or not. Of course, after so many years of training and dedication, one must have some natural ability. When I was in my 20s and 30s, my main emphasis was on attacking and offensive techniques … how to completely finish off an opponent in the fastest and most powerful way. In my 40s and 50s, I practiced more blocking and development of different methods of controlling the opponent without facing his power. Today, I focus on improving my spirit. When you reach a certain age, it is the spirit that keeps you going. Your body is left behind, and your mind truly knows the limitations of your body. It is then that your spirit really pushes you forward. Although my stamina may not be the same as it was many years

ago—and that is natural—the techniques I use are still the same. Their physical application is not based on power and speed but in deceptiveness. As long as you have a good, strong foundation developed through years of hard training, a good healthy spirit will keep you going. When you are young and strong, you can be very powerful and fast. As you age, you must learn how to adapt your body and not expect that the same physical qualities that made your karate strong will be important now. This is partly what is meant by the motto, "The man makes the art." You are always changing how to train, the techniques you select, and the way you see your art as your body and mind change with age. Karate-do is my life, and I put all of the necessary time and effort to do my best by correctly promoting the art in all its different aspects.

Q: What are the most important points of your teaching days?
A: Important aspects of my teaching involve how and what is being taught. I feel it is important to teach children the importance of a good education. Not just karate kicks and punches, but the importance of excelling in their regular school as well. Education will be with them for the rest of their lives and will have a big influence in what they will become as adults.

"I feel it is important to teach children the importance of a good education. Not just karate kicks and punches, but the importance of excelling in their regular school, as well. Education will be with them for the rest of their lives and will have a big influence in what they will become as adults."

The physical techniques of karate-do should be used as a vehicle for that. For adults, I feel it is important to instill a sense of confidence and the importance of responsibility. These aspects of our karate training can be translated into how we conduct ourselves in our everyday lives. Better and more mature karate practitioners will become better human beings. And with better human beings, we all have a better world to live in.

Karate Masters

"Life is always changing, so systems change. And that is a natural way. What is important is to understand and respect the changes and differences in the different ryu. Knowing and practicing different styles of karate can be beneficial as long as the instructor teaching those styles understands and passes on the real essence to the students."

Q: With all the technical changes during the last 30 years, do you think there are still pure karate styles?

A: While there have been many changes to the karate tournament system throughout the years, and things may have changed and modernized, the elements of good karate have remained the same ... strong basics and strong spirit. These two simple concepts can make any activity better over the years. Different ryu are important in budo. Ryu is a system developed by a martial arts master through years of training, experience and dedication. Today, we don't have that much time to dedicate to the art, so whatever was developed by the ancestors should be taken very seriously. It is not correct to take those different perspectives lightly. Life is always changing, so systems change. And that is a natural way. What is important is to understand and respect the changes and differences in the different ryu. By understanding those differences, we will always be able to remember our roots and at the same time appreciate what other styles have to offer. Knowing and practicing different styles of karate can be beneficial as long as the instructor teaching those styles understands and passes on the real essence to the students. Once again, it boils down to the teacher and how he shares the knowledge with the students.

Q: What is your opinion of full-contact karate and kickboxing?

A: Full-contact and kickboxing are very different to me. I don't know their systems or rules, so it's hard to comment on them. I do know that my focus has changed as I have gotten older; I just wonder how age will affect those who practice full-contact karate and kickboxing, which are competitive combat systems and not an art of life. About the other more modern versions of no-holds-barred competition, I really don't know enough to comment.

Q: Do you think that karate in the West has caught up with Japanese karate?
A: Japanese karate-do isn't as fancy as other Western fighting methods, but it does attract a steady clientele of well-educated people who understand there is more to karate than just kicks and punches. Other styles seem to be fads, and those who are serious eventually find their way back to traditional karate. There are examples of world famous competitors who only practiced sparring and criticized kata training and the traditional aspects of the art. And guess what? Now they are teaching traditional kata and traditional karate. They should have thought a little more when they were younger and didn't have such a narrow mind, because their level as karate teachers would be higher today.

Basically, everyone does kicks and punches in any karate, regardless of their nationality. But I think the Europeans move very quickly and are extremely fast on their feet, while the Japanese don't move too much. Japanese fighters are more static and base their offensive in pure speed. Europeans tend to fake a lot before an attack, which makes them very deceptive. Nowadays, it is almost impossible to hit someone with a clean shot. The competition level is very high, and elite competitors control the fighting distance. Europeans train more and are very versatile in their approach to kumite, so they have a different kind of confidence than seen in other parts of the world. Americans are very independent and train well also. Americans will be very strong in Olympic karate in the years to come, but they still have a long way to go when compared to the European countries.

I don't think it is necessary for a person to train in Japan. Today, there are many good instructors here in the United States and all over the world. I do think that if you have the opportunity to visit Japan it is a good idea to

"I don't think it is necessary for a person to train in Japan. The atmosphere and environment will definitely help you to better understand the proper art, but from the physical point of view, it is not necessary. Just take a look at the names of Japanese instructors outside of Japan. There are many, and they are very good."

Karate Masters

"Karate is several things at the same time: It is a great physical activity, a martial art, a self-defense method and a great sport. We need to correctly educate future instructors because they will be the ones carrying on the art and the sport without losing the values of budo."

experience a different culture. The atmosphere and environment will definitely help you to better understand the proper art, but from the physical point of view, it is not necessary. Just take a look at the names of Japanese instructors outside of Japan; there are many and they are very good.

Q: Karate is nowadays often referred to as a sport. Do you agree with this?
A: I agree with the idea that karate today is also a sport. I also feel it is very important that an instructor knows the difference between sport karate and self-defense because it will make a difference in how and what an instructor teaches. Karate is several things at the same time: it is a great physical activity, a martial art, a self-defense method and a great sport. We need to correctly educate future instructors because they will be the ones carrying on the art and the sport without losing the values of budo.

Q: Do you feel that you still have further to go in your studies?
A: I don't think that anyone ever reaches a point in which they have learned all there is to know. I travel and give seminars in many countries, and I always learn something new all the time from the students. Maybe not a new technique but maybe I need to use a new approach to teach a certain person a karate movement and this simple fact makes me improve my teaching ability and therefore the general knowledge of that particular movement.

Q: How do you see Japanese karate in America and the rest of the world at the present time?
A: Unfortunately, compared to other martial arts systems, there is not a high percentage of traditional Japanese karate schools in the United States. I think that many people feel uncomfortable when they first begin, but the

longer they train, the more they want to know. They realize there is a deeper meaning to traditional training. I guess that to truly understand the real value of traditional karate-do, the practitioner needs to spend years training in the proper way and under a competent instructor. It is only after years of practice and a certain level of maturity that an individual will be able to perceive all the benefits of budo and not just stay on the surface of the physical movements, the tournaments, et cetera.

Q: What's your opinion about makiwara training?
A: I think makiwara training is sometimes misunderstood. Some people simply think it is just to strengthen your fist and develop callused hands so other people are impressed when they look at your hands. Real makiwara training is much more than that. Proper tension should be felt throughout your body by using the connection between your wrist and your hip to achieve a correct whole body feel at the moment of impact. That feeling should be duplicated when you punch everytime, because that's the right kime. You need to use the makiwara properly so your body develops that important aspect of all techniques in karate—kime. Without kime, there is no technique in karate-do.

"A good instructor should show techniques slow and fast. This is the time to demonstrate good solid basics. This is also part of your training. In fact, if you teach five classes a day and you perform 100 gyaku-tsuki per class, by the end of the day you have punched 500 times."

Q: Do you think a practitioner's personal training should be different from what he teaches?
A: I think instructors should have at least one class a month dedicated to training themselves in those important areas they need to develop. I also think that instructors can get personal training while they teach. A good instructor should show techniques slow and fast. This is the time to demonstrate good solid basics. This is also part of your training. In fact, if you teach

Karate Masters

"Your karate-do should be technically balanced. If you can do good kata, but you cannot perform good kumite, then there is something wrong. And vice versa; being good at kumite but performing poorly at kata is a sign of unbalanced training."

five classes a day and you perform 100 gyaku-tsuki per class, by the end of the day you have punched 500 times. Of course, it is advisable that the instructor doesn't use the class for his own training; but whatever he has to do in class should be used for his own benefit, too. When he performs for the students, he is receiving the benefits of doing the techniques over and over. It is wrong when some instructors, after showing the techniques a few times for the students, instead of going and correcting the pupils, they keep repeating the technique for their own benefit. And that's not right. The instructor's main objective in class is to teach and to correct the students, not to train himself. He should allocate time for his own personal training and development.

Q: When teaching the art of karate what is the most important element: self-defense, sport or tradition?
A: Self-defense, sport and tradition are all important elements of the art. You don't want to separate them. Which one is more important depends on your own personal goals. What is important is that each one relies on good solid basics. If you are more focused on developing self-defense techniques, then make sure your foundation is good. If you want to compete, make sure your kihon is good enough to get you there, et cetera. A good and strong foundation is the base for anything you want to do. Kata and kumite should be divided 50-50. The karate-ka should balance his training because the path to perfection—a perfection that is never achieved, by the way—is based on balance. This balance should keep the practitioner on the right track, preventing him from going too much into one single aspect of the art. Your karate-do should be technically balanced. If you can do good kata, but you cannot perform good kumite, then there is something wrong. And vice versa; being good at kumite but performing poorly at kata is a sign of unbalanced training.

Q: What do you consider to be the major changes in the art since you began training?
A: The basic difference between today's training and when I started is that today's training is easier. It's not as strict as it was in the past. When I started, your instructor was your master; you never questioned him. You addressed someone by saying, "*Ouss*"—a word that had a different meaning back then. If Mr. Funakoshi, Miyagi, Motobu or Mabuni Sensei saw our training today, I think they would be shocked ... truly and really shocked.

Q: If it could be anyone, with whom would you train?
A: If I had the chance to train with anyone, it would have been Motobu Sensei. He was a big person, he was very fast and he specialized in scooping techniques. I wish I had that opportunity.

Q: What would you say to someone who is interested in learning karate-do?
A: The first thing I would tell someone is that it is not like what you see on TV or at the movies. All that stuff doesn't belong to the art of karate-do. Budo and the martial arts in general are deeper in meaning that what people see in movies. Sometimes movies are good because they bring exposure to the martial arts. Sometimes they are bad, because they misinform and give the wrong impression of what martial art training is all about.

"Budo and martial arts in general are deeper in meaning than what people see in movies. Sometimes movies are good because they bring exposure to the martial arts, but sometimes they are bad too, because they misinform and give the wrong impression of what martial art training is all about."

Movies show action. They are exciting, and they draw people to the martial arts. But one preserves the essence and the spirit and tries to lead the individual further on. So it is with adapting instruction. With my pupils, I introduce a weapon into training at the green belt level. I introduce the bo first, because it is a very good weapon for developing overall coordination, and the student now has something new and exciting. So his techniques begin to improve from practicing with the bo while interest is held. Then you introduce sai and tonfa; they develop the wrist. Again you strengthen the student's karate technique while maintaining interest. You are drawing

Karate Masters

"Kumite in the dojo or in competition and streetfighting are two different ways of fighting. Training in kumite will help keep you in shape for any type of fighting; however, actual kumite techniques are not a part of streetfighting. Self-defense techniques are completely different that those used for kumite."

the student closer to reaching a deeper understanding of budo while trying to avoid the plateaus that affect everyone in training.

Adapting teaching methods can greatly aid the development of the student. If you practice seriously, your body will know the techniques. If something happens, your body will react automatically; proper practice is the most important thing to remember. It won't matter if you are in an airplane, in the snow, if it's day or night; if you have practiced, your body will have the strength, balance and coordination to use the techniques without having to think about it. You body will have a mind of its own.

Q: You have been involved in teaching actors for movies; is that correct?
A: Yes, it is true. I instructed Arnold Schwarzenegger in sword techniques for *"Conan, The Barbarian."* I was also involved in other productions like *"Dune,"* *"Dragonheart"* and others. It is always a fun and interesting experience, but it is not real martial arts, though.

Q: What keeps you motivated after all these years?
A: Teaching others motivates me. It is an opportunity to share with others what I have learned, so I want to be in good condition to do the demonstrations and to bring the art into other people's lives. I have also taken up golf. I have found that golfing motivates my mind and my spirit. It's very interesting. Also, iaido training has always been a key motivator for me. Martial arts training offers an opportunity to expand knowledge—not just the knowledge of budo—but knowledge of different cultures and people. As this knowledge grows and people are introduced to the benefits of budo and how it can enrich their lives—how it fits into the lives of people from different cultural backgrounds—we all benefit ... not just in the martial arts, but also in terms of the largest goals of the budo, which are peace, understanding and harmony.

Q: Do you think it is necessary to engage in freefighting to achieve good fighting skills in the street?
A: Kumite in the dojo or in competition and street fighting are two different ways of fighting. Training in kumite will help keep you in shape for any type of fighting; however, actual kumite techniques are not a part of street fighting. Self-defense techniques are completely different than those used for kumite. If you approach a self-defense situation as you would a competition, you are going to be in big trouble. Every karate-ka should know this and study both aspects separately. Those qualities developed in competition—reflex, speed, proper distance, et cetera—will help you in a self-defense situation, but forget about jumping around and scoring with a gyaku-tsuki. You need a more decisive approach and more decisive techniques.

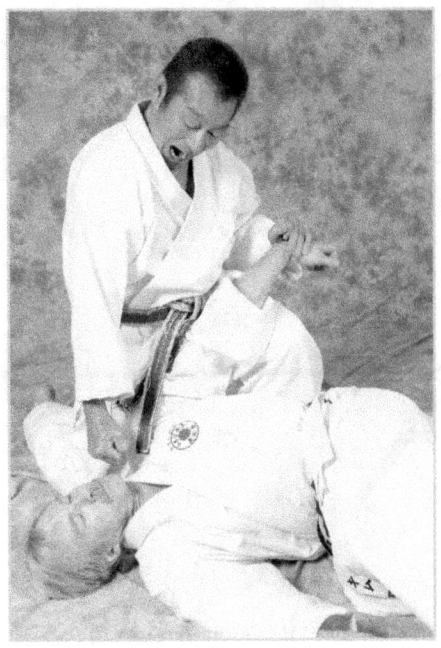

"I think bunkai is very important. It brings karate to another level. When you understand bunkai, a lot of things are revealed to you. You need to know how to look at kata and its bunkai."

Q: How do you feel about *bunkai*?
A: I think bunkai is very important. It brings karate to another level. When you understand bunkai, a lot of things are revealed to you. You need to know how to look at kata and its bunkai. Even deeper meanings are found in its *onyo*, which involves a deeper and analytical use of the same techniques used in kata and developed in bunkai.

Q: What is the philosophical basis for your karate training?
A: My basic philosophy for my karate training is to keep good health and spirit in my life and use it as motivation to train. When you can do this, your karate training becomes an integral part of a healthy life, on or off the dojo floor. For many people, karate-do starts in the dojo and finishes in the dojo, but this is wrong. Yes, karate-do started for you the first day you entered in a dojo, but it should be with you all the time. There has to be karate-do in everything you do.

Karate Masters

"To understand the spiritual aspects of karate through discussion is difficult. It is not something you can talk about and know. It doesn't work that way. I always tell people to just do it. It is only when they practice themselves that they gain insight into what karate is all about."

Q: Do you have a memorable experience that has inspired your training?
A: Many years ago, I was in a car accident. I was in the hospital for three months with a paralyzed hip. I had no leg movement; needless to say; that was a very tough situation for me ... not only physically, but emotionally. Returning to the practice of karate motivated me, brought my spirit up and helped me to work hard in physical therapy, which was a big, challenging phase. My doctors said I recovered from my injuries three times faster than they thought I would and were amazed I was able to walk again in such a short time. I owe it to those qualities developed through hard karate training. The practice of karate-do is the development of body, mind and spirit using physical techniques. These are the basics of karate-do, but they can also be used in everyday life.

Q: How can a practitioner can increase his understanding of the spiritual aspects of karate?
A: To understand the spiritual aspects of karate through discussion is difficult. It is not something you can talk about and know. It doesn't work that way. I always tell people to just do it. It is only when they practice that they gain insight into what karate is all about. Karate-do, as any art in budo, can only be realized through personal practice and not through words said by someone else. It is also important to understand the fact that when we are young sport competition may be a relevant aspect of our training. When we get older, the idea or being better than anyone else is kind of ridiculous.

Q: How much training should an older karate-ka do to improve and get better at the art?
A: Students who begin karate as an adult can be easily educated on the philosophy and history of karate, but their coordination and body movement

may be limited due to their age. They should train as much as they can, but not worry about accomplishing fancy techniques and high kicks. They should train using step-by-step techniques and concentrate on doing the basics very well. They will improve quickly and be able to develop a very mature form of karate-do.

Q: Is there anything lacking in the way the martial arts are being taught today?
A: When I first began training, instructors only thought of making strong bodies with strong techniques. Today, many instructors are thinking about making a good income. I understand that this is how times have changed and that's how many need to survive in today's world. True feeling and right motivation are the foundations of budo. There are things in tradition that are worthy to hold onto. They connect us with our past and make us better. Money should not be the main reason we do things.

"The important attributes of a student include a strong body, motivation to keep learning and a good understanding of the true meaning of karate. The most important aspect every karate-ka should keep in mind is to train hard."

Q: What advice would you give to students on the question of supplementary training?
A: Supplementary training depends on the individual. I feel that each person must know his body and must adjust his training to suit his own needs. All supplementary training is in addition to karate training, so each individual needs to recognize his weak points and try to improve those areas. It's a personal thing, but I must say that everything that helps your karate grow is good for you. But be careful. For instance, running is good, but you don't want to become a professional runner; weight training is good, but your don't want to become a bodybuilder or develop such a large amount of muscle in your body that it prevents karate techniques from being performed properly. You want to be limber and do stretching, but you don't want to stretch so much that your joints become loose and weak. It's very important to strike a balance. Whatever supplementary training you do is to improve your karate—not take time away from it.

Karate Masters

"I have a responsibility not only to myself but to my students and organization to show and say things correctly. I am still learning things, and there are still ideas out there that I don't understand. I have been more vocal on training children and self-defense because I am more confident in those areas."

Q: What do you see as the most important attributes for a student?
A: The important attributes of a student include a strong body, motivation to keep learning and a good understanding of the true meaning of karate. The most important aspect every karate-ka should keep in mind is to train hard. Also, training in kobudo and other weaponry art like iaido will help the student very much. Iaido is particularly important because of the many Japanese martial arts' philosophies involving the use of the katana. This weapon is a symbol for all budo practitioners.

Q: Why do a lot of students start falling away after two or three years of training?
A: I believe some students stop training because they are not motivated by their instructor. While students must be responsible for their own training, many instructors try to control their students too much. A healthy balance on both the part of the instructor's input and the student's willingness to learn is needed. On the other hand, the student should understand that martial arts training doesn't bring rewards the way we receive them in our daily jobs. We work and we make money. In budo, the gain is not visible; it is not that clear. The process is indirect and things should be discovered.

Q: There is very little written about you in magazines; you obviously do not thrive on the publicity like some martial artists. Why?
A: Not much has been written about me because I have been selective about what is published. If I am quoted in a publication, or if photos of one of my demonstrations are published, the information must be exact; techniques must be correct. I have a responsibility not only to myself, but to my students and organization, to show and say things correctly. I am still learning things and there are still ideas out there that I don't understand. I have been more vocal on training children and self-defense because I am more confident in those areas. Eventually, I would like to write a book about my

thoughts on the philosophy of karate and how to develop good spirit. I would like it to be helpful to everyone, not just karate people. True karate-do goes beyond rank, black belts, trophies and tournaments. In some way, I would like to share this.

Q: Have you felt fear in your karate training?
A: I have been fearful thinking about someone attacking me. Because of my karate training, I know what I can do to an attacker. Because of my karate training and who I am, I would have to fight back. Win or lose, it would be a shameful situation. Fear is an important part of the training of karate-do, but you should control this emotion and use it properly for your own benefit. Sometimes fear is a great thing because it forces you to be prepared for whatever may come. You may feel fear and then you know you have to prepare yourself to the best of your possibilities. Then the better you prepare, the better you will do in anything in life. Fear is not a bad thing. It is good if you know where it comes from and know how to use it for your own advantage.

"The teaching of karate's history and philosophy may be lost and the traditional system of training may be diluted. This is why it is so important that today's instructors have a good understanding of our roots; this will enable them to pass it on to the next generation."

Q: What are your thoughts on the future of karate-do and the Olympics?
A: I think the future for karate looks good, and the Olympics can be a huge step forward, but only if we do it the right way. I hope sponsors will support our athletes, coaches, judges and referees in the process. The negative aspect of karate in the Olympics could be that the focus of training will be towards the Games and will move away from budo ethics and morals. The teaching of karate's history and philosophy may be lost, and the traditional system of training may be diluted. This is why it is so important that today's instructors have a good understanding of our roots, so they can pass it on to the next generation. The sportive aspects will bring more practitioners to karate, but it will be on the instructors' shoulders to teach the true essence of budo in order to perpetuate the art in the proper way, which is for the generations to come. O

Koss Yokota

A Balanced Spirit

THERE IS A QUIET AUTHORITY ABOUT YOKOTA SENSEI ... NO MOVEMENT OR WORD IS WASTED. THERE ARE MANY TEACHERS OF SHOTOKAN KARATE, HOWEVER, KOSS YOKOTA STANDS APART IN HIS APPROACH TO TEACHING, CONTRIBUTIONS TO THE ART AND EMPHASIS ON ACTUAL BUDO PHILOSOPHY.

FOR YOKOTA SENSEI, THE ART OF KARATE-DO ADDS UP TO A BASIC ATTITUDE—AN ATTITUDE THAT PLACES THE HIGHEST IMPORTANCE ON RESPECT AND SELF-KNOWLEDGE. THE SENSE OF "FAMILY" THAT HE FEELS TOWARDS HIS STUDENTS IS VISIBLE IN HIS PATIENT LISTENING AND QUIET UNDERSTANDING. ALTHOUGH HE IS A MAN OF MANY INTERESTS, YOKOTA SENSEI ALWAYS THINKS IN TERMS OF KARATE. TO HIM, A *KENDO-KA* IS A KARATE-KA WITH A SWORD AND A *KYUDO-KA* IS A KARATE-KA WITH A BOW AND ARROW. "KARATE GOES BEYOND PHYSICAL EXCELLENCE," SAYS YOKOTA SENSEI. "IT STRIVES FOR SPIRITUAL ATTAINMENT. UNFORTUNATELY, MANY PEOPLE ABANDON THEIR BASICS BEFORE THEY ARE READY. SOMEONE LIKE PICASSO COULD NOT HAVE ACHIEVED HIS SUPREMACY IN IMPRESSIONISM HAD HE NOT MASTERED THE BASICS OF THE ART."

Q: How long have you been practicing the martial arts?
A: I started my martial arts in 1960 with judo. I was 13 years old. My father was a black belt in Kodokan judo. When I asked him which martial art I should learn, he encouraged me to take up judo. There was no judo club at the junior high school I was attending, so I went to the district police station where they had judo and kendo training. This was mainly for the policemen, but it was open to the public. I went for three years and got a black belt. A new student—who was a little different from most—joined the class towards the end of the period. As soon as he was thrown down, he jumped up like a bouncing ball and took a different stance that was much wider than a normal judo stance. I asked him why he was doing this, and he said that he was getting into a karate stance. Even though I knew about karate, I had very little knowledge about it, so I asked him about it after the training. He told me that he was a karate practitioner and was taking judo to better his fighting skill. At that time, I believed that judo was the deadliest art, so I asked if he agreed. To my surprise, he said karate was much deadlier in a

Karate Masters

"I wanted to expose myself to full-contact for further understanding of kumite, and indeed it was a good experience. Kyokushinkai is known for a very rigorous training. I was very fit in 1981, but the training was very physically demanding. I enjoyed the training, but I never thought of switching to kyokushinkai or any other style."

hand-to-hand combat. He showed me how he could attack me and knock me down while I was trying to grab his hand or *gi*. If I could grab him, I had a chance to throw him down, but his fast punch and kick would surely get me first. So, this opened my eyes, and I switched to karate in 1963. Again, my high school did not have a karate club, so I joined the YMCA Karate Club in my hometown, which was Kobe. The club, although I didn't know it, was a JKA organization. This is how I got into the world of shotokan karate.

Q: In how many styles of karate or other methods have you trained?
A: Basically, I am a true blue shotokan practitioner, but I practiced goju-ryu in the early 1960s. When I started karate training, I wanted to get as much training as possible, so I went to two different dojo (JKA and Goju-kai) for one year. In addition, I practiced *kyokushinkai*, full-contact style between 1981 and 1982. I was going through the instructor's training at JKA, so I was training four times at JKA and two times per week at kyokushinkai. I wanted to expose myself to full-contact for further understanding of kumite, and indeed it was a good experience. Kyokushinkai is known for a very rigorous training. I was very fit in 1981, but the training was very physically demanding. I enjoyed the training, but I never thought of switching to kyokushinkai or any other style. For my body and mind, shotokan suits me best.

Q: Sensei, who were your first teachers?
A: My first sensei was Master Sugano, 9th dan JKA in Kobe, Japan. I trained under him between 1963 and 1966, as well as from 1981 to 1983. Unfortunately, he passed away three years ago at the age of 72. My instructor in the U.S. was Okazaki Sensei, 9th dan and chairman of the ISKF. I was one of the assistant instructors at the Philadelphia ISKF headquarters dojo in the 1970s.

Q: Tell us some interesting stories of your early days in karate training.
A: I have many "interesting" stories. Let me give you three, and I hope I do not bore the readers. A few months after joining the Kobe YMCA in 1963, I joined the Osaka Athletic Club where goju-ryu had a dojo. This is an unorthodox way, which I would not recommend to anyone, but I did not know any better then. I simply wanted to train every day. They practiced shotokan on Monday, Wednesday and Friday and goju-ryu only on Tuesday, Thursday and Saturday. I trained at two dojo for one year and enjoyed the different ways of teaching at each dojo. However, eventually, I had to quit one of them. I found out that training in different styles at two dojo can get you in big trouble. One of the students at the YMCA was a friend of mine, and he found out that I was also training at Goju-kai. He is the one who warned me. In fact, he told me, "They will kill you." Nevertheless, despite my fearlessness or ignorance, I kept on practicing at the two dojo. I figured that I could keep it secret, as the dojo were located in two different cities and were 40 miles apart. However, I did not realize that all the traditional karate style dojo held annual tournaments in the region, which was Kansai. Even though I was only a mere white belt, I had to be at the tournament to assist the senior students or the *senpai*. Obviously, it was extremely difficult to serve the senpai from both dojo simultaneously without being funny, as I had to "go to bathroom" so often. After that, I decided to drop one of the dojo, and I stayed with shotokan.

The second anecdote is when I flunked my very first test. Luckily, this was the last time I failed an exam. After six months of training, we were allowed to take a *kyu* test. I assumed the test would start from the higher rankings, so I showed up at the dojo around the time it started. The first thing I had to do was fill in the test application form. As everyone else got there before me, my application was on top of the pile. The examiner's assistant called my name first, but I was in the dressing room still changing my clothes. I had to run out while I was still putting my belt on. It was a combined test with many dojo of the region, so there were more than 100 students in the hall. It was very embarrassing. I did not know exactly what was expected in the test, and I had figured that I could watch the other students and learn. As it turned out, I was the first one to go. So, not only I could not watch other white belts taking an exam, but I was not mentally prepared. As a result, I did not do any *kiai*, I showed no *kime* and I moved too slowly. Naturally, out of 30 to 40 beginners, I was the only one who did not pass. I don't know if this story is interesting, but I always tell it to the students before their first test in the hope that they will feel more relaxed.

The last story is funny and hard to believe. To get my instructor's certifi-

Karate Masters

cate, I went back to Japan and stayed there between 1981 and 1983. During the day, I taught English at the YMCA so I could pay my bills. While there, I met this American guy, a fellow English teacher. Without knowing I was a karate practitioner, he started to boast about his skills in the Chinese martial arts. He said Japanese styles, particularly shotokan, were rigid and no match for kung-fu. So, I told him there was a karate club in the YMCA, and I suggested that he visited there so he could take a few lessons. He said he would, and he kept his promise. He showed up at the club, and he was shocked to see me in a *gi* with a black belt. I asked him to show us the fluid style he was talking about. He showed us some movements, but he definitely was not an expert. I asked him to do a little sparring, but he declined and left the dojo in a hurry. Though I saw him again at the language school, he never spoke about his kung-fu skills or anything about the martial arts. The funny part comes later. In 1984, after I moved to California, I was speaking to my assistant instructor, Joe, a high-tech sales man who traveled often, and he told me about an incident he had at LAX on his last trip to L.A. While having a drink in one of the bars at the airport, he ended up sitting next to a tall American guy who said he just returned from Japan. Joe asked him if he practiced any martial arts while he was in Asia. He said he did and started boasting about his kung-fu skill. Then he asked Joe if he practiced any martial arts, and Joe said, "Yes, I practice shotokan." The guy looked somewhat uncomfortable but asked "Who is your instructor?" When Joe mentioned my name, this guy dropped his jaw to the floor. He excused himself and left the bar very quickly. Joe could not figure out why this guy took off like a bat out of a cave. When I heard the description of the guy (a tall guy wearing cowboy boots, etc.), I was sure who he was. I told him of the incident at my old dojo, and he understood exactly what had actually happened. We had a good laugh on the unlucky guy.

Q: How did the Westerners respond to traditional Japanese training when you started teaching?
A: Karate was little known in the 1960s and early 1970s. Judo and jiu-jitsu were more popular, so I initially taught both judo and karate. When the students saw the karate techniques—particularly the kicks—I got instant respect. Many of them were familiar with boxing, but kicking was unknown and maybe a little bit mysterious. They were impressed not only by the kicking techniques but also by the sophisticated body movements like rotation, jumping, squatting and lying down ... movements that are uniquely found in karate.

Q: Were you a natural at karate? Did the movements come easily to you?

A: No, I was not. I am not flexible and my reflexes are not any better than anyone else's. I had to practice a lot to make the movements natural to me. During my 20s and 30s, I spent six to eight hours training in the dojo. I continue my daily training even now.

Q: How has your personal karate changed and developed over the years?

A: In shotokan, *kime* is important, but no one really taught me how to make it sharp like a whip. During my 20s and 30s, I was using too much muscle power to generate

"You can be a coach who is fat and out of shape in football or baseball. A coach does not have to perform better than the players to become a respected coach in those sports. But in karate and all of the martial arts, this must not be the case."

kime. When I was doing this, some of the muscles I was using were going against other muscles. Thus, my power was off. In addition, my kime was too long, and I could not attain a whip-like snap effect that was sharp and powerful. With this flaw, my technique did not flow naturally, and it made me slow and less powerful. I began to realize this more and more when I was nearing 40. I did not want to be an instructor who could only say, "I used to be good." You can be a coach who is fat and out of shape in football or baseball. A coach does not have to perform better than the players to become a respected coach in those sports. But in karate and all of the martial arts, this must not be the case. My belief is that a karate instructor, at least a certified one, must be able to perform better than any of his students who may be younger or physically bigger and stronger.

When I neared 50, I decided *ki* may be the answer, so, in 1997, I moved back to Japan. I wanted to focus on ki, so I gave up karate training for three years. I joined the famous Master Nishino's dojo in Tokyo. He has written many books on ki and some of them were translated in English so you may have read one of them. Master Nishino could throw people around without touching them. He simply used his ki. To make a long story short, I was the only student he could not throw around. However, I could not learn how to throw the people with my ki alone. Nevertheless, I do not regret that

Karate Masters

"I changed my affiliation to JKS (Japan Karate Shotokai), a new shotokan organization that Master Asai formed in 2000. He was the technical director at the JKA in the 1990s, and he was well known in Japan for his unique style of karate."

I spent two years attending to ki in his dojo. I learned the breathing exercises, and I believe there was a positive effect on my karate. When I returned to California in 2000, my karate was better, or at least more relaxed, despite the fact that I had not trained in more than three years.

I changed my affiliation to JKS (*Japan Karate Shotokai*), a new shotokan organization that Master Asai formed in 2000. He was the technical director at the JKA in the 1990s, and he was well known in Japan for his unique style of karate. I knew him since the 1980s and was always impressed by his whip-like technique. He had a lot of exposure to Chinese style martial arts. At the seminar we had in the Bay Area this summer, Master Asai, who was 69, was impressively more flexible and quicker than all of us. I believe I can expand my karate by practicing the Asai style of shotokan.

Q: What are the most important points of your teaching philosophy?
A: I tell my students all the time that thinking is most important in karate training. It is very easy and becomes comfortable for a student to get in automatic pilot mode. A student tends to follow an instructor's commands blindly without thinking about the technique he is performing. Improvements will not occur only with repetitions. Each student has different challenges and must make appropriate efforts during the movements to improve himself. To be able to make such an effort, a student needs to know what and how to correct the flaws and mistakes. In Japan, an instructor rarely makes any comments. In the 1960s, we had to learn only from watching the senior students, senpai or sensei. I used to picture my sensei's movements and attempt to copy them. The system and expectations were such that only the talented and lucky ones would advance. Many did not improve and kept their bad habits, but it was OK with sensei because there were hundreds of students and he expected only a few good ones. Non-

Japanese instructors often take time and effort to explain and comment on the technique and this can be helpful. When an instructor points out the important element, students reply by saying "*Osu*," but I wonder how many are really making a conscious effort to do that. Each student should not only listen but also apply that point to himself in each step and movement he takes. Again, simply repeating a technique or kata, even 10,000 times, will not necessarily improve karate skills. It is obvious when you repeat a bad technique 10,000 times that you will have a very solid bad technique. This is not only true in basics but also in kata and kumite. All students must know the application of each movement and apply that technique in that context. If you do a kata without thinking, that kata will be not too far off from a dance. If a movement or an application does not make sense in a kata, the student must challenge the movement and investigate it until it does. If an application does not work or looks unrealistic, he needs to find out why. It is a waste of time to do a kata in which the movements lack the meaning of fighting or some other reasonable meaning. This approach is needed more in kumite. It is more difficult here as one needs to think in a hurry during kumite. The student has more time in kata, as your imaginary opponent is much more patient and generous in giving you time to think. In kumite, most of the time, you do not dictate the time. You need to think of the distance, timing and target, in addition to the stances and the very technique to apply. But, of course, you only have a few seconds—or less—to decide. So, it becomes more important to think through the technique and other factors both before and after the kumite exercise. With well thought out preparation, you can apply better and get more improvement from the exchanges. A student will understand better why his technique worked or did not. I recommend that students plan ahead so they know what to do during their next kumite exercise because this will give them a better chance to improve. This is the only sure way, unless you are a natural karate-ka, to make steady and visible improvements.

Q: With all the technical changes during the last 30 years, do you think there is still pure shotokan, shito-ryu, goju-ryu, et cetera?
A: I have some opinions on two areas of this subject. One pertains to the changes that occurred within shotokan itself and the other pertains to the changes that occurred to the other traditional karate styles.

As far as shotokan is concerned from my observation, technique has been fairly consistent during the last 30 years. If we examine the last 50 or 60 years since the teaching days of Master Funakoshi, I think it has changed somewhat. So, if you call Master Funakoshi's karate pure shotokan, then I have to say we no longer have pure shotokan. However, if you consider JKA style as the standard shotokan, it has not changed too much, although one exception may be tournament kumite. As soon as Master Nakayama became the chief instructor after the death of Master Funakoshi, he brought in many changes. For one thing, Master Funakoshi was totally against tournaments. The first All-Japan JKA championship did not happen to start by chance right after Master Funakoshi's death. Master Nakayama modified many karate techniques and training methods, such as kata, the dropping of bo practice, et cetera. He made the JKA method very standardized. So, among the Japanese instructors, shotokan basic technique stayed pretty much the same during the last 30 years. Master Kanazawa left the JKA many years ago, but his technique is definitely JKA style. The only exception is Master Asai. He spent several years in Taiwan and Hong Kong to teach karate in the 1960s. During his stay in those countries, he learned the technique from the Chinese styles and incorporated them in his karate. Therefore, his karate has more complex body movements. In addition to the long stances, shorter stances are frequently practiced, such as *nekoashi-dachi*, which is rarely practiced in other shotokan styles.

Inter-style competitions are becoming more popular. This is good and bad for the different ryu. I experienced the situation as a competitor in 1982 when I represented my prefecture in the All-Japan Athletic meet in the karate division. The practitioners from all traditional karate styles were there. This was a learning experience as we shotokan stylists got to see and compete against the top competitors from other styles. In kumite, I was somewhat surprised, as all of the competitors fought in the similar ways, and I could not tell the difference between the various styles. For instance, nekoashi-dachi, a typical stance for goju-ryu, became impractical and disadvantageous in a tournament-style kumite. It is a shame that the tournament rules forced them to change their fighting style. I was also frustrated in kata competition. Naturally, judges were comprised of the instructors from different styles. Different styles emphasize different aspects of kata. For instance, in shotokan, power and strength shown in kime movements were very important, whereas smooth but faster movements were favored by shito-ryu. So, there were big differences in the five judges' scores. This showed the inconsistency of judging standards. This was more than 20 years ago, and I do not know if the judging has been standardized since then or not. Regardless, it is my opinion that through the inter-style tournaments, the uniqueness of each ryu, particularly in kumite, has become less noticeable with dilution of the technique and less emphasis on the unique fighting methods of each style. The degree of dilution and changes varies from one style to another. The biggest change might have occurred among the goju-ryu practitioners and much less to other styles, including shotokan. This is mainly because goju-ryu technique, by my understanding from a limited experience and research, centers around short-distance fighting. Thus, there are short stances and many open-hand techniques. A few changes I see in shotokan are stances and protective gears. Hopping around like a boxer seems to be very popular now. When we competed, we took a *zenkutsu-dachi* and never hopped. I am personally not in favor of any protective gear. It does not make a kumite any safer, and it permits or promotes less accurate technique.

This subject may be controversial, as some karate-ka may disagree with my opinions, but whether one considers the changes as improvements or deterioration, each ryu has become less distinctive during the last 30 years because of the inter-style tournaments. And this is a fact.

Q: Do you think different ryu are important?
A: Yes, different ryu are important when you practice karate as martial arts. There cannot be one ryu that transcends all styles, as our bodies and minds are all different. Can we say European fencing is better than Japanese kendo or Chinese sword fighting? Certainly not. Each karate ryu has the basic concepts of fighting style and methodology. Some emphasize close fighting like goju-ryu and others long-distance fighting like shotokan. Then the techniques such as stances must change according to the varied distance from the

"It is a shame that the tournament rules forced them to change their fighting style. I was also frustrated in kata competition. Naturally, judges were comprised of the instructors from different styles. Different styles emphasize different aspects of kata."

Karate Masters

"Each karate ryu has the basic concepts of fighting style and methodology. Some emphasize close fighting like goju-ryu and others long-distance fighting like shotokan."

opponent. Different masters had different ideas and skilled technique, but no one master was perfect. There is always something you can learn from another style.

As I mentioned above, there is no style that is best for everyone. One style is good in some aspects but weak in others. This is why it is good to have many different styles. Though you cannot usually compare the styles, you can find a wide range of teaching qualities in different dojo. The quality varies because the skill level and experience of instructors vary. You may find an excellent shotokan dojo with an excellent instructor, but you may also find a bad one in the same city if the instructor is not certified or has little teaching experience. The same can be said of any style. The strength and weaknesses of a style should not be judged by the performance of one dojo or even by a group of dojo. If you wish to compare or examine the technique and methodology of a certain ryu, you need to go to the source, which means you go to the headquarters or the original master.

Q: What is your opinion of full-contact karate and kickboxing?
A: I practiced kyokushinkai for a short period of time so I have some familiarity with full-contact karate. In the context of kumite, there is a big difference between traditional (non-contact) karate and full-contact karate. Experience in full-contact karate certainly gives a traditional karate practitioner a totally different perspective on kumite. In full-contact, your punches

and kicks start at the target and you drive through the target. On the contrary, in non-contact, your technique must stop right before the target. This very point is the huge difference in the concept and execution of technique. Non-contact practitioners often do not know for sure if the technique they completed could knock the opponents down. The feeling of contact you get from hitting a human body is quite different from punching a makiwara or a punching bag. Unfortunately, there is not enough kime in the techniques of the non-contact black belts to knock down their opponents. This may be because there isn't enough power or they miss the target. Interestingly, in a tournament, a competitor gets a half-point (*waza-ari*) or even a full point (*ippon*), even if a punch or a kick does not result in a knockout, and that can give a student a false sense of skill and power. In recent tournaments, most scoring techniques result from *chudan-gyaku-zuki*. In fact, it is extremely difficult to knock someone down with a punch to chudan even in a full-contact tournament. If a punch to jodan makes accidental contact, we have seen the receivers get knocked down. However, I have rarely seen competitors knocked down with an accidental chudan punch in non-contact tournaments. In full-contact tournaments, therefore, the competitors prefer the kicks to the head or the legs. The non-contact practitioners may be shocked in a street fight when they find that their "lethal" punches or kicks to the mid-section do not knock the enemies down. On the other hand, in full-contact, hand attacks to the face and head are prohibited. This is a serious flaw and leads to the unrealistic (too close) distance between the fighters. I cannot say much about kickboxing because I have no experience with this style. However, in kickboxing, they use gloves and allow contact to the face, so it is closer to real fighting—even if the threat is much less than fighting with bare knuckles. So, my conclusion is that practicing both styles of kumite is a must for serious karate practitioners who wish to develop fighting skills that are useful in a real fighting situation.

Q: How would you describe the life and dedication of Master Funakoshi Gichin and Nakayama Sensei for the art of karate?
A: I certainly have a tremendous amount of respect for both masters because they truly dedicated their entire lives to karate-do. Without master Funakoshi, I may not be practicing the karate style I love. After retiring from the teaching position, he could have had a peaceful and financially comfortable retirement life in Okinawa. In his mid 50s, he moved to the mainland, leaving the "family" behind to propagate karate to mainland Japan. Even though the move was within the same country, it was a big move nearly 100 years ago for a resident of a small southern island to migrate to

the capital of Japan (Tokyo). He chose to live under an unattractive living condition (financially), plus he faced a lot of ignorance and prejudices toward karate in a society in which karate was unknown. I truly respect Master Funakoshi for his selfless dedication and love for the arts. There were other karate masters from Okinawa who visited the mainland to introduce karate, but Master Funakoshi was the first one with a commitment to live there. It is always the hardest for a person who tries to do something new or unknown. I was only 10 years old when he passed away so I never had an opportunity to train under him or even meet him.

Master Nakayama was great because he built a JKA empire, which then was the world's largest traditional karate organization. It was not only the largest but also the most solid karate organization in the 1970s and 1980s. He established a *kenshusei* system and dispatched many talented instructors to the world in the 1950s and 1960s to propagate karate. I believe this is the main reason why shotokan became the brand name among the traditional karate styles around the world. JKA was also most respected as the best fighting style in Japan for many years. It is a shame that Master Nakayama passed away so young. He was really the axis that gave the tight cohesion among the JKA instructors, not only in Japan but also around the world. Unfortunately, the organization suffered breakups after his death. Shotokan now has many different organizations headed by ex-JKA masters like Kanazawa, Asai, Abe and Yahara. I only had a few training sessions with Master Nakayama in the 1970s and 1980s while we were in *Hoitsugan* and when he visited the U.S. However, he made a big impression on me, as he was a true gentleman and a karate master. I sincerely miss his leadership and teaching.

Q: Do you think that karate in the West is on the same level with Japanese karate?
A: My answer varies depending on what kind of karate we are discussing. There are several different kinds of karate. You have the martial arts, self-defense, sport and exercise. If we take the sport or tournament karate, the Western competitors are getting very close to the Japanese, especially in kumite. As far as the martial arts karate is concerned, there have been some extraordinary masters in Japan. The Western world, to my knowledge, has not produced these types of masters yet. This is true with the other martial arts such as aikido, kendo and kung-fu in China. Those masters are very few, even in Japan. The readers in the Western world would have difficulty believing it, but it is true that these masters did and do exist even now and they truly possess the super human level of expertise.

Q: Do you feel that there are any fundamental differences in approach or physical capabilities between Japanese and Western karate-ka?

A: No, there is no difference between Japanese and Western practitioners. In fact, average Japanese are shorter and lighter than Westerners, so these attributes are typically considered disadvantages in fights. On the other hand, the Japanese have a few cultural and environmental advantages. For example, the Japanese tend to stick to one thing once they start. In general, they do not give up easily, and this is a good trait for a martial artist. Thus, when a college freshman joins a varsity karate club, he will most likely continue for four years or until he graduates. Even in a town dojo, most of the new students will continue for years and rarely quit before one year (the minimum time to show respect to the instructor) is up. There are also a few undesirable cultural traits in Japan that affect karate-ka. One is a sectionalism that prevents karate-ka of one style associating or training with the practitioners of other styles. There is more openness to other styles and martial arts among the karate-ka in the U.S. In the U.S., you'll find a strong desire for students to attain their black belt. This desire by itself is not wrong or bad. Actually, the desire is good as it works to motivate students to train. What I have a problem with is that there are so many unqualified *yudansha* (black belts) in this country. Another thing I find peculiar in this country is that practitioners want to be a sensei too soon. A qualified instructor must not only have the ranking of 3rd dan or above, but he must also have the proper age for maturity, which is usually about 30, and enough karate experience, normally 10 years or more. Teaching a class is a difficult task, so I do not understand why they wish to teach so soon. Maybe there is a perceptual glory (positive image) in being a karate instructor, but I

"The Western world, to my knowledge, has not produced these types of masters yet. This is true with the other martial arts such as aikido, kendo and kung-fu in China. Those masters are very few, even in Japan."

Karate Masters

"There are also a few undesirable cultural traits in Japan that affect karate-ka. One is a sectionalism that prevents karate-ka of one style associating or training with the practitioners of other styles. There is more openness to other styles and martial arts among the karate-ka in the U.S."

want them to realize that it comes with a big responsibility and obligation to the students.

Q: Karate is nowadays often referred to as a sport. Would you agree with this definition or do you think it is only budo?
A: As I mentioned earlier, there are different kinds of karate. It can be a sport (tournament), martial arts, self-defense or an exercise to improve health. They are all fine, and it is up to the practitioners to choose which karate they wish to practice. When I was younger, I enjoyed tournaments, but I graduated from them 20 years ago. Now, I train for martial arts (budo) and health purposes. I teach martial arts karate at my dojo but, if some of the students want to participate in tournaments, I do not object to it. Even though we do not practice anything in particular to prepare for a tournament, I encourage the young students to get some experience and enjoy the excitement. The unfortunate thing is that many of the tournament competitors believe there is not much difference between sport karate and budo karate. I feel this is my job to teach my students how budo training is different from tournament karate training.

Q: Do you feel that you still have further to go in your studies of karate and budo?
A: Absolutely yes. My goal is still far, and I train daily to improve.

Q: In general, how do you see karate and shotokan around the world at the present time?
A: I am pleased that karate is becoming more and more popular—in general—around the world. Shotokan now has many different organizations. I hope each one will make a serious effort to improve techniques and raise the bar, rather than being comfortable with them and simply keeping them like a family heirloom. I believe it is healthy to have some competitions—not necessarily in a tournament format—between the organizations in shotokan. I also hope shotokan practitioners will continue to expand their knowledge and skills by exposing themselves to different karate styles and other martial arts.

Q: Does training with weapons improve empty-hand karate?
A: Yes, because weapons are extensions of your arms. I have trained extensively with weapons, particularly the nunchaku. It certainly helped me with my karate. My instructor, Master Asai, trained with nine-sectional chains to get his famous whip-like arm technique. It is my personal opinion that all practitioners who are 3rd dan and above should be using at least one weapon in their overall training schedule.

Q: What's your opinion of makiwara training?
A: The makiwara is a good training tool that teaches you how to make a tight fist and align your arm to your body and it toughens the knuckles. The benefits you get from makiwara training are all important in a real fight, and you do not learn them in a non-contact kumite. Thus, I recommend that all black belts should get some experience with a makiwara and sand bags. It is very important for them to experience the actual impact of hitting a solid target and learn how to deliver the power through the target. However, I personally do not recommend a heavy workout of more than 15 minutes with a makiwara. It is my opinion that many people tighten their arm muscles too long when training on a makiwara, as I see some practitioners push the makiwara after the impact. What I mean by too long is that the length of time is longer than what is necessary for a knockout punch.

In addition, one must not forget that a human is quite different from a makiwara, a sandbag or a waterbag. To experience this, a practitioner must get involved in full-contact fighting in which he can land his punches and kicks to the opponents in full force and experience the real hitting.

Karate Masters

Q: How should a sensei prepare and schedule his personal training to progress in the art?
A: Asai Sensei gets up at 4 every morning to train for two to three hours. He trains alone and keeps this ritual every morning, 365 days a year. I cannot duplicate his dedication, but I train every day to improve myself. Some instructors join the students during a class as they teach and believe they are training. Though some exercise may be good for health purposes, they must realize that unfocused exercise without intense mind concentration cannot be true training. Therefore, the training for an instructor must be done either alone or in a class taught by someone else. Of course, you will receive better training from someone who has more experience and higher ranking, but you can still train and learn in a class taught by a lower ranking instructor.

Q: When teaching the art of karate, what is the most important element: self-defense, sport or tradition?
A: I cannot say what is the most important element for everybody, as it varies according to different practitioners. I believe each element is important in different ways and should be respected. At our dojo, budo and tradition are considered the important aspects in our training. Tradition teaches not only etiquette but also the character development (shotokan *dojo-kun*) that is very important to me. The way of karate-do is applied to every aspect of one's life and this is budo karate.

Q: What's the proper ratio of kata and kumite in training?
A: The three major components in karate training—*kihon* (basics), kata (forms) and kumite (sparring)—are all equally important and should receive an adequate amount of attention. However, as far as the ratio of time for each element is concerned, it will change as the level of a practitioner changes. Naturally, beginners will have to spend more time in kihon to learn the techniques than in kata and kumite, which is the application of the techniques. The advanced students will spend more time in kata and kumite, but they should never skip kihon. Between kata and kumite, the ratio also varies but not as drastically as it did with kihon. Kata teaches you the sequences of attacking and defending moves or combinations, body shifting and turning, and some non-standard techniques that you generally do not practice often in kihon. Each component accomplishes particular aspects of karate training and all three are intertwined and support each other. For instance, kata should not be practiced without kumite in mind. I already mentioned that kata, without knowing the meaning of each movement, might be a dance. At

the same time, kumite practice should never stop at standard *ippon kumite*, *jyu ippon* and *jyu kumite*. Instructors must be creative and, for the most part, they should include kumite with two or more opponents or require that the student or students use a certain technique from a kata ... whether they are the attacker or defender.

So, kata and kumite should not be considered as two separate and non-related components. They are two sides of a same coin, so to speak. It is an interesting and important subject to discuss the purpose and the meaning of each element and all instructors should a have clear understanding of them.

Q: Sensei, do you have any general advice you would care to pass on the karate-ka?
A: I hope many karate-ka will make karate a lifelong endeavor. Train every day, but keep the practice segments short so your interest stays

"Naturally, beginners will have to spend more time in kihon to learn the techniques than in kata and kumite, which is the application of the techniques. The advanced students will spend more time in kata and kumite, but they should never skip kihon."

high for a long time. It is like boiling water and keeping it hot. You need a lot of heat initially to boil some water. Once the water is at the boiling temperature, you can keep it boiling with much less heat.

Q: Some people think that it is critical to train in Japan. Do you agree?
A: I think you can learn a lot from training in Japan. However, I do not think it is absolutely necessary unless you wish to be a top competitor or an above average instructor. If you train locally under an excellent instructor—especially if he is Japanese—you can get the same quality training as you

Karate Masters

"Kata and kumite should not be considered as two separate and non-related components. They are two sides of a same coin, so to speak. It is an interesting and important subject to discuss the purpose and the meaning of each element and all instructors should a have clear understanding of them."

would get in Japan. Some karate-ka boast about visiting there, say for one week every summer. But visiting one week or even a few weeks will not bring a complete understanding of training in Japan. What they will learn will be limited to the superficial aspects and not the true karate life. You need to make a commitment and live there at least a year or two. Then, and only after that amount of time, will you learn something. Therefore, you need to be pretty serious about karate to make such a commitment and only a few can do it. Also, there are many dojo in Japan with various degrees of professionalism and skill levels; therefore, any dojo would not do. In addition, if you are going to make that kind of commitment, I suggest that you attend the headquarters dojo to get the most training. The biggest benefit of a *honbu* dojo is that you find many high-ranking instructors teach there. Thus, you can receive different kinds of training from various experts and get a holistic view of karate training.

Q: What do you consider to be the major changes in the art of karate since you began training?
A: As I mentioned earlier, the popularity of tournaments is making karate more like a sport. This is a double-edged sword. I am happy that karate is becoming more popular and now more people practice. On the other hand, I find a tendency in general—even in Japan—to put a heavier emphasis on tournaments. This means that they are mainly practicing the techniques that are usable in a tournament. It is a shame that those practitioners are forgetting the budo and its traditions.

Q: Whom would you like to have trained with that you have not?
A: I have too many to mention, but I will share four late masters who fall into this category. Many of them are not known in the Western world. There are many books written about some of them in Japanese, but it is a shame that you can find only a few of them in English. I think the Westerners are missing much, as they cannot enjoy the stories of fantastic masters.

The first is, of course, Master Funakoshi. I wish I could hear his philosophy on karate and life directly from him in person. Luckily, there are a few books on him and his life, so I do not need to explain anything about him.

The second is Mr. Kenichi Sawai (*iken* style of kung-fu). He was the only Japanese student of a great master of kung-fu, Master Wang. He made a big impact on kyokushinkai during the 1970s and many kyokushin students picked up this style of kung-fu that Master Sawai taught.

Master Harumichi Hida (Kenkoho), an extraordinary person who developed superhuman power through his breathing and some simple exercises, is the third person. He became so strong that he would break *bokken* by simply swinging them toward the ground sharply. He also developed such a keen sense in his late years that he could shoot an arrow and hit a target without fail. This was amazing because he did this while he was blindfolded. Even though he was excellent in judo, kendo and other martial arts, he never called himself a *budo-ka.* He formulated his own exercise that brought him the superhuman physical and mental conditions, and he was most proud of this.

The last master I shall share is Master Yukiyoshi Sagawa (jiu-jitsu). He was supposed to be so good at jiu-jitsu that even Master Ueshiba of aikido did not dare challenge him. His students could not grab him or his gi for more than a split second before they were thrown about like pieces of cloth. The master trained until one week before his death, and he died when he was in his 90s. In his last training session, he still had multiple students attacking him. But, in an instant, they found themselves flat on their backs. He was born in 1902 and passed away a few years ago.

Q: What would you say to someone who is interested in learning karate-do?
A: I say, "Welcome. Start today." But at the same time, I will advise the student to take time and check the instructor's qualifications and experience before signing up. Starting one's training in a proper dojo is a must. If a student learns poor or wrong technique, it will be very difficult to correct or unlearn them later. It is said in Japan that it is better not to practice for two years while you search for an ideal instructor.

Q: What keeps you motivated after all these years?
A: I guess I just like shotokan karate. It seems the more I practice the more challenges I find. I never get bored.

Q: Do you think it is necessary to engage in free fighting to achieve good self-defense skills for a real situation?
A: First we need to define free fighting. If it means street fighting, we do not need it to achieve self-defense skills. If it means free sparring, then my answer is yes, on one condition. Free sparring does help in self-defense situations, but it does not achieve self-defense skills. Let me explain. We must understand there are two different kinds of training. One builds technique and the other uses the technique. Free sparring is a training device or method to use the technique you learned in basics and kata. Therefore, if you do not have the technique, you cannot use it in free sparring. This is why free sparring is not recommended to beginners. On the other hand, if you only practice basics and kata, you cannot learn timing, distance and other aspects of fighting such as fear. They can be learned in sparring, and the ultimate method in dojo sparring is free sparring. I must note that free sparring is not the same as free fighting or street fighting. Being good at free sparring does not guarantee self-defense skills. I have already touched on the subject of the flaws of dojo kumite. In street fighting, you will encounter situations that are not found in dojo training. For example, there may be a multiple number of opponents, they may have weapons, they may be wearing heavy coats so a *chudan* punch or kick will not have much effect, the ground may not be even or flat and you may have to protect your wife or

children. All these factors will play key elements in a fight. Therefore, the best defense is not necessarily the skills that result from free sparring. Instead, the best "technique" is to avoid the predicament. If you have no enemy, you will have a victory in every battle. The best defense is to avoid the fight by giving the money willfully in a hold-up, or an apology to the guy who bumped into you, or a smile instead of a finger to a driver who cut in. You should be proud that you have not been in a street fight. Some people may consider stepping away from a street fight a sign of cowardice, but it is not. You are being smart. It is not worth risking your life in a silly street fight over an insignificant cause. However, when you know that you have to protect your life or a family member's, it will be different. In this case, you do not run and you must be able to fight to the death (literally). This may happen only once in your lifetime. What is important here is your mental determination, and this cannot be learned over night. You must have the feeling of *ikken-hissatsu* (one punch to kill) at all times during your karate training, so that you can bring that feeling when you really need it in a life-threatening situation. In that case, your experience in free sparring may help to some degree, but it becomes obvious that the attitude you show will become critical. For example, when I mention attitude, I'm talking about the intention that you will fight until you die or kill the enemy. Your enemy can feel your seriousness, and he will most likely back off, as he

"Free sparring does help in self-defense situations, but it does not achieve self-defense skills. We must understand there are two different kinds of training. One builds technique and the other uses the technique."

Karate Masters

"If you have no enemy, you will have a victory in every battle. The best defense is to avoid the fight by giving the money willfully in a hold-up, or an apology to the guy who bumped into you, or a smile instead of a finger to a driver who cut in."

does not want to die either. This is what I call budo karate, and this is the philosophy I want my students to understand.

Q: What is your opinion about mixing karate styles? Does the practice of one nullify the effectiveness of the other, or on the contrary, can it be beneficial to a student?

A: I can understand your question in two ways. First, you are asking for my opinion on a student practicing different styles. The second is an idea of making one style that covers various different styles. In essence, a student can learn from other styles to expand his own karate training. So, I recommend that all advanced students take advantage of an opportunity to participate in seminars held by other styles. I believe it takes 10 years or more to master, or at least understand sufficiently, one style. Thus, an average student who trains two or three times per week must have the correct expectation. Even though it is possible for a practitioner to be very good at two or more different styles simultaneously, obviously, it will be extremely difficult. It makes more sense for an average practitioner to focus his time and effort to master one style. I believe it is better for a budoka to be excellent at one than be mediocre in several.

As far as I am concerned, we should keep the traditional styles or ryu independent and practiced separately. Personally, I am against the idea of mixing them up for the reason I stated. However, karate is a fluid art and each style does change as it is handed down through the generations. In the process, there may be an exceptionally talented master who may be capable of incorporating two or more styles and establish his own style. That is possible but nevertheless unlikely. Then, how about mixing karate with another martial art? It is sort of a natural move for a martial artist who is familiar with multiple kinds of bujutsu. I know that it has already been done to some extent. Master Ohtsuka, the founder of *wado-ryu*, was a jiu-jitsu master before he learned shotokan from Master Funakoshi. Though I have only limited knowledge of wado-ryu, I understand that Master Ohtsuka took the essence and combined shotokan karate, jiu-jitsu and kenjutsu. Unfortunately, I have never taken any lessons in wado-ryu, so I cannot make a determination as to whether this style is more effective than shotokan. I also have heard of *jukenpo*, which is a mix of jiu-jitsu, karate and kung-fu. I understand it is practiced in Japan as well as in the U.S., but it is a minor organization and it has not earned wide popularity. Of course, that does not necessarily mean that they are illegitimate or ineffective. I cannot make any judgment or comparison, as I do not know of those styles at all. I cannot say such a mixed style is or can be better than bujitsu, and I will refrain from expressing my opinions. Hopefully, I will have some exposure to such styles in the future to expand my knowledge and experience.

Q: Modern karate is moving away from the bunkai in kata practice. How important do you think bunkai is in the understanding of kata and karate-do in general?
A: First, I want to point out the true meaning of bunkai. It is translated as "application," and its literal meaning is "to break apart" or "to dissect." So, it means that we are to break apart or dissect the entire flaw of one kata

into pieces or parts to analyze and examine the meaning (application) of those parts.

Now, let's get back to the question. My belief is that kata without studying bunkai or knowing the meaning of a movement is nearly a dance. Though bunkai is important, there is a pitfall with it. As some of the instructors either do not understand the meaning of the movements or try to be creative, they come up with strange and unrealistic applications to the movements. It is true that there are many moves that are difficult to apply in a real fight and do not look like they make sense. I think there are two or three major reasons for this. One is the actual application is hidden in the moves, and the bunkai seems difficult on the surface. After understanding the moves or a kata itself, one can apply the correct moves in bunkai ... and only then. A good example of this is the *tekki* kata. A lot of people assume this is a kata to practice *kiba-dachi* and the principle of moving only sideways while fighting opponents from the sides and front. That is only partially correct, and one should not be trapped in the movements alone. It will make sense when the practitioners finally understand the meaning of a kata as a whole, and this will come after encountering difficulties in understanding certain movements. Then one may ask, "Why did the kata creator hide the applications rather than making it more obvious?" This is a good question, and I can write a book on the subject. I only give a hint and encourage the readers to do their own research and investigation. There are several reasons for hiding the true applications, but one of them is that a creator had a theme in a kata. In order to transcend the important technique or move, he purposely ignored some of the true applications. In tekki, kiba-dachi and body shifting are the major themes. Of course, upper body rotation at the hips is another theme, but it is not as important. Body shifting through the use of kiba-dachi is an important subject for all traditional karate, and everyone must investigate this and learn it. Our body is constructed in a way that it is natural to move our legs forward. Therefore, it is easier to make *zenkutsu-dachi* and move forward and backward; however, it is much more difficult to assume good kiba-dachi and move sideways. The key here is to learn how to shift your center of gravity to initiate and power the body shifting. For this reason, the creator chose to use only one stance—kiba-dachi—and the movements are only in lateral directions, rather than mixing it with zenkutsu or other stances. Therefore, the body movements to the front and back are purposely omitted. This is a very important point, and all shotokan people must practice *tekki* until they understand this very technique. There are three tekki kata: *shodan, nidan* and *sandan*. Nidan and sandan have interesting upper body movements and technique. As far as the secret technique of body shifting is concerned, this can be learned by practicing tekki shodan. The students must also investigate the importance of *namigaeshi* in this kata. It is supposed to be a blocking technique using your feet, but there is a hidden technique within this movement. I will not go into this interesting subject at this time, but I will encourage the readers to investigate it on their own. We also need to study the history of kata to understand the meaning better. The other reason for the difficulty in bunkai is that some of the movements are put in or added for the form or physical exercise, like the final move of *heian godan*. It could be just a *gedan-barai* with the right fist and the left fist could go to the left hip rather than be held up high above the head. If you interpret this movement as a jodan block from the rear, it is unrealistic and impractical. With the final move you execute the right-fist *uchikomi* and then immediately grab the opponent's gi with your left hand and pull up strongly. The right hand move that is done simultaneously means a punch to chudan that leads to a throwing technique. In order to develop a strong pull up motion and to gain the momentum of the upper body movement to the back as you shift from zenkutsu-dachi to *kokutsu-dachi*, the left fist is pulled up high in an exaggerated motion. Let's look at the stance, the *kamae*, you take in the middle of heian sandan. No one fights with a stance in which both feet are together with the fists held at the hips. It is difficult for a beginner student to deliver a *hiji-uke* (elbow block) and get in a kiba-dachi at the same time. So, you start from the closed-feet stance with the fist held at the hips to make it easy to deliver the next move. So, don't believe it if any one says it is a move to break away from an armlock around your body. In addition, we must know that the

"One may ask, 'Why did the kata creator hide the applications rather than making it more obvious?' This is a good question, and I can write a book on the subject. I only give a hint and encourage the readers to do their own research and investigation."

Karate Masters

"We also need to study the history of kata to understand the meaning better. The other reason for the difficulty in bunkai is that some of the movements are put in or added for the form or physical exercise."

heian kata was created by an Okinawan master as the introductory kata for the beginners. Therefore, this kata is conceptually different from *bassai*, *kanku* and other shotokan black belt kata. The movements were picked from those "real" kata so that the beginners can get used to kata movements before they start on the "real" kata. You can easily see that many movements of kanku-dai are found in heian yondan, and some movements of bassai are found in heian godan.

Therefore, it is natural that we find the applications to be difficult or impractical in many bunkai. Then, there is another cause for bunkai difficulty. The applications are no longer practiced in the recent training, such as in a blocking technique against a bo. *Jitte* is a good example. For most shotokan practitioners, bo practice is no longer part of regular dojo training. If this kata is taught to fight against the opponents' kicks and punches instead of a bo, the bunkai will probably not make sense.

I am not an expert in kata and its history. The ideas and concepts I described above are only my opinions and understanding. I could be wrong, and I am also aware that I need to study further to expand my understanding. I also admit that other concepts and understanding may apply to the movements and bunkai. Many a time there are multiple aspects to one bunkai and technique. One answer may not be the ultimate explanation but could be only one of many explanations to that aspect.

I encourage each student to examine all of the movements in all kata and try to understand the applications and true meanings. If a student has a problem, he should ask the instructors or research it on his own until he finds the satisfactory answers. Kata is an accumulation of the excellent moves that were used by the experts of the past and it is a textbook of fighting movements. Kata teaches you some intricate moves and sequences that you normally would not practice in basics. At the same time, it cannot be helped but kata does change gradually, as they were handed down from one generation to the next. Though the changes may happen moderately, they do change over the years and from one instructor to another, so the study of the kata from the historic sense is also very important and necessary.

Q: What is your philosophical basis for karate training?
A: The philosophical basis for my training is budo, a way of life. This is a way for me to grow and improve as a karate-ka and simply as a human being.

Q: Do you have a particularly memorable karate experience that has remained as an inspiration for your training?
A: I was inspired every time I was with Master Asai. It was amazing to watch him move. He has a very fluid motion with flexibility and power that none of us can match.

Q: After all these years of training and experience, could you explain the meaning of the practice of karate-do?
A: There is no big deal with the meaning of practicing karate-do. It is an everyday endeavor to better myself, as a karate-ka and as an individual. But we find it very difficult to keep practicing it daily and continuously for many years without giving up. That is the real challenge and meaning of karate-do practice, I think.

Q: How do you think a practitioner can increase his understanding of the spiritual aspect of karate?
A: First, we must define the meaning of "spiritual." If you mean this in a religious sense, it is a much harder subject and I defer the exploration at this time. I only mention that I believe there is a connection between budo and the spiritual aspect of religion. In fact, some masters like Master Ueshiba and Master Hida have described their spiritual experiences in their books.

"Spiritual" can also mean more of a mental state of karate. The good example is high spirit and kiai. If one practices karate as a martial art, this high spirit is critical. Without high spirit, something important is missing in karate ... like a gi without a belt. My spiritual search starts with our shotokan *dojo-kun* (five credos). The first one is: "Seek perfection of character." As I mentioned earlier, this is why my karate training is a lifelong endeavor. The second one is also hard. The English translation is, "Be faithful." Unfortunately, it is a poor translation. The meaning of the second credo is, "Keep the way of Makoto." That can be translated as truthful, real, genuine and ingenious, but it cannot be translated fully. For instance, by keeping the way of Makoto, we must not lie or be irresponsible. Also, winning or losing in a tournament or passing or failing an exam will not be as important as the process, which is much more important for the way of Makoto. By following dojo-kun, you will have perseverance and become courteous, humble, honest, truthful and responsible. As we get closer to perfect, I think we will come very close to the spiritual sphere.

Q: How much training should a "senior" karate-ka be doing to improve?
A: All of the "senior" (high ranking) karate-ka should be training every day. That is the responsibility that comes with a high rank. However, the amount of time one spends will depend on the individual's desire and capacity. Regardless, it should be a lifetime endeavor.

Q: Is there anything lacking in the way karate is taught today compared with those who were being taught in your early days?
A: Karate is changing, even in Japan as the tournament karate is becoming more popular. Thus, the introduction of a sports mentality is unavoidable. The budo aspect was emphasized more and the rules and dojo etiquette were followed much more strictly in the past. When I was a junior student, we were not allowed to cut a class even when we were sick. Having a cold was not a good enough excuse. Recently, even at a Varsity Karate Club, a student is allowed to be absent if he is sick. budo means a way of life and a sickness is a part of your life. Thus, we train with fever and headache. The formality, unfortunately, is disappearing as well. In many dojo, line-up rituals in *seiza* and bowing are no longer exercised. Bowing etiquette between the students and to the sensei are enforced and followed less. Such etiquette is a crucial part of budo, so it is my opinion that we must never forget or ignore it.

Q: What do you consider to be the most important qualities of a successful karate-ka?
A: The ability to enjoy the training, learn every day, and the ability to share one's knowledge and skills with the junior students and enjoy doing it.

Q: In regards to supplementary training, what advice would you give to students?
A: This is a very important subject. First, good flexibility is required in

karate. Thus, I recommend daily stretching exercise unless you are super flexible already. I have to be very careful how I explain this so that what I say will not be misunderstood. This may be a surprising statement, but—other than the stretching exercises—I do not recommend any supplementary training. I found the muscles used in cycling and running are quite different from the ones used in karate technique, and you will see the ill effect in your karate technique from such exercises. You can say similar things for other exercises such as swimming and weight lifting. Please note that I am not saying karate-ka should not swim or do some weight lifting for enjoyment. I am saying that if you have average strength and physical ability that other exercises are not necessary and do not improve your karate. A karate practitioner must perform karate techniques and use particular muscles in certain methods to produce power and movements. By just making some muscles stronger, it will not necessarily make your karate technique more powerful. Moreover, your karate technique may suffer. This is because well-executed karate techniques require the intricate and harmonious use of various muscles. Strengthening a part of some muscles—and not all that are used for a technique—is not harmonious. Thus, a practitioner's motion may become slow and inaccurate. I heard a story about a one-time great golfer, Gary Player. During his prime, he wanted to make his swing stronger so he could hit farther. To achieve his goal, he chose to be a lumberjack. He believed that swinging a heavy ax was similar to a golf swing and would increase his hitting power. Unfortunately, his golf form was totally destroyed, and he could not come back to the U.S. Championship to win. I can appreciate the lesson taught here. I am afraid a lot of people do not understand the complexity of body movements and requirement of harmonious operations of different muscles and their groups. A good example is Mike Phelps, the Olympic gold medallist. He does not do any weight training as a supplement. Instead, he swims many hours daily. By doing just that, he won Olympic gold medals and set some world records. He must have known that the weight exercises could deform his swim form (harmonious and coordinated muscle movement) that would generate the world-record speed. I am sure that weight exercises with scientific and medical planning under a well-educated coach can be beneficial for some swimmers and karate-ka. Olympic swimmers may have such luxury, but how many karate-ka can afford that? If you have one extra hour or even 30 minutes to exercise, you are better off practicing karate in that time. I want to say again that there is nothing wrong with casual jogging, bike riding and weight lifting for leisure and pure enjoyment. However, if you are very serious about improving your karate skills, you must evaluate all of your exercises and the amount of time you spend. You want to avoid anything that may have a negative impact on your karate technique. If you do not need to do the stretching, I recommend walking as a supplementary exercise. I do not mean a slow casual walk in a park, but it should be done in a correct form with good posture and correct muscle movements at a rapid pace. Walking is the base of almost all moves we have in karate body shifting. Interestingly, watching people walking tells you a lot about their physical abilities, as well as some aspects of their personalities.

I would like to expand a little further on supplementary exercise. There are some traditional exercises such as rubber tube, bunny hopping, push-ups, sit-ups, et cetera. I used to make my students do all of them and did them myself until recently. The more I studied sports science and medicine, however, I found that those exercises, done without good guidance and correct instructions, are more harmful than beneficial—not only to karate-ka—but to anyone who does them. I suspect most of the old-time karate-ka do not like to hear that the rubber tube exercise, sit-ups and push-ups can bring harmful and damaging results to karate technique. There still is a lot to be learned for all of us and that makes it challenging and interesting.

Q: What do you see as the most important attributes of a student?
A: Persistence and curiosity; why, how and what are very important. I found the new students who are uncoordinated tend to stay longer and achieve higher ranking than the more talented. I assume the physically talented new students don't find karate training as challenging. Thus, they find it less exciting and stimulating. They tend to drop out before they reach a black belt rank. A student who can continue his training until his 80s and 90s is the winner.

Q: Why is it that a lot of students start falling away after two or three years of training?
A: This is a good question. As instructors, it is our responsibility to examine this problem seriously and find the ways to prevent it. I can think of two major reasons. The talented students will train hard for two or three years, and they can achieve shodan in that time period. Many students believe that they have reached their ultimate goal in karate, thus they are not motivated to train more. Instructors must lead those talented students to the higher expectations and goals. The students need to be told that shodan means a "starting" dan. The other reason is the fact that the advancement to the next rank, nidan, requires much more time and effort than what was required for shodan. Going from shodan to nidan is only one level, but it is nothing like going from sec-

ond *kyu* to first *kyu*. It will take a minimum of two years to advance to nidan. This discourages the students who used to see the advancements every three to four months. Without appropriate encouragement and instruction from the instructors, shodan students could easily get discouraged ... even to the point of giving up. It is necessary for the instructors to encourage the students to try for the next rank, but I believe it is much more important to teach them that karate-do practice means a lifetime endeavor and rank advancement is only a part of karate and not the ultimate goal. It is also ultimately the instructor's responsibility to improve himself continuously so that he can provide exciting training to the advanced students for many years.

"The talented students will train hard for two or three years, and they can achieve shodan in that time period. Many students believe that they have reached their ultimate goal in karate, thus they are not motivated to train more. Instructors must lead those talented students to the higher expectations and goals."

Q: There is very little written about you in magazines. You obviously do not thrive on the publicity like some martial artists. Why?
A: I have never been active in article writing or doing seminars. In the past, I did not have a desire to express myself outside our dojo. However, recently I began to think it is my responsibility to share my thoughts and understanding with others. I have read many articles written in different magazines, and I find some vacuum in the area of understanding karate and the martial arts. If I have another opportunity in the future to present my views and thoughts, hopefully I can contribute something to the karate education.

Karate Masters

"In the past, I did not have a desire to express myself outside our dojo. However, recently I began to think it is my responsibility to share my thoughts and understanding with others."

Q: Have there been times when you felt fear in your karate training?
A: Only a few times in JKA training. For example, when I faced some of the top JKA instructors, such as Tanaka, Kagawa and Yamamoto. They are all either Japanese or world champions. It was scary, but at the same time, I was happy to have a chance to face them. I had more fear in full-contact kumite. Even though the punches to the face are supposedly "controlled"—if you are lucky—your opponent is throwing his kicks full force to your legs and head and he's trying to knock you down with his punches. It is really a different feeling when your opponent is intending to maim you. You do not know this feeling until you experience it.

Q: What are your thoughts on the future of karate-do and what's your opinion about karate entering the Olympic Games?
A: Karate will change and that is a natural process. It is our responsibility to

keep karate at its best and improve it so we can hand down the arts to the next generation.

I personally oppose adding karate to the Olympics. I am sure the Olympics will make karate even more popular, and this can be a welcome effect to many instructors. However, I am afraid the downside outweighs the benefits. This is very clear when you observe what has happened to *taekwondo*. If you stayed up late and saw an Olympic match on TV, I don't need to go any further. But that is what you have to expect if karate would become an Olympic event. The ill effect is also visible in judo—though at a smaller degree. I have already explained about the downsides of the inter-styles tournaments earlier. In addition, there will be other problems. One is the judging problem that we witnessed at the gymnastic events this summer. The other is the use of drugs and unethical or illegal methods that are used to win. I personally want to keep karate in a "pure" Budo state as much as possible.

Q: Is there anything else you would to add for the readers?
A: I am solely responsible for what I said and commented here. The opinions and thoughts I expressed here are not necessarily those of JKS or its instructors. They are based on my 40 years of martial arts training and experience, and they are solely my own. Thus, if my explanation and/or descriptions are incorrect or inaccurate, I will take the full responsibility. O

"A true martial arts practitioner, like an artist of another kind—be this a musician, painter, writer or actor—is expressing and leaving parts of himself in every piece of his craft. The need for self-inspection and self-realization of 'who' he is becomes the reason for a journey in search of that perfect technique, that great melody, that inspiring poetry, that amazing painting or that Academy Award performance. It is this motivation to reach that 'impossible dream' that allows a simple individual to become an exceptional artist and master of his craft."

—Jose M. Fraguas

www.ingramcontent.com/pod-product-compliance
Lightning Source LLC
Chambersburg PA
CBHW081343080526
44588CB00016B/2364